PRECOGNITIVE
DREAMWORK
AND THE LONG SELF

"Eric Wargo takes us on an exciting journey of discovery into the interconnected web accessible by the time-traveling aspect of our subconscious. He weaves past, present, and future together with insights from ancient wisdom, visionary writers, discoveries in physics, and a variety of precognitive dreams. You will be inspired to dig deeper—to partner with your 'Long Self' to gain insight on the past and respond to the future to enhance your journey through life. As an active time traveler, you are part of the evolution of consciousness and a global caring society."

DALE E. GRAFF, PHYSICIST,
FORMER DIRECTOR OF PROJECT STARGATE, AND AUTHOR OF
TRACKS IN THE PSYCHIC WILDERNESS

"Here is the book for which I have been waiting, a paranormal practice manual to recommend to readers who ask for one thing: *a practice*, a way to cultivate their own superhuman capacities and will them out of the Matrix of Depression that is our modern world. Integrating the best insights from ancient and medieval memory theater, Freud's *The Interpretation of Dreams*, J. W. Dunne's *Experiments with Time*, and the contemporary neuroscience of memory, Wargo shows us *how* to become our own mutants, how to shape and make ourselves from the future along what he alternately calls the 'tesseract brain' or the 'Long Self.' His message is a fantastic one: You are not puny and insignificant. You are vast—a Time Lord, a sci-fi special effects master, a highly evolved cosmic being. Wake up! (and record your dreams). We need you. And we are in this, and *out of this,* together."

JEFFREY J. KRIPAL,
AUTHOR OF *MUTANTS AND MYSTICS*

"Eric Wargo is a new kind of intellectual whose refinement has emerged from his thoughtful response to the dogmatism that opposes new queries in science. Wargo's profoundly exciting and thorough book on the question of dream precognition not only advances an important area of study but demonstrates the quality of intellectual dialogue that increasingly finds expression today within parapsychology. His writing and tone reawaken the reader to the excitement of radical and discerning inquiry."

MITCH HOROWITZ,
PEN AWARD–WINNING AUTHOR OF *OCCULT AMERICA*

"Eric Wargo takes a new and refreshing look into dreams and their meaning by investigating their relationship to time and precognition. This book conveys a clear and concise message that expands on the fact that dreams are much more than they seem, which is a valued consideration by any serious oneirologist."

LEE ADAMS,
AUTHOR OF *A VISIONARY GUIDE TO LUCID DREAMING*,
FOUNDER OF TAILEATERS,
AND HOST OF THE *COSMIC ECHO* PODCAST

PRECOGNITIVE
DREAMWORK
AND THE LONG SELF

Interpreting Messages
from Your Future

A Sacred Planet Book

ERIC WARGO

Inner Traditions
Rochester, Vermont

Inner Traditions
One Park Street
Rochester, Vermont 05767
www.InnerTraditions.com

Sacred Planet Books are curated by Richard Grossinger, Inner Traditions editorial board member and cofounder and former publisher of North Atlantic Books. The Sacred Planet collection, published under the umbrella of the Inner Traditions family of imprints, publishes on the themes of consciousness, cosmology, alternative medicine, dreams, climate, permaculture, alchemy, shamanic studies, oracles, astrology, crystals, hyperobjects, locutions, and subtle bodies.

Cataloging-in-Publication Data for this title is available from the Library of Congress

ISBN 978-1-64411-269-4 (print)
ISBN 978-1-64411-270-0 (ebook)

Printed and bound in the United States

10 9 8 7 6 5 4 3 2

Text design and layout by Debbie Glogover
This book was typeset in Garamond Premier Pro with Gotham Condensed, Gill Sans MT Pro and ITC Legacy Sans Std used as display typefaces

To send correspondence to the author of this book, mail a first-class letter to the author c/o Inner Traditions • Bear & Company, One Park Street, Rochester, VT 05767, and we will forward the communication, or contact the author directly at **eric.wargo@gmail.com**.

For Laura, Emily, and May

Contents

PART 6

SPACETIME TRAVEL IN THE BORDERLANDS (GAMES FOR ADVANCED PLAYERS)

Acknowledgments

I completed this book manuscript just as rumors of a deadly virus were emerging from China, with ominous stories of whole cities locked down and dire prognostications that the pathogen would spread across the world. Within three months, many of us in the United States, including in Washington, DC, where I live, found ourselves in a surreal, transformed reality: isolating at home, wearing masks whenever we went out, fearful of human contact outside our immediate families.

The COVID-19 pandemic became what is likely to be the defining event for the generation too young to remember 9/11. It revealed an America starkly polarized about the role and authority of science and brought in its wake long-overdue reckonings over racism and racist violence. Only time will tell how the tumultuous, tragic, and at times surreal events of the year 2020 will turn out to have shaped our dreams in previous years and decades. Even as I was preparing my manuscript for submission, friends and colleagues were sending me uncanny dream portents of their transformed lives under lockdown. I included a few of them in the book.

I am thankful to everyone who helped me bring this book into the light of publication during the stresses of this period. Patrick Huyghe gave me valuable advice and encouragement. Hussein Ali Agrama, Jess Taylor, and Alex van Oss read drafts of the book and provided feedback that improved it in many ways, as did the expert editing of Kayla Toher at Inner Traditions (thanks for being patient with my quirks!). And I could not have written this book without the friendship and insights of Jeffrey Kripal, who has long championed my work and helped spread the gospel of precognition and time loops. I have benefited immensely from conversations with Jeff, his students at Rice University, and participants at Jeff's Beyond the Spinning Symposium at the Esalen Institute's Center for Theory and Research in January 2019, a few of whom have now become good friends. Jeff also put me in touch with Richard Grossinger, who facilitated bringing the book out with Inner Traditions.

I am especially indebted to all the people who shared their precognitive dreams with me. With permission, many of their stories appear in the following pages. Most important were the dreams and insights of super-precog and dreamworker extraordinaire Tobi Watari, whose astonishing narrative you will read herein. Tobi exemplifies the citizen-science approach to precognition that I am advocating in this book. Although she and I continue to debate the finer points of the theory, many of the principles I have formulated here emerged out of our long-distance collaboration over the past few years. Tobi deserves much credit for helping me hone and clarify my ideas. She also went over this manuscript with a fine-toothed comb and saved me from more than a few gaffes. (All errors are my own, of course.)

Most of all, I thank my long-suffering wife, Laura, our daughter Emily, and our newest daughter, May, who came into the world just as this book was being finalized. They are dreams come true.

INTRODUCTION
They Dreamed

I am in a world which is in me.

PAUL VALERY

All over the world, all throughout history, they dreamed. They dreamed about wars and assassinations before they occurred. They dreamed about plane crashes before they hit the news, and about crises happening to friends and loved ones far away. They dreamed about jets crashing into tall towers in New York weeks, months, and even years before it happened in real life. And they dreamed about plagues and the need to shelter in their homes, long before anyone had heard of coronavirus or COVID-19.

But they also dreamed in advance about the little things, including the happy or just haphazard things, that punctuated their lives. They dreamed about things like births, reconnecting with an old friend, seeing a rare animal, committing a social faux pas, needing to deal with a plumbing problem, or reading some really interesting story in a magazine or online.

By "they," I mean regular people from all walks of life, ordinary dreamers. We are all ordinary dreamers, even if we don't tend to remember our dreams, or only do so once in a blue moon. Dreaming is something we do at least two hours a night, possibly even the whole night. It's thrilling, sometimes life-changing, when we realize that we may in fact be time traveling in our sleep, actually interacting with our future.

In her second year of university, Valerie* had a vivid dream that her parents' house had been burgled and that men were in the house. It was striking enough that she called her mother the next day to tell her—something unusual at that point in her life, as her limited budget didn't allow her to call home more than once every couple weeks.

"When I described my dream, my mum went quiet and said, 'Have you been speaking to your sister?'" Valerie's sister, who was at another university, had called their mother the same day, having also dreamed (the same night) of a burglary at their parents' house—although details of the two dreams were different. "We agreed this was quite weird and left it there."

But two days later, Valerie's mother called her and said, "Your dream came true." She explained that burglars had ingeniously "entered" the house using a fishing rod to take the car keys off a side table by the door and had stolen their car. Some neighbors' houses were burgled the same night, in most cases through actual physical entry. It was evidently an organized gang of thieves operating in the neighborhood. It was the first time their house had been burgled in twenty-eight years living there—and it seemed that both Valerie and her sister had gotten a whiff of this rare event a few days beforehand in their dreams.

This was just one of several precognitive dream experiences that Valerie sent me. Readers of my blog *The Nightshirt* and my previous book *Time Loops* frequently email me such stories—I love to hear them. And after I've had a couple drinks at parties and admit that I spend my free time writing about ESP, acquaintances are often forthcoming with their own stories about life-changing brushes with precognition.

---

*Unless otherwise noted, dreamers' names are pseudonyms and stories are used with permission. Exceptions are dreams from published sources.

For example, knowledge of his inner, secret time traveler has been a kind of talisman for Ray, a radio producer in his late twenties I met at a Washington, DC, social event. After his bottom baby teeth fell out in second grade, two of his adult teeth came in double for some reason, and he had to have them removed. The night before his dental surgery, he dreamed the extraction was already over (Sigmund Freud would call that wish fulfillment) and that his dentist gave him a little box containing his extracted teeth. "When I opened the box, one of the teeth was a tiny little square," he said. "The other tooth was long and pointy and spear-like. It looked like an animal tooth."

The next morning his parents brought him in for his surgery; he was put under anesthetic and awoke when it was over. "Just like my dream, my dentist gave me a little box containing my extracted teeth. And the contents of the box were identical to what I'd foreseen in my dream the night before. The second tooth was so long because it contained the root of the tooth." Like most second graders, Ray didn't know that teeth had roots, so this was quite surprising. But way more surprising was the fact that he'd dreamed the whole scene the night before.

Two decades later, Ray says this experience had a huge impact on him. "Realizing I could predict the future with my dreams was beyond exciting. It made me feel like a mutant from *X-Men*. Like I had this secret power that no one else could comprehend." It colors his life to this day. "I still think I have some of that power!"

He's right—he does still have that power. In fact, I believe we all do.

People who are curious about the topic of precognition generally want to know whether you could get rich using this ability, for instance by dreaming of winning lottery numbers. It's not unheard of—the physician and writer Larry Dossey tells the story of a New York housewife who was able to pay for a roof repair after praying for lottery numbers, which came to her in a dream and proved to be right.[1] One precognitive dreamer I correspond with followed a waking psychic flash instructing her to purchase a lottery ticket, and she won seven dollars. (Hey, it's something.)

An equally common story, though, is to dream of correct lottery numbers but somehow be prevented from purchasing a ticket—and then living with regret—or simply dreaming about a lottery win but being wrong on important details, like who will win.*

One of my favorite dream-stories was sent to me in June 2019 by a man in England named Thomas. He had recorded a striking dream that his parents had won £230,000 in a lottery but that he couldn't retrieve the money as it was stuck in a milk bottle. He awoke with the feeling that this was prophetic somehow, and urged his parents to purchase a lottery ticket. When Thomas called his father a few days later, he learned they had bought the ticket, but none of their numbers had been a match. But then a week later, in another phone call, his mother casually mentioned that his dad's cousin had won in the lottery, on the same day he had had his dream. Thomas breathlessly asked how much the cousin had won, feeling that he already knew the answer; £230,000, she said—quite a major windfall for their family and much needed, since the cousin had retired. He asked what his dad's cousin had done for a living. "He was a milkman," his mother said.

Thomas had written his dream down and thus was able to have his family independently confirm the dream's highly improbable correspondence to what he later learned about his relative's stroke of good luck. He told me that this and a few other similar dreams have helped convince his wife, a scientist and natural skeptic, that the phenomenon of dream precognition is real and not fantasy. I would argue that he did, very much, "win the lottery"—but that his winnings were not money. They were an expanded sense of his own mind.

A dream journal kept for a month can be precious for what it reveals; a dream journal that spans years becomes priceless. That's something astronomer Paul Kalas could attest to. In 2008, Kalas made national headlines with the first picture of an extrasolar planet using

---

*A waiter in York, England, named Fatih Ozcan won a lawsuit in 2014 against his former manager at a Turkish restaurant, whom he claims purchased a winning lottery ticket after he (Ozcan) had dreamed the manager would win. Surveillance video showed Ozcan and his boss buying the ticket together, so the judged ruled that the boss needed to split the $1.7 million winnings with the dreamer (Moye 2014).

visible light, taken by the Hubble Space Telescope. The planet orbited the star Fomalhaut in a highly elliptical orbit and had been predicted by his own earlier discovery in 2004 of a very anomalous debris ring around the star. What was so unusual about the debris ring was that it was distinctly off-center with respect to the star. The only possible explanation for this anomaly was that a large planet with an elliptical orbit had cleared the debris closer to the star; its orbit would be found somewhere on that elliptical boundary. Thus, the debris ring led to finding the planet.

Fortunately for our purposes, Kalas's interest in inner space mirrored his interest in outer space; he had kept a dream diary for years. After his initial discovery of the off-center Fomalhaut debris ring in 2004, he looked at his dream journal and found that nine years earlier, almost to the day, he had written that he dreamed of seeing a picture of a debris ring around another star that he had been studying at the time (Beta Pictoris), and was "surprised at the circular structure; the star seems displaced relative to the center."[2] Above the text was a drawing that closely resembled the Hubble images later revealing the off-center debris ring around Fomalhaut.

In other words, Kalas seemed to have precognized one of his major career discoveries in a dream, exactly nine years beforehand. Calendrical resonances—dreams prefiguring an experience on the same or nearly the same date years later—are a frequent discovery in precognitive dreamwork, as we will see. This discovery led the astronomer to find other cases of dream precognition in his journals and to write about the topic of precognitive dreams in his book *The Oneironauts*.

RIVER LETHE

If you have spent any time at all thinking about time and what our culture teaches us it is supposed to be—"flowing" in a single direction, with events fixed in the past but open-ended and unpredictable in the future—then a precognitive dream is utterly verboten. It is a cause for cognitive dissonance. To avoid cognitive dissonance, most scientifically educated people who notice an uncannily specific correspondence between a dream and a later experience may puzzle over it briefly but will then boot it out of their memory. It's like there's a River Lethe that surrounds and washes anomalous experiences from our biographies. It happened to me too, as I'll be admitting with some chagrin when I describe my own learning curve about precognitive dreaming in part 1.

This forgetting is abetted by purveyors of scientific skepticism, self-appointed guardians of Enlightenment rationality. When faced with claims of precognitive dreams, skeptics argue that the mind, biased by hindsight and the eternal search for meaning, finds patterns in random noise. We misremember our dreams, they say, contorting them to fit later events. Or we disregard all the times our dreams don't seem to come true and then think it's remarkable that they occasionally do, even though statistics predict this should sometimes happen—known as the law of large numbers. Thus, when you do notice what appears to be a prophetic dream, skeptics say, it is just a statistical coincidence, or evidence of your own more-biased-than-you-know perceptions.[3]

While it is certainly true that humans are subject to biases, including expectations and cherry-picking evidence to support our preferred worldviews and beliefs, very little (if any) actual evidence has ever been marshaled to falsify or disprove precognitive dreaming. This is crucial to bear in mind the next time you hear the skeptical claim that the notion of prophetic dreams has been debunked. There are individual cases when ostensible prophetic dreams have been shown to be misreported or falsified—for instance, it's not true that Abraham Lincoln dreamed of seeing his own body laid out on a catafalque a week before his ill-fated visit to Ford's theater; the story was made up by one of Lincoln's bodyguards to sell to a newspaper after the assassination.[4] But most so-called debunking of psychic dreaming amounts to citing evidence that our memories *can* be distorted and our perceptions *can* be tricked, and that since we don't understand statistics, our estimates of the impossibility of coincidences are often wrong. A skeptic will then assert, circularly, that these kinds of cognitive fallibility must account for ESP claims, since to assert ESP really exists goes against science.[5]

It's really a kind of gaslighting. Saying that anything goes against science just because it violates our assumptions is actually what goes against science. As I hope to demonstrate in the chapters that follow, the skeptics' argument of last resort, the law of large numbers, goes right out the window when the astonishing frequency and regularity of precognitive dreams is taken honestly into account. Many, many people report having had dreams that come true: 17 percent to 38 percent in some surveys.[6] That number likely underrepresents the percentage who have such dreams, since most such dreams go unnoticed, and it is likely that most that are noticed are never reported. People don't trust their own perceptions, or they fear the ridicule of their families and peers. In the mid-1960s, when the writer J. B. Priestley solicited BBC viewers to send him precognitive dream experiences to discuss on a TV show, he was inundated with mail (receiving around 1,500 letters), and a common refrain—mostly from women, interestingly—was that their no-nonsense spouses refused to take their stories seriously.[7]

The dearth of public examples of the phenomenon perpetuates the silence. Nobody likes to feel like a kook or a freak. Consequently, a negative feedback loop keeps us largely unaware of dream precognition and the topic relegated to disreputable books on the paranormal and cautious divulgences to misfit writers at parties. That fear needs to be overcome in order to see clearly how common dream precognition is and then how to work with it, and so one of the purposes of this book is to banish that fear. When dreamers begin attending to their dreamlife by recording their dreams and looking for signs of precognition—doing precognitive dreamwork—they are generally astonished to find that their dreams really do accomplish the impossible: reach into their futures. And people who already notice precognitive dreams occasionally now notice them happening all the time.

Imagine being able to explore the hidden structure of spacetime itself using only a notebook, a pen, and a pillow. That is, quite honestly, what you're about to do. The great adventure of precognitive dreamwork is a journey of discovery that directly concerns what physicists in the shadow of Einstein have called the block universe. Your brain, it turns out, is the perfect instrument for studying aspects of our higher-dimensional reality, way more complex (yet way cheaper) than anything sent into orbit by NASA.

THE ORIGIN OF THIS BOOK

This book is the result of ten years of investigation of the precognitive dream phenomenon. I wrote it to help people. The more I spoke on the topic of precognition after the publication of my first book, *Time Loops,* the more I discovered that there is a large silent community of people out there—I don't know yet if they make up a majority, but I suspect they do—who have consciously had precognitive experiences, usually in dreams, which they don't know how to explain and are seriously perplexed by and sometimes are even fearful to talk about.

Sometimes they are amazed by their experience and, like Ray, would love to have it happen again. They may assume wrongly that it's not something in their power. Sometimes they are troubled. They may have had a premonition of a loved one's death and then felt like it was their fault or missed a premonitory warning until it was too late. (We will be dealing with these and other pitfalls of prescience—but to cut to the chase, no, it's not your fault if you dream of a tragedy that comes true, of if you fail to purchase winning lottery numbers you dreamed of, and there are important reasons why it can't be your fault.) So I saw there was a need for a kind of guide to answer common questions about precognitive dreaming and to reassure experiencers, as well as to help dreamers make the most of this dazzling feature of our God- or Nature-given brains.

In *Time Loops,* I showed a lot of scientific evidence for precognition and addressed the theoretical as well as the nuts-and-bolts, mechanistic questions of how it may work—interesting to nerds. Space limitations prevented me from delving too deeply into dreams and dream interpretation. I also wanted to omit conclusions about precognition that had been derived mainly from my own experiences as a dreamer; it was important to argue from published evidence that readers could examine for themselves to draw their own conclusions. This book is a lot less technical and a lot more personal. It draws not only from published accounts and dreams sent to me by readers of my book and my blog *The Nightshirt,* but also from my own dreams. In fact, I will set the stage in part 1 by describing my own path from semi-skepticism toward astonishment and finally to acceptance of the reality of precognition—my "precog's progress"—through some of my own early experiences with precognitive dreaming. My first priority is to inspire readers to explore the topic of precognitive dreamwork on their own, so I need to demonstrate how easy and rewarding it is. I also think the process by which we arrive at our conclusions reveals a lot about the quality of our thought and our sincerity. By showing my work, I want to impress on any skeptics daring to read this that they can no longer dismiss this subject as mere credulity, superstition, and bias. I also think being open invites discussion and debate.

All of the principles of precognitive dreamwork I list in this book (they are assembled in an appendix) are conclusions I can confidently make based on my experience and study so far, but they are not etched in stone and they are not exhaustive. I welcome alternative interpretations—collegial push-back and discussion among dreamers is the only way progress is going to be made around this topic. We are a long way from fully knowing the rules of precognitive dreaming with anything approaching certainty. Join me in helping map this unexplored and uncharted landscape.

The core argument of this book goes well beyond what is asserted in many popular books on ESP. Namely, precognition is not some rare and extraordinary occurrence that only signals us about catastrophes or major upheavals, nor is it a rare talent possessed by just a few among us. Instead, precognitive dreams are common, probably nightly affairs that go almost entirely unnoticed for a number of interesting reasons.

Contrary to a common belief, precognitive dreams are seldom "numinous"—they don't announce themselves. And they are also imperfect—they are very rarely video-quality. Paul Kalas's dream, seemingly precognitive of his Fomalhaut debris-ring discovery, was uncannily specific in certain respects, but it also had the elements of imprecision and displacement that caught Sigmund Freud's attention a century earlier in his writings on dreams. In Kalas's dream, the anomalous star was different from the one in real life; in the dream, he viewed the picture in the office of a colleague, which was not the case when viewing the actual Hubble picture; and so on. As in Thomas's dream about a lottery win in his family or Valerie's dream about the burglary of her parents' home, the similarity between Kalas's 1995 dream and his 2004 discovery was (as he argued, and as I would argue) too precise to chalk up to the coincidence or retroactive force-fitting that skeptics assume must be operative. But if information really was refluxing from his future into his past, there was also some funny kind of distortion at work.

Those distortions, and other related peculiarities of dreaming that interested Freud, are the subject of part 2. They contribute to our overlooking the vast majority of our precognitive dreams. One irony is that Freud himself, who firmly disbelieved in the possibility of dreams foretelling future events, seems to have precognized one of the most important upheavals in his later life in the very dream that prompted him to write about dreams in the first place. It's a mindbogglingly loopy business, precognitive dreaming and dreamwork, so buckle up.

One of the loopiest aspects of the topic is that events foreshadowed in dreams are often brought about by our own actions, sometimes in response to the dream. The chicken-and-egg quality of such experiences has led some to think these occurrences fall outside the realm of physical causation altogether. Carl Jung famously argued that dreams confirmed by subsequent events are symptomatic of the "acausal connecting principle" he dubbed synchronicity.[8] His writings have been powerfully influential in getting generations of readers to pay attention to remarkable alignments between their mind and the outer world. The downside has been that his theory has caused dreamers to overlook or minimize their own role in bringing about these alignments, seeing these meaningful coincidences as orchestrated by timeless archetypes or else as communications from some discarnate intelligence. We will address

Jung's ideas and the interesting role he plays in the story of precognitive dreamwork in part 3.

The most perplexing kinds of precognitive experiences are premonitions of death and disaster. Although much less common than precognitive dreams about more trivial occurrences, disaster premonitions generate the biggest questions. If the future already exists in some way that enables us to get a preview or warning about an event, then does that mean the event is not subject to change? Do precognitive experiences doom us to have the experiences precognized? Are we responsible (or perhaps, pre-sponsible) if we foresee some negative outcome and fail to prevent it? In part 4, we will grapple with premonitions, fate, and what our precognitive ability means for our cherished beliefs about free will.

Other books have invited readers to explore their psychic side through dreaming, but this book aims to be the first comprehensive guide to identifying and working with precognitive dreams that is grounded in a coherent theory of precognition and how it works. It covers several topics that have never before, to my knowledge, been covered in such a book, including why dreams about future experiences are often distorted and what those distortions mean; how precognitive dreams relate to memory; how to detect precognitive dreams through free association; why dreams sometimes bundle multiple future experiences together in a single narrative; and why, contrary to most writings on the subject, precognitive dreams show us our future thoughts about actual experiences rather than possible or probabilistic life options subject to change. ESP is often likened to radar scanning the future for dangers, but I'll be trying to convince you throughout this book that this is a misleading metaphor, one that reinforces a false picture of how precognition really operates. It's way, way weirder than radar.

Here's the first of many spoiler alerts: precognition is not (at least not mainly) about getting rich in the lottery or in Las Vegas. Dreams tend to come true in ways we can't anticipate—if you dream about winning the lottery, you might be wrong about exactly who wins, as Thomas found. The rewards of precognitive dreamwork are much bigger than material riches, though. Precognitive dreamwork can enrich our relationships to other people, for one thing—friends, family, even complete strangers. Even bigger are the spiritual rewards. Precognition is a new *gnosis,* a path of insight, one that connects us with our higher—although I prefer to say *longer*—Self.

We humans are vastly more than we imagine when we think we are just our consciousness at the present moment, severed from a past that is lost to oblivion and facing a completely unknown and indeterminate future. Precognitive dreamwork is the most powerful—and fastest—way to get acquainted with your Long Self. Think of a video editing program, with your life as a ribbon of frames that your consciousness scrolls across from left to right. Your whole life, birth to death, is speaking to and through your narrow, conscious "cursor self" right now. Dreaming is the doorway—the royal road as Freud would call it—to a greatly expanded sense of your life on Earth—seeing that whole timeline rather than the myopic now that typically dominates our attention.

There's an even more mind-bending implication of all this that we'll be addressing in part 5: if you are able to be influenced by some future experience via a dream—even just one that you took a minute out of your morning to write down—then by extension, present dreamworthy thoughts and experiences shape your past. Let that sink in a moment: your present thoughts and experiences shape your past. Consequently, the business of keeping an annotated dream diary lays the foundation for an even more sublime autobiographical project that I have come to call precognitive lifework: the reexamination and reexploration of one's own life in light of the trans-temporal wormholes, i.e., our dreams, that transect it and periodically bring us face to face with our younger and older selves. It's a process that actually makes our prior history through self-discovery, and one emotion in particular—amazement—may be the motor of this self-creation. In the process of examining this possibility, we will delve into various unexpected and amazing curiosities of the precognitive dreamworld such as time gimmicks, symbols of precognition within a dream.

If you win the lottery or otherwise get rich because of the principles in this book, fantastic—and please tell me about it. (My email can be found below.) But I believe the biggest rewards of precognitive dreamwork do not come with a dollar value. Besides giving you impossible, oblique glimpses of where you're going, precognitive dreamwork radically expands your understanding of who you already are and how you got to this point in your life's path. It's (ironically) as much a retrospective as a prospective endeavor. In fact, I'll be comparing it to a kind of archaeology, or even paleontology, of your life story.

Lastly, in part 6, we will explore precognition in altered states of dreaming such as sleep paralysis, lucid dreams, and out-of-body experiences. We will also explore some of the ways we can tap into our precognition in waking life, through liminal states such as hypnagogia, active imagination, meditation, and creativity. These are games for advanced players, but the rewards for the persistent are transformative.

WELCOME, TRAVELER

Science says precognition is impossible, yet it is as real and as common as breathing. That flushing in your face, that catch in your breath, is the feeling and the sound of cognitive dissonance gripping you. Let it arise, and also watch as it passes away. You will then have to face the fact that much of what mainstream psychology has told us, or just assumed, about the workings of the mind-brain will have to be revised in the coming decades. So will our understanding of time and causation. It doesn't mean psychology as we know it is dead, nor physics. It means there's a lot of work ahead, and some old assumptions will need to be jettisoned. It's time for a housecleaning. That's a normal part of science—part of all domains of human knowledge, in fact—and it's a good thing.

You can help. A growing army of precognitive dreamworkers able to wave their fat dream diaries in skeptics' faces is what might, in the end, change the culture and the conversation around precognition and ESP more generally, thereby leading to a revolution in how we view the mind. This book tells you how to create your own precognitive dream corpus, and why that corpus is in fact, quite literally, a time machine.

When I was a kid, I dreamed of building a time-traveling spaceship (or space-traveling timeship?) out of the junk in my parents' basement. A few years ago, when I looked at my binders full of dreams, full of symbols of my past and childhood, but many of them starred or with strings of exclamation points in the margins because they turned out to refer to experiences *after* the dreams, I realized that I'd built that ship. It wasn't sleek and metallic, nor a steampunk clockwork contraption like in H. G. Wells, but it was a time machine all the same. I'm still adding to it, and I'm still learning how to navigate the depths and shoals of my life with it.

This book is for the dreamers, to help you build your own space-timeship. If you don't think of yourself as a dreamer or a "precog" yet, I hope and expect that by following the guidance in this book, you will awaken to what you always were. In fact, I'd like to preemptively welcome you to your future, where you are already a precog with a fat notebook full of time-defying dreams under your belt.

AN INVITATION TO THE DREAMER

I am always eager to hear precognitive dream stories, and I am especially eager to hear readers' results following the guidance in this book. Please email me your experiences at eric.wargo@gmail.com. (Confidentiality is ensured.)

PART I

A PRECOG'S PROGRESS

1
Unmanned
My Psychic Due Diligence

On the morning of September 11, 2001, my alarm awoke me around six o'clock. Before rising from bed, I rolled over, groggily reached for my notebook and pen, and scribbled a few notes on the only dream I could remember from the night before.

In the dream, I was driving past a pair of identical, single-story, perfectly square buildings on a street near where I grew up in Lakewood, Colorado. They had gray steel lattice- or corduroy-like facades, and I thought that, despite their ugly, drab appearance, they were possibly mosques. There was another, identical, third mosque some distance away down the street, almost like an afterthought. Like many dreams, I was both in the setting and narrating it to someone after the fact. I wrote in my notebook that I was describing these mosques to a very skeptical high school friend who was annoyed somehow at my story, but I held firm that "I'm telling it like it is."

That was it. That was all I could remember . . . but I wrote it down.

I had no association with the "mosques" in my dream. Islam was not on my radar at all at that point in my life. I did however have a powerful memory associated with their setting. On the stretch of street where the dream-mosques were situated, there is in reality a one-story medical office building built in the 1960s or early 1970s. About twenty years before this dream, my father had briefly had his clinical psychology

16

practice in that building before moving his office to a larger bank building nearby. Late one rainy night, my father had to go to that office to
meet a client of his who was having a suicidal crisis. My father's sharing
this fact the next morning remains a vivid memory, as it is the only time
I was ever aware of him needing to counsel a client after hours or give
support to someone contemplating suicide.

The low one-story-ness of the "mosques" in the dream was also
notable. My dreams have periodically featured distinctly low buildings
(i.e., the opposite of tall buildings) as well as ruined towers, which a
decade or more of reading in Freudian dream symbolism had suggested
were symbolic of castration. Men frequently have anxiety dreams about
threats to their masculinity or power, so these distinctly low buildings
of Islamic worship seemed to me, with just a moment's free association,
like castration symbols. Thus, the ideas of castration, suicide, and crisis
were all folded into my associations to these buildings.

I was then living in Vienna, Virginia, a moderate commute by train
to nearby Washington, DC, where I had just started a new editing job
for a small nonprofit. In fact, my then-wife and I had only moved to
Virginia from Georgia, where I had been finishing my Ph.D., a week
and a half earlier, on September 1.

It was a couple hours after my dream and less than an hour after I
had sat down to work at my office that the suicide attacks in my city
and Manhattan began to unfold. I first heard about them when my wife
called me on the phone frantically, saying, "They're crashing planes into
buildings!" I pictured an out-of-control Cessna hitting a bank. A few
minutes later, my coworkers started gathering around the small television in the office, and we watched stunned as CNN showed replays of
the second jetliner crashing into the South Tower of the World Trade
Center. We stood aghast as the smoldering towers collapsed, one by one,
in pillars of gray smoke. (Since I did not yet feel like I worked in the
nation's capital, I did not immediately process that the attack on the
Pentagon also being reported had occurred about five miles south of my
office, which was in the northwest DC neighborhood of Tenleytown.)
Already, as the tragedy played out before us, the CNN chatter included

talk of Al-Qaeda, the Islamic terrorist group that had threatened such attacks on American soil.

It was only some time later, probably the next day, that I saw my dream notes from the morning before the attacks and noted the weird, albeit oblique associations to the terror attacks. I was not yet accustomed to looking for precognitive material in my dreams—at that point, I didn't even know precognitive dreaming was a thing. And my dream was not some unmistakably literal premonition like you might read about in a typical ESP book. I didn't dream of planes crashing into buildings, for instance, or specifically of a terror attack in Manhattan. (I later learned that many, many people did report such dreams, however.[1]) Yet I found it weirdly coincidental that the dream had contained a pair of identical, square-floorplan buildings, side by side, with gray facades exactly like the distinctive corrugated facades of the Twin Towers; that there was a third, similar building some distance away;* that the buildings were associated with Islam;† and that, though not ruined, they seemed somehow like they had been brought low via castration, in a dream setting I specifically associated with suicide. If there is anything the suicide attacks of that day felt like, it was as a castration of the United States.

NO TELEOLOGY

Historically and in almost every culture on Earth, people have imputed significance to some if not all dreams, regarding them as portents of future events, as messages from the gods or spirits, as indicators of our spiritual or physical well-being, or as a kind of semaphore represent-

---

*I am thinking of the Pentagon as the likely precognitive referent here, although one will recall that a third building of the World Trade Center, Building Seven, also collapsed, although I cannot recall whether I became aware of this on the day of the disaster.

†Since I had been recording my dreams electronically for several years at that point, I was able to verify that I had never before dreamed of mosques, nor for that matter anything with Islamic overtones. This was confirmed by doing a word search for *Islam, mosque, Muslim,* and *Koran.*

ing thoughts or feelings we are not aware of in waking life. Freud, the great psychiatric dream pioneer, took the latter view: that dreams represent our unconscious thoughts and feelings—feelings that, when denied, can make us ill or deflect our behavior in strange and sometimes unpleasant ways.

In a nutshell, Freud's theory was that dreams used symbolic disguises to represent our anxieties as well as to fulfill wishes we have repressed. On the basis of recording and analyzing many of his own and his patients' dreams, Freud argued that the "manifest content" we remember of a dream conceals a latent thought or thoughts, disguised by the operations of displacement—an object standing or substituting for another object—and condensation—dream elements containing multiple meanings.[2] The way to uncover these operations and restore the original meaning in the dream was to free associate about it—that is, to reflect honestly on what each noticed element, character, situation, and so on called to mind.

Freud's 1899 book, *The Interpretation of Dreams*, where he lays out this approach in detail along with his theoretical rationale, was a heroic attempt to reconcile the universal folk wisdom that dreams are meaningful with the then-new scientific study of mental processes. It was to turn-of-the-century psychiatry what Einstein's papers on the special theory of relativity were to turn-of-the-century physics and what Darwin's *On the Origin of Species* had been to biology four decades earlier. *Scientific* needs an asterisk by it in Freud's case, however, because most of today's sleep researchers and neuroscientists would not consider Freud's approach scientific—we'll see why later.

Freud has sometimes been presented as a skeptic on all things psychical—he famously argued with his protégé Carl Jung about psychic phenomena, for instance—but the real story is more complicated. Privately, Freud was curious and open-minded about many "occult" phenomena like telepathy and even wrote about them late in his career. Some of his patients described dreams or manifested verbal slips that seemed to reflect some kind of mind-to-mind contact. But one thing the doctor could not accept was any form of foreknowledge not rooted in ordinary inference. If his theories pushed the envelope of what science would admit into its purview, such as the meaningful constructions of the unconscious mind or the latent sexual basis of many of our thoughts and motivations, he still would not buck scientific orthodoxy by pushing against rule numero uno of the Enlightenment: effects cannot precede their cause. You can call this the no-teleology rule—teleology being an old term for what physicists now call retrocausation.

Isaac Newton and his Enlightenment friends had a very sensible reason for banishing teleology, or any influence from the future of a system on its past. Any idea of a system's purposiveness was, in that more religious time, assumed to be a function of God and His divine plan. So to create science as we now know it, it was important to be resolute: it's no fair to bring God in; you need to account for as much of nature as possible without invoking miracles. Whatever we may think of the no-teleology rule and the materialist scientific paradigm it produced—I'll certainly be challenging it (or stretching it) in this book—we must honor it here at the outset. We have materialism to thank for all of the advances of science in the past three centuries. The electricity that powers our homes and cities, the medical miracles that keep many people alive into their eighties and nineties, the robots that explore the solar system, and so on and so on (and yes, some bad things too, like atomic bombs), all were made possible by the scientific method and its refusal to yield on this issue of teleology and the divine purpose teleology seemed to imply.

This is where Freud was coming from. An alleged premonitory dream seemed like it could only be an effect (the dream) preceding its cause (the foreseen event) in time, and thus smacked of the supernatural, which by definition has no place in nature. So Freud was happy to dismiss cases of ostensible dream premonitions as faulty memory or construction of a false dream memory after the fact—similar to the debunking tactics still relied on by most skeptics. For example, in an 1899 paper "A Premonitory Dream Fulfilled," he debunked the claim by a female patient, Frau B., that she had dreamed of encountering an old friend in front of a certain Vienna shop on the night before that encounter actually happened. She was, he authoritatively explained, really dreaming of her lover, who happened to have the same initials as her old friend. After encountering her old friend in the street, Freud explained, her unconscious distorted her memory of the dream. In that more gender-unequal time, Frau B. was, Freud wrote, "obliged" to accept his causally kosher reinterpretation of her experience "without raising any objection to it"[3]; unfortunately, we have no record of what she really thought.[4]

Freud did not even address ostensible precognitive dreams in *The Interpretation of Dreams,* so unworthy of scientific attention were they. Instead, he resolutely insisted that to find the repressed wishes he thought dreams represented, we can only look in the individual's recent or more distant past. Even though later writers and thinkers in Freud's tradition nuanced and modified the psychoanalytic approach to dream interpretation in various ways, they mostly continued to direct our attention to the past, either to the individual's personal past or to the collective cultural past—for instance, Jung's archetypes of the collective unconscious. We'll be circling back to both of these important dream pioneers, Freud and Jung, later.

HEAD IN THE SAND

I had been keeping a dream journal pretty systematically for about six years by that day in September 2001, and my interest in dreams was largely framed by Freudian dream interpretation and its major offshoot, Jungian dreamwork. At that point, I was also beginning to think about dreams' possible relationship to memory—a topic we'll also be coming back to, but again, pointing presumably only to past experiences. I thus simply had no mental category for any kind of dream that went in the wrong direction by (seemingly) foreshadowing a future event or experience in my life. Like most scientifically educated people, I was fundamentally and unthinkingly in agreement with the no-teleology rule. That an event could cause or influence something coming before it, such as a dream, was simply beyond the bounds of rational consideration.

So I swept that dream under my mental rug. I didn't yet know that there is a large and growing body of research, including sound scientific research, both on precognition and on the physics of retrocausation that would make it possible.

And I was a slow learner, because the same pattern happened on a few other occasions over the subsequent decade: I would notice an uncanny correspondence between a dream and an experience the next day, and each time it happened, I treated the dream with the same mildly curious but ultimately disinterested "ignoral" as I did after my dream on 9/11. This was facilitated by the fact that, on every other occasion, the experience seemingly foreshadowed in my dream was far less momentous or horrible than a terror attack. It's one thing to imagine that especially terrible events, such as massive death and destruction, could ripple backward in time somehow to brush some mysterious psychic antennae—such premonitions are at least staples in folklore. It's another thing to think our dreams might bring us previews of objectively mundane experiences like a phone call at work.

One morning in 2008, I dreamed that a former coworker of mine was going to be interviewed on a major radio program. In the dream, I was jealous, because he was going to be interviewed on a topic that I, not he, was expert in. Later that same morning, I got a call from an NPR (National Public Radio) reporter asking to interview me about an article I'd recently written about a new study that had just been published. I was then an editor at a professional organization of scientific psychologists, and I often summarized new findings in our organization's magazine. This was the first time I had ever been approached by the media for an interview, but while I was initially excited at the prospect of being on the radio, I had to decline the offer: I had not actually conducted the research, and to really understand the findings, the reporter would need to talk to the psychologist who had done the study.

The real situation was strictly a mirror image to the one in my dream, yet it was still uncannily similar, and it was about a type of occurrence (being sought out by the media) that was totally unfamiliar to me at that point in my life. But as on 9/11, I just noted this weird coincidence between the dream and the circumstance the following day, puzzled over it for a while, and then paid it little more attention. Remember that River Lethe I mentioned? It's a real thing. And this, from someone (me) who claimed to be interested in dreams and who had even kept a detailed electronic dream journal for well over a decade! Consider this book my penance for having kept my head in the sand for so long.

THE ROYAL ROAD TO RIDICULE

It was an article in *The Journal of Personality and Social Psychology* in 2011 that pulled my head out of that sand a little bit, and launched me on the ten-year journey that led to the book you now hold in your hands. The article itself had nothing to do with dreams, but its larger implications for dreams were obvious.

The article was called "Feeling the Future: Experimental Evidence for Anomalous Retroactive Influences on Cognition and Affect," and its author was a well-known psychologist at Cornell University named Daryl Bem. It presented the findings of a series of experiments Bem had conducted with a large participant pool of Cornell undergraduates over the course of several years. By ingeniously reversing the usual order of stimulus and response in a set of psychological protocols—putting the response *before* the stimulus instead of after—he showed that the behavior of the participants appeared to be affected slightly but significantly by stimuli that were randomly chosen and presented to them later—a series of apparent causality-defying and temporality-defying findings.[5] For instance, participants scored better on a word-recall test if they studied the word list *after* they took the test. In his most publicity- (and joke-) worthy experiment, participants were more accurate at guessing which of two curtains on a computer screen had a picture behind it if the picture turned out to be erotic, rather than something bland and unexciting. (The pictures were randomly selected by the computer after the participants made their choices—there was not anything yet behind the curtains.)

Such findings usually only ever see the light of print in small journals devoted to parapsychology that mainstream psychologists never read and probably don't even know about, but this paper by Bem appeared in one of the highest-ranking journals in the field, and reactions verged on apoplexy. If ESP rankles some scientifically minded people, it *most* rankles scientific psychologists, who (I was discovering) harbor an almost violent hostility toward the topic.*

Colleagues at the psychology organization where I worked were considering writing a complaint to the editors of the *Journal of Personality and Social Psychology* protesting the publication of Bem's "Feeling the Future." They felt that such findings, being preposterous, should not sully the pages of any journal in the field, let alone one of the top-ranked psychological science journals. Bem had been a maverick all his life, so he was probably untroubled by the response he was getting—I'm sure he expected or even welcomed the controversy. But to me it was a shock, and an education: I was learning that ESP is the royal road to ridicule, and it triggered in me a natural underdog alert that goes off whenever I sense someone with a radical and original idea being bullied by an organized and dogmatic opposition.

At that point, I knew very little about parapsychology or the rather large body of evidence for time-defying psychological effects that had already been accumulated by several other scientists. What I did know was that it went against the spirit of scientific inquiry to reject or ridicule any finding solely on the basis of one's prior beliefs and assumptions. Bem's paper had passed peer review, the ritual that scientific consensus decrees is the needed filter for new findings. Isn't science about constantly testing our assumptions and being open to changing our minds when new evidence challenges those assumptions? So I quietly began my due diligence in reading more about a topic that, while impossible-sounding on one hand, was also undeniably intriguing.

---

*A 1979 survey of 1,188 U.S. college professors across the natural and social sciences and the humanities found psychologists to be the most psi-skeptical (Wagner and Monnet 1979).

IS ESP REAL?

I learned that since the 1930s, parapsychologists at Duke University,[6] and then later at Princeton University[7] and private think tanks like Stanford Research Institute (SRI) in Menlo Park, California, as well as at other small labs across the United States and around the world, have amassed statistically overwhelming evidence of extrasensory perception or ESP, a term encompassing not only precognition (seeing or knowing events in the future) but also telepathy (mind-to-mind communication) and clairvoyance (seeing things that are hidden or at a distance). Some of the most compelling evidence for ESP was gathered in the 1970s by CIA- and Department of Defense-funded researchers at SRI, who developed a clairvoyant modality called remote viewing and went on to train military personnel to psychically spy on Soviet weapons development, locate downed airplanes, and probe the location and health of hostages during the last decade of the Cold War—the storied Project Star Gate.* But despite some brilliant successes, the researchers never figured out how remote viewing works, and in the end Project Star Gate could not withstand the skepticism it attracted from certain factions in government. The program officially ended in 1995, due largely to an increasingly ESP-hostile, fundamentalist Christian climate in the military. (Many literally saw it as demonic.[8])

I also learned that there is particularly strong scientific support for precognition. Studies in what is called precognitive remote viewing, for example, show that participants can describe pictures they haven't yet seen and that haven't even been selected yet by the experimenter with a much greater degree of accuracy than chance would predict. An especially interesting variant of precognition is presentiment, or "future feeling": in the mid-1990s, an engineer at the University of Arizona named Dean Radin conducted experiments in which he found

---

*The results of this work were declassified in 1995, and since then, many of the people involved have written detailed accounts. See May, Rubel, and Auerbach 2014; Smith 2005; Schnabel 1997; Targ 2004. The Soviets, we now know, were engaged in similar research, with similarly striking results (see May, Rubel, and Auerbach 2014).

autonomic responses in participants like changes in heart rate and skin electrical conductivity in advance of arousing stimuli.[9] Radin and several other researchers have found that experiment participants physically react to loud noises, randomly selected disturbing or arousing pictures (versus neutral pictures), or other stimuli fractions of a second, or in some cases a few seconds, beforehand. These experiments had paved the way for Bem's studies. More recently, inspired partly by Bem, researchers like Northwestern University neuroscientist Julia Mossbridge have reported finding behavioral pre-sponses to stimuli as much as ten seconds in advance.[10]

Meta-analyses assessing the strength of the evidence across multiple studies, even accounting for the so-called file-drawer problem, the tendency of negative results to go unpublished, show high, often astronomically high, statistical significance for the existence of precognition[11] and presentiment.[12] A meta-analysis by a team that included a UC Davis statistician concluded that "psychic functioning has been well established. The results of the studies examined are far beyond what is expected by chance. Arguments that these results could be due to methodological flaws in the experiments are soundly refuted."[13] Some have even argued that other forms of ESP like clairvoyance or remote viewing are really disguised forms of precognition—for instance, previewing feedback that will be received after the experiment, rather than seeing something that is really happening at a distance. I find this argument compelling, for reasons we will see later.

Yet the claim that there is no laboratory evidence for ESP is one of those memes that is rehearsed endlessly by skeptics with a stake in discrediting the field, goes unquestioned by the public who have no basis to doubt the skeptics' claims, and thus gets reinforced year after year. Psych 101 textbooks may relegate parapsychology to a short section on pseudoscience, as an object lesson on the pitfalls of careless thinking and various forms of experimenter bias, such as the tendency for researchers to produce results that accord with their beliefs or expectations. The student is assured that ESP (mockingly held to stand for "error some place") has never been demonstrated in the lab, that its claimants are frauds or are sadly self-deceived, and that its very premises belong to an older, more superstitious age.* The meme stays in the picture.

It would be too simplistic to accuse all skeptics of dogmatic closed-mindedness or chalk up their psychic skepticism to blind adherence to the materialistic paradigm. What people like my psychologist colleagues see in their mind's eye when they hear "ESP" is not earnest inquiry into an exciting and mostly unexplored dimension of human functioning but, rather, a little old lady being scammed out of her meager pension by a quack faith healer, or devastated parents giving up hope for finding a missing child because a TV psychic erroneously said she was dead (a weirdly repeated pattern in the career of the late TV psychic Sylvia Browne[14]). Skeptics see themselves as society's immune system against trickery and exploitation of the gullible. They also see themselves as champions of rigor in a field—science—that like any other has its careless and occasionally outright deceptive practitioners.

The recent replication crisis in psychology, for instance, arises from a growing awareness that much of what has been published in major journals over the last few decades is subpar science. Many exciting psychological findings that make brief splashes in the popular press and get disseminated in TED talks go on to be quietly debunked a few years later. Because it seemed so preposterous to so many psychologists, Bem's article was catalytic in sparking a movement toward greater openness about methods and toward publication of negative, not just positive, results. The irony in all of it is that Bem's own studies seem to have replicated well, despite some skeptics' early claims to the contrary. In 2015, Bem and his colleagues conducted a meta-analysis of ninety studies, from thirty-three laboratories in fourteen countries, that had sought to replicate the findings in his controversial 2011 paper, and found overwhelming—in most cases, decisive—support for the precognition effects he described. The odds against getting these results by

---

*William James, an influential early psychologist and thinker, himself actively researched psychic phenomena and remained committed to their reality his whole life, a constant embarrassment for modern scientific psychologists who regard James as one of the founding fathers of their discipline.

chance were estimated at over a billion to one, with a negligible probability that it could be an effect of negative experimental results being unpublished.[15]

More research is needed—more research is always needed—but ESP, in at least some forms, is real.

WHAT ABOUT THE PHYSICS?

Another thing I quickly learned in my journey researching precognition was that the Enlightenment's no-teleology rule has been on the ropes for a long time among physics's deepest thinkers. Just in the past two decades, some truly mind-bending experiments have been conducted that reveal causality to be way weirder than we ordinarily suppose, at least on very small scales. Interacting with a photon during a measurement can actually influence the photon's prior properties, for example.[16] Research in the nascent field of quantum information theory is showing that causal order can be indefinite and information can even be sent backward in time in the mysterious guts of a quantum computer. As I was finishing this book, a team at the Moscow Institute of Physics and Technology reported they had effectively "reversed time" using a public quantum computer program available from IBM.[17] Playing with time and causation is a major frontier in quantum computing research, with extraordinary potential technical applications.

As a parallel, there is growing evidence from the burgeoning field of quantum biology that our brains could have quantum computing properties, scaling up these spooky characteristics of the microworld of photons and atoms and subatomic particles. Even if we don't yet know exactly how the trick is done, it is looking increasingly plausible from a physical and biological standpoint that quantum computing at the molecular level could enable neurons to get information about their own future activation, and thus that animals may on some dim, preconscious level always be pre-sponding to stimuli ahead, just like the experiments of Bem or Radin suggest.[18] For instance, it would help explain Rupert Sheldrake's famous animal ESP experiments in which pets seem to know when their owners are coming home, and the like.[19]

It's still all very speculative, but just put yourself in Nature's shoes: if feeling the future is possible at all, then evolution surely, given billions of years, would have found a way to capitalize on such a valuable effect in a consistent fashion. The nervous system's ability to be influenced by experiences ahead in time, as I suggested in my book *Time Loops,* could be the basis of precognitive dreams. And donning the futurist hat I sometimes wear when I blog on edge-science topics at *The Nightshirt,* I even have a strong hunch that retrocausation will turn out to be the missing X factor behind some more basic mysteries in biology, including the arising of life from lifeless physical processes.[20] Retrocausation might not only allow the brain to communicate with itself—send itself messages—backward across the fourth dimension; it may turn out to be relevant to the survival of even the simplest living organisms.

Because they haven't received these memos about causality and the truly wild frontiers we are entering with quantum computing and quantum biology, skeptics still assume that precognition is a topic wholly belonging to the supernatural, to the disreputable world of back-alley fortune-tellers, and just generally to Carl Sagan's "demon-haunted world."[21] But we all know what happens when we assume. The evidence from experiments like Bem's, coupled with the science trends I outlined in my previous book, all point to a remarkable conclusion, one that has no place now in mainstream psychology but will likely have an important place there in the future: we are actually four-dimensional beings, and our behavior at any given moment is shaped not only by our past but also by what is yet to come. We are informed by our future. Parapsychology experiments may just show us the tip of the iceberg of how we—and all creatures—really inhabit time.

Dreams, I believe, show us a much bigger portion of that iceberg.

2
Vaal and Redemption

How a Star Trek *Episode Taught Me*
Memory Goes Backward

After the Star Gate program was closed and declassified in 1995, some of its guiding lights took their show on the road, teaching classes and workshops in remote viewing. Several have published memoirs as well as guidebooks teaching their methods.[1] Like many who get interested in psychic phenomena and ESP research, I also wanted to try my hand at it. Who isn't interested in finding out if they are psychic? So in the years after my semi-conversion experience reading Daryl Bem's "Feeling the Future," I devoured these guides and followed their instructions, interested to explore and exercise my own remote-viewing abilities.

Remote viewers love "protocols," so for an easy, beginner's protocol, I asked my wife to print out random pictures from the internet while she was at work during the day, seal them in envelopes, and set one on the table next to my bed each evening I wanted to do a trial. It is before sleep at night that it is easiest for me to relax into a hypnagogic state, when psychic flashes are liable to arise, so that was when I attempted to sketch my impressions of what was in the envelope.

I'll confess I had very few hits doing this at first. Not to be discouraged, though, I followed the advice of one remote-viewing pioneer, Dale Graff, who had been Project Director for Star Gate and had written two excellent books about his experiences incorporating dreams into his remote-viewing practice.[2] Instead of going ahead and opening the envelope right after trying to psychically peer inside it, I waited until the next morning to see if my dreams might have delivered useful images or information overnight. This produced interesting and, in a couple cases, amazing results.

My first attempt was the most striking of the lot. Late on a Friday evening, I meditated in bed and imagined the scene of opening the brown envelope over breakfast. Then in the morning, I arose and groggily jotted a few notes on the main dream I could recall from the night before: something about a lush, green, idyllic landscape that was somehow maintained by an advanced futuristic technology. In this landscape dwelled a group of people of very strange or unfamiliar ethnicity. This detail was significant enough that I wrote it down, describing them as "dark skinned but not Black/African." It was also significant that they were reluctant to leave their Eden, despite the urging of an affable, white, heroic military man. That man was communicating by phone to some ship that was under attack—I pictured a sea-vessel on fire some distance away at an ocean port or harbor. There was also a vivid scene of two of the people, a man and a woman, facing each other at close distance, gazing into each other's eyes almost theatrically, as if they were about to sing a duet.

Over breakfast, I opened the envelope to reveal a picture of a pair of hands in a palms-up gesture nearly touching at the wrists. Initially, it seemed to bear zero resemblance to my dream, so I chalked it up as another remote-viewing failure. However, there was something familiar about the picture. What came to mind was the nearly identical gesture of greeting used by the Polynesian-style natives in a *Star Trek* episode I remembered from my childhood, an episode (as I quickly found out via Google) called "The Apple."

Much of the original *Star Trek* series is burned into my neural wiring as a result of a childhood spent watching reruns of that series every afternoon after school during the 1970s. "The Apple" was a typical gnostic *Trek* episode from the show's second season, about an ancient planetary computer named Vaal that kept the inhabitants of its planet, Gamma Triguli VI, in an innocent and ignorant (but idyllic) state of nature. When commanded by Vaal, they brought offerings of fruit and placed them inside a stone serpent's head that served as a temple interface to this subterranean control system.

Although I had not seen this episode in well over three decades and couldn't remember most of the other specific details, a few elements from the show, including the natives' greeting, had always stuck with me, and my mild disappointment over a failed remote-viewing attempt gradually turned to interest and anticipation: the picture in the envelope triggered an association to that episode . . . and the themes of my dream also seemed connected to it.

It was Saturday and I had nothing more pressing, so I immediately streamed "The Apple" on my computer to refresh my memory. It was even campier than I remembered—Star Trek historian Marc Cushman likens it to the Enterprise visiting Gilligan's Island[3]—but I didn't care one bit. The major points of the episode matched very closely all the elements I recorded from my dream, including the idyllic landscape maintained by an invisible technology, the inhabitants who were reluctant to leave their Eden, and the predicament of an affable military commander (Kirk) communicating by "phone" (communicator) with a distant ship (the Enterprise) that was under attack. Strikingly, there was also a tender scene between two of the villagers, gazing into each other's eyes and wondering at the mystery of love—but in fact, looking for all the world like they were about to break into a duet.

The most specific match was the appearance of these natives: they were all clearly Caucasian actors, as was the norm in TV of the time, and all wore wigs of silvery-white hair, yet they were made up with deep bronze-orange tans. They were notably "dark skinned but not Black/African," just as I had recorded in my dream journal.

I need to note that in selecting the picture of the hands making the spreading palms-up gesture, my wife could not have anticipated any association to this Star Trek episode. Although she had been a fan of Star Trek: The Next Generation, she had never seen most episodes from the original series, and to this day has still never seen "The Apple." (Honestly, she's not missing much.)

LONELY ISLANDER

As I reveled in my strange, oblique dream-remote-viewing success and enjoyed watching "The Apple," I realized that what I'd been doing hadn't really been remote viewing at all, at least as the practice is ordinarily assumed to operate—and this is the point I want to make with that story. My dreaming mind hadn't peered into the shut envelope. Instead, it had picked up on the most emotionally salient event in the landscape of my near future: watching an old *Star Trek* episode in a state of eager excitement to confirm a psychic hit. The dream had been about precisely what I was *right then* doing, hours *after* the dream.

My second attempt at dream remote viewing, a few days later, followed the same pattern and the result was almost as striking. I placed another of my wife's sealed envelopes next to my bed and again mentally requested a dream about what was inside it. I woke up the next morning and recorded some images of a sandy cave with some artifacts, including a long object that seemed to be a bone flute. After breakfast that morning, I drew from the envelope a photograph of an enormous white dog sitting next to a teenage girl in front of a warehouse—again, seemingly nothing to do with my dream. But again, just a moment's free association on the picture came to the rescue.

The picture immediately called to mind a memory of a book I hadn't read since my childhood: *Island of the Blue Dolphins,* by Scott O'Dell. Unlike "The Apple," I couldn't remember O'Dell's story very well at all—just that it was about a Native American girl who fended for herself and her canine companion for years after being abandoned on an island in the Pacific. But I'd never forgotten the cover of the Dell paperback from the 1970s, which showed the girl standing and holding a spear with the big white dog sitting beside her.

A quick Google search was able to confirm my recollection of the book's cover and publisher. (As a bibliophile, I've got some kind of sixth sense when it comes to publishers and book cover art.) I was also able to read part of the book online, and one of the first scenes I read—which I had not remembered at all from childhood—was about the girl,

Karana, and her dog, Rontu, being trapped overnight in a spooky cave that contained idols and a skeleton of one of her ancestors. The skeleton was holding a pelican-bone flute.

So here again, it was a distinct hit from my dream. And, despite my conscious intention to peer directly into a closed envelope and see what was inside it, my dream had showed me instead a surprising and rewarding reading experience the next morning, one that had been stimulated by the target of that remote-viewing attempt.*

A skeptic would likely try to claim that my watching "The Apple" and my reading a random chapter or two from *The Island of the Blue Dolphins* on the mornings after my dreams were only an effect of those dreams and not their cause. They might point out that, at least in the *Star Trek* case, my dream images could have been drawn from memory since I had remembered many aspects of the episode from my childhood, and even could suggest reasonably that the scene of Karana and Rontu in the cave with the bone-flute-playing skeleton had somehow been retained in my unconscious for nearly a half century (called cryptomnesia—consciously forgotten but unconsciously remembered details encountered earlier in life). But that would leave unexplained why I specifically had those two dreams when I did—in each case, on the night before a previously unseen picture drawn from an envelope made me think of that TV episode and that book for the first time in decades.

Subsequent experiences replicated this pattern: when attempting to remote view a target using my dreams, my dream sometimes contained objects or themes that associated to what I did in the process of interpreting my results, not (directly) to the image in the envelope. In short, I wasn't perceiving anything, either with the senses or with any

---

*I quickly ordered O'Dell's novel on eBay, with the cover that I remembered, because honoring psychic successes is important—a topic we'll return to. eBay gets a lot of money from me honoring psychic hits connected to old books. I subsequently became mildly obsessed with the true story of the Nicoleño woman Juana Maria (the basis for Karana) and the archaeological investigations on San Nicolas Island, which centered on a sand-filled cave.

extrasensory faculty. What it seemed to be was something more like memory, but in the wrong direction.

These experiences did more than help confirm for me the reality of psychic functioning. They also taught me a lot about the counter-intuitive way dream precognition (and, I would argue, remote viewing) really works.

UNSTUCK IN TIME

The first investigator to figure out that something like "memory for things future" was at the heart of psychic dreams was John William Dunne, an English soldier turned aeronautical engineer in the first decades of the twentieth century. Dunne was not a scientist by train-ing, but he became interested in questions of time and consciousness as a young man after observing many instances when his dreams seemed confirmed by things he saw or learned shortly thereafter. Often, they were things he soon read about in the news.

For instance, in 1901, after a stint fighting in the Boer War, Dunne contracted typhoid fever and needed to convalesce in a hospital on the Italian Riviera. While there, he dreamed of being in a village near Khartoum, in the Sudan, and encountering three deeply tanned white men dressed in attire he associated with colonists from the south of the continent. In the dream, he wondered how they had gotten all the way to the Sudan in the north. The next morning's paper brought him news of a cross-country trek by a group of three colonists from the southern tip of Africa all the way to Khartoum—the first time such a journey had been made by white men.[4]

Dunne's most famous precognitive dream was one he had while he was back in the South African bush fighting with his regiment the fol-lowing year. He dreamed that a volcano on some French-speaking island was about to erupt, and that 4,000 people were about to die. In the dream, he was frantically trying to convince the French authorities of what he knew, but they didn't seem interested. When the next batch of mail reached his camp, it included a newspaper story about the eruption of Mount Pelée in the Caribbean. The dramatic headline reported that over 40,000 people had been killed—very similar to his dream, except he was, as he later wrote "out by a nought."[5] In fact, whether because of his dream or just the numerical dyslexia that afflicts many people when reading long number strings, Dunne misread the headline to read 4,000 and he remembered it that way for years afterward, until he reread the clipping for purposes of writing his classic 1927 book on precognitive dreaming, *An Experiment with Time.*[6]

Just a few years after Dunne began noticing dreams that seemed to predict future events, Einstein's discoveries provided the beginnings of a possible explanation for this impossible-seeming phenomenon. According to the theory of relativity, time is a dimension like the three dimensions of space. Einstein's teacher Hermann Minkowski realized that his student's theories led to the conclusion that there is a singular continuum, space-time—or what is often called a block universe.[7]

In such a universe, future events already exist, as it were, and past events still exist. Although we can't directly perceive it, objects including our own bodies are really cross sections of four-dimensional worm-like entities winding and twisting through the block universe from birth to death. (The particles our bodies are made from, like atoms, may last much longer.) The four-dimensional path of a particle or a body through the block is called its world line. Grasping that we are really four-dimensional beings opens various possibilities for how we— or at least our brains (what Dunne called our brain line[8])—might send messages to ourselves back from our future. Effectively, through the particles making up our bodies and nervous systems, we are already connected to that future, like wires to and from our fate. We'll loop back to the physics of retrocausation later on, in part 3.

FUTURE LEARNING EXPERIENCES

After his years of soldiering were cut short by heart disease, Dunne pursued his childhood dream of designing and building airplanes. The Wright Brothers' first flight occurred in 1903, and Dunne became one of the first British pioneers in the new field of aeronautical engineering. He designed, built, and flew innovative tailless aircraft and promoted the nascent British aircraft industry to his country's military. And in his spare time, he decided to approach the problem of his dreams the way an engineer would: by methodically recording them so he could carefully compare them with subsequent events without relying on his memory. Partly, he wanted to rule out the kind of retroactive memory distortion that skeptics of the time, like Freud, assumed was operative. His experiment—which he encouraged readers of his book to replicate for themselves—was systematically recording his dreams and then comparing them in the days afterward to events that occurred in his life. Dunne's book is filled with numerous striking correspondences between his dreams and later (usually but not always imminent) experiences.

To take one example, in 1904, he dreamed that a horse escaped its enclosure and came running after him. The next day, while fly fishing with his brother, he saw a horse behind a fence in a setting that exactly resembled his dream. While he was telling his brother his dream, the horse they were watching broke free and approached them—a terrifying moment weirdly predicted by the dream he had just been relating. Fortunately, unlike in the dream, the horse changed its mind and galloped off.

Most of his dreams, however, continued to show him things he would read in the news. The same year, for instance, Dunne dreamed of many people crammed together on a balcony, bathed in smoke; that afternoon's paper brought news of a fire at a factory in Paris that had killed many female workers who had attempted to flee out to a balcony. And in the autumn of 1913, he dreamed vividly of a train going over an embankment and lying on its side below the Firth of Forth Bridge in Scotland; a few months later, on April 14 of the following year, he read the news that a famous mail train, the Flying Scotsman, had derailed coming off the Forth Bridge exactly where he'd pictured the derailment in his dream.

What's so valuable about Dunne's science-minded effort to study his own dreams is that he was able to rule out any actual connection between his mind and a distant newsworthy event, forcing him to conclude that what his dreams brought him were previews of his own experience of reading about those events in the news. He was previewing news stories of volcano eruptions, train disasters, and cross-country treks, in other words, and not somehow seeing the events themselves.

How could he tell? Sometimes, when there was a discrepancy between the news report and the actual event, that discrepancy served as what an epidemiologist or forensic investigator might now call a tracer, showing that the dream always matched the news report, not the event. For example, the actual death toll in the Mount Pelée eruption ended up being something like 36,000, not over 40,000 as the newspaper had claimed. The discrepancy told him that his dreaming brain had not brought him direct information about the faraway disaster, but had presented a kind of imaginative dramatization of the newspaper story (even if his dream death toll was dyslexically missing a zero).

Another powerful piece of evidence came in 1912, when Dunne dreamed that a test-pilot friend, Lieutenant B., crashed a monoplane and walked away from the wreckage toward him, explaining it was the "beastly engine."[9] He later found out B. was killed in a test flight along with another pilot the very same morning he had the dream. There was no information about the cause of the crash, but B. had previously expressed concern about the engine in the plane, making engine trouble a reasonable assumption. Yet, when investigating the crash later, Dunne discovered it had to do with a lift wire that had snapped—something the unfortunate aviators would have realized as they were plummeting to earth. Thus, it is unlikely that Dunne was telepathically tuning in to his doomed friend, or receiving some kind of afterlife communication from him. He was precognizing reading the distressing news about B. and, as dreams will do, supplementing what he read with a supposition of his own that proved false.

"I'M GOING TO HAVE TO SCIENCE THE SH*T OUT OF THIS"

This distinction—between a real event out there in the world, in the future, and a future learning experience such as reading of an event in the news—may not seem important, but it is probably the most essential for understanding the nature of precognition and precognitive dreaming. In fact, it is Principle #1 for our book:

Precognition isn't about events in the future;
it is about our own future experiences,
including reading or learning experiences.

Why is this distinction important? Because real events may not match the way we learn of them, for one thing. Just as Dunne discovered with his Mount Pelée case, the news may be wrong or may be missing essential information. Our dreams, notably, fill these gaps with our own assumptions, not with the facts. It's one of several reasons why precognitive dreams are seldom precisely literal or exact representations of future events: dreams represent our subjective thoughts and emotional reactions in response to surprising learning experiences ahead, and thus they typically do not represent events as we would see them through some kind of God's-eye camera. We'll be circling back to this idea (and other reasons for dreams' distortions and inaccuracies) throughout the book.

One of the most compelling modern cases of recurrent precognitive dreaming clearly demonstrates the principle Dunne discovered with his own dreams. A Houston woman named Elizabeth Krohn was struck by lightning in the parking lot of her synagogue in 1988 and since then has been plagued with astonishingly accurate dreams of imminent catastrophes, especially air disasters and newsworthy near-disasters. Eventually, she learned to send herself time- and date-stamped emails of these dreams to facilitate later authentication, and to prove to herself she's not crazy. For instance, on January 15, 2009, about six and a half hours before Captain Chesley "Sully" Sullenberger piloted his US Airways jet to a safe water landing in the Hudson River after losing engine power, Krohn dreamed that a Southwest or US Airways jet crashed in the water in New York City and that somehow the passengers survived and were standing on the wings. Images showing just such a scene—people spread out across the wings of a jet floating in the water—went viral after the event. On February 2, 2015, she dreamed that a passenger plane with propellers went down in Asia and that its right wing was straight up before the crash. On February 4, 2015, a TransAsia Airways propeller plane was captured on a driver's dashcam video crashing right after takeoff; images of the propeller plane crossing the road, with its right wing straight up, similarly went viral.

These and several other of Krohn's amazing precognitive dream hits are detailed in the book she cowrote with Rice University historian of religions Jeffrey J. Kripal, *Changed in a Flash*.[10] Kripal points out that Krohn's dreams matched not the events themselves but the media accounts—specifically the photographs that Krohn was about to encounter on TV or the internet. As far as I'm concerned, Krohn's dreams put firmly to rest the idea that prophetic or premonitory dreams bring information about events per se, unfolding in objective future reality. They are previews of the dreamer's own future experiences, especially learning (reading, viewing, web-surfing) experiences.

An extension of this principle—and another reason why it is so important to distinguish objective events from subjective learning experiences—is that it is possible to precognize things that are totally fictitious, like scenes from novels, TV shows, or movies. We live in a media- and myth-saturated world, and as a result, very many precognitive dreams concern our interactions with the media in one form or another. My dreams about "The Apple" and *Island of the Blue Dolphins* would be examples of this, as would one of my all-time favorite Dunne dream hits.

On October 4, 2015, I dreamed about a rocket launching, but there was something strange about the command module atop the rocket: it looked more like an open tent. When I awoke and wrote this down, I noted that it reminded me of the flimsy canvas cover of a Vietnam-era river-patrol boat (PBR)—totally inappropriate for a spacecraft. I wondered if the dream might turn out to have something to do with Ridley Scott's new movie *The Martian*, which I had tickets to see that afternoon.

I knew few details about *The Martian* other than the basic premise shown in trailers: astronaut Mark Watney (Matt Damon) is stranded alone on Mars, "sciencing the shit" out of his situation, as he says, and there is a mission to rescue him—an effort that, I could guess, would ultimately succeed after a series of tense challenges. When the climactic scene unfolded, I was way more excited about the confirmation of my Dunne dream than about the movie. To lighten the weight of an escape rocket on the Martian surface, Watney removes all the heavy glass windows from its cabin, duct-taping clear plastic in their place. When he blasts off into orbit, protected only by his spacesuit, the makeshift windows of the capsule flap furiously like a tent in a windstorm.

I suppose I should have said "spoiler alert" before I gave away that detail from the climax of Ridley Scott's movie, but in fact there are a lot of spoilers in this book, and that's only appropriate for our topic of precognition. The precognitive faculty loves to home in on startling revelations ahead, things like the twist endings of movies we're not supposed to know in advance, and the kinds of things that aren't included in movie trailers. So fair warning: if you don't like spoilers, you might not like precognitive dreamwork. But if, like me, you sometimes read the last pages of a book first, well, then, you're in your element.

I later confirmed I could not have drawn my canvas command module image from some memory of one of the trailers for *The Martian,* as this particular scene was not depicted in them. My dreaming brain had simply concocted a makeshift image from associations in my TV- and movie-watching memory to pre-present this unexpected, exciting, and totally fictitious scene several hours ahead in my timeline. As I sat in the dark theater flushed with excitement over this cinematic fulfillment of my dream, I felt a lot like Ray, the radio producer in the introduction who dreamed about totally unpredictable details of his tooth extraction in second grade and then felt like an *X-Men* mutant*: I too felt like I had secret powers nobody knew. If Matt Damon scienced the shit out of his predicament as a castaway on Mars, I *psi*-enced the shit out of *The Martian.*

---

*Jeffrey J. Kripal at Rice University likens psi to the mutant powers of the *X-Men,* and considers this (and other comic books) to be a crucial modern mythological framework for both experiencing and even studying the paranormal (Kripal 2011, 2017).

Pseudoscienced, a skeptic would almost certainly retort.

As we will see in the next chapter, replications of Dunne's "experiment with time" are chock full of amazing precognitive dreams, and the mass of this evidence, despite how "anecdotal" each case may be individually, adds up to a compelling and surprisingly consistent picture that makes the skeptics' arguments about the law of large numbers look increasingly unconvincing. It is really a law of large desperation.

3

Psychic Citizen Science

Taking the J. W. Dunne Challenge

Nonscientists have always played a role in the advancement of scientific knowledge. Amateur astronomers have discovered new comets and other heavenly bodies. Amateur paleontologists have contributed to our understanding of fossil life. The internet and smartphones have increasingly enabled ordinary people to help gather scientific data about epidemiology, climate change, and wildlife populations and migrations. Even some significant recent discoveries in medicine have been made by patients doing their own research, scouring the medical literature, and connecting the available dots to find new effective treatments for their conditions.[1]

Citizen science did not enter the *Oxford English Dictionary* until 2014, but Dunne's *An Experiment with Time* fell squarely in this long and hallowed tradition. The book was an invitation and challenge to readers to conduct his experiment in their own lives, thus crowdsourcing evidence for what he imagined could be a Copernican revolution in our understanding of the mind. Dunne envisioned a new science, which he called Serialism, that made a central place for consciousness within the new spacetime cosmology of Einstein and Minkowski. The data could be gathered by ordinary dreamers with nothing more than a pen and bedside notebook. Many readers took up his challenge.

The challenge, as Dunne formulated it, is deceptively simple: record your dreams every morning on waking, and then revisit your records from the past few nights at the end of each day, looking for possible connections between your dreams and experiences during that interim.

That second step is the single most important key to precognitive dreamwork. Many people write down some of their dreams, at least when they are striking or feel somehow important, but very few people think to go back to their dream records after a short duration. Without doing that, you are much less likely to catch yourself having dreamed about a subsequent experience. We'll see lots of cases in this book of people only discovering a precognitive dream long after the fact, when revisiting an old journal. Ideally, you should make this revisiting a routine part of your day.

There is a common but totally false belief that precognitive or premonitory dreams feel different from other dreams—that they feel numinous somehow, or otherwise special. This can lead people to (a) be lazy about writing down those special-feeling dreams, because they think they will remember them, and (b) not bother writing down dreams that seem unimportant or trivial. Consequently, the importance of the dream journal is necessary to underscore. Principle #2 of our book is:

Precognitive dreams do not necessarily feel special or numinous. Record all your dreams.

Memory is unreliable when it comes to pretty much anything, and dreams evaporate on waking like the morning dew. Thus, it is necessary to keep a notebook and pen by your bedside and get in the habit of noting down as much as you can remember of all of the dreams you remember from the previous night. I also keep a small LED headlamp from REI next to my notebook for when I wake up in the middle of the night. If you tend not to remember your dreams, you may find that just having that notebook by your bedside causes you to start remembering them. It is like setting an intention or priming a pump. The only physical work involved in dreamwork is the writing-down part, but it is absolutely crucial.

"All the dreams you remember" does not equal all your dreams.

What was not known in Dunne's day is that we dream throughout the night. The most vivid ones, the ones we usually think of when we describe ourselves as having had a dream, are the relatively elaborate and typically bizarre narratives and scenes that are generated by the brain during REM sleep. We spend on average about two and a half hours each night in this relatively shallow sleep state, and our brains are highly active during it. A given dream recalled on waking is liable to be just a small fraction of our cortical activity during REM. It is now known also that dreaming is not confined to this phase of sleep but probably occurs, although less vividly or memorably, throughout the night.[2] So whatever we can recall of our nightly dreamlife, it is likely only a fraction of the dreams our brain has generated while we were asleep, the bulk of which are going to be forgotten despite our best efforts.

The latter is an important point to bear in mind throughout this book, because it helps explain one of the biggest perplexities of precognitive dreams: their apparent tendency to focus on random or seemingly mundane occurrences in our lives, not only or mainly the big upheavals as we might expect. As we'll see later, this may be a kind of statistical illusion produced by the fact that we are only consciously remembering a small portion of our dreams, as well as the fact that our dreaming brain may be metabolizing (or digesting) all of our salient experiences over the subsequent days.[3] Nature may have never intended us to consciously remember most of our dreams—even though, ironically enough, they are directly concerned with forming memories, as we will see later.

You may awaken with a few images or details and a sense that much of a dream is lost. That's okay. Just write down as much as you can remember, even if it seems trivial. It helps, if you have the time, to lie in bed quietly upon waking and summon a dream's fading images to mind, rather than rise immediately to start the day—but obviously, between jobs, school, and kids, many don't always have that luxury. For me, weekends and days when I work at home and can afford to keep hitting the snooze button for a while are particularly rich for capturing interesting dreams in the transitional (or liminal) hypnopompic state prior to waking. Whatever you can remember and write down upon waking is valuable, and don't feel bad that your net only captures a small number of the many fleetingly glimpsed fish in your dream sea.

If you have the time, it is ideal to use your handwritten bedside jottings to make a more detailed record of the dream later, preferably in the morning when it is still somewhat fresh in memory. It is helpful to keep dream records on a word processor, if you have a computer and have the time, because this facilitates inserting notes and interpretations later. I always keep a Word file open on my laptop where I write my dreams and then can later insert any notes or thoughts relevant to them. Write down every noticed detail, every noticed element, every noticed emotional reaction, and so on. We will see later why each detail in a dream is like a word or term in a larger text; if you noticed it, it means it is significant, no matter how stupid or trivial it appears on the surface. The longer you wait to record a dream, the more these details will be forgotten, and the more the dream-text will be like a faded parchment or papyrus fragment with whole words or sentences missing, merely hinting at a larger lost whole. Keeping a laptop by your bedside, of course, can cut out the middleman of your notebook; if that works for you and won't bother a sleeping partner, it is a fine solution.

However you choose to record your dreams, and even if you share some of your dreams with loved ones or friends—something I highly recommend—it is important that your journal or computer file be private. Dreams and especially your associations to them are highly personal affairs, often touching on embarrassing or unshareable memories, thoughts, and feelings. When recording your dreams and dream interpretations (including your free associations, a topic we will cover in more detail later), you need the freedom to be honest with yourself and note down thoughts that you may not feel comfortable having others read. Your dream journal is a private space. Thus, do not use a shared notebook or a blog, for instance. A lack of privacy will exert an inhibiting effect on your dreams and the connections you allow yourself to make and write down.

Be somewhat systematic in your filing system, but don't go overboard. If I'm recording a lot of dreams, I'll make a new file for each month, naming the file by date and year; if I am in a dry spell, I might start a new file every season or every year. Just be consistent in how you name your files, and store them all in one place to facilitate going back to them and searching them. I also print mine out periodically and keep them in binders so I have a hard copy that is easily thumbed through.

In physics, an inverse-square law holds that the intensity of radiation or gravity diminishes as a function of distance. Precognitive dreams may obey such a law, very roughly, in time. People generally find that most, although definitely not all, precognitive material in dreams relates to events and experiences over the next few days following the dream. However, inevitably a selection or file-drawer effect plays into this: the simple likelihood of drawing a connection between a dream and a waking experience dwindles with temporal distance from the dream. At this point, it is hard to say if there is any kind of probability curve defining some temporal sweet spot when you are likeliest to identify a waking experience relating to a prior dream. This is one of the many, many open questions that we need armies of precognitive dreamworkers with fat dream journals to help figure out. While the bulk of my precognitive hits occur within about three days of a dream, it is not uncommon to find hits up to a couple weeks after a dream, as well as at yearly intervals (we will discuss calendrical resonances in more detail later).

Dunne recommended returning to your dreams up to two days afterward and thereafter discarding dream records. He lived before word processors, and since no one would have the time to check all their dreams on an indefinite daily basis, he felt you had to set limits to make your search most effective. In our day of computer files, it is easy to keep permanent, detailed dream records—they no longer take up space—as well as to search them electronically and potentially perform other kinds of analyses if you are really hardcore. But it remains the case that nobody has the time to compare their entire dream journal, which may grow a bit each day, to their entire life, every day. You can see how that could begin to consume one's life! You have to make compromises. Revisiting your dream records from the previous three days for a minute or two each evening is minimally sufficient.

EMINENT COMPANY

In taking the J. W. Dunne challenge, you will be in some brilliant and eminent company. Some of the most influential writers of the mid-twentieth century, including T. S. Eliot, C. S. Lewis, and J. R. R. Tolkien, were powerfully inspired by Dunne's book, and some undertook his experiment. Most fans of Tolkien's fantasy epics *The Hobbit* and *The Lord of the Rings* don't realize that the timeless worldview of his Elven races was based largely on the serial-universe cosmology developed by Dunne on the basis of his dream experiences.[4] So far, no dream diary has emerged among Tolkien's papers that would prove he carried out Dunne's experiment systematically, but his friend C. S. Lewis, author of *The Chronicles of Narnia*, probably did. Lewis hints as much in a posthumously published novel called *The Dark Tower*, which is partly devoted to Dunne's ideas.

A writer who we know for certain carried out Dunne's dream experiment is Vladimir Nabokov. In midlife, Nabokov developed a strong interest in dreams, based partly on a doozy of a precognitive one he had had when he was a teenager. In 1916, the seventeen-year-old Nabokov inherited a vast fortune from his uncle Vassily, including an estate outside of St. Petersburg. He seemed to be set for life . . . yet fate just as quickly snatched his wealth away in the revolution the following year. With his family he was forced to flee the country. However, at this point the young writer had a dream in which his dead uncle appeared to him and promised he would return one day as "Harry and Kuvyrkin." Nabokov pictured a couple of circus performers. Forty-three years later the increasingly well-known novelist, now living in Ithaca, New York, received amazing news that the film rights to his recent novel *Lolita* had been purchased for a very large sum by Stanley Kubrick's production company, Harris-Kubrick Pictures. Nabokov was, for the first time since his youth, again a rich man, and thus his dream had come true. When Anglicized, the Russian name Kuvyrkin would be Kubrick.

Five years later, in 1964, Nabokov encountered Dunne's book, and it naturally captured his interest. Over the course of a month of systematically recording his dreams, the novelist recorded several more Dunne dreams, albeit targeting less momentous experiences. He had his first hit on the second night of his experiment, and it was, appropriately enough, about Dunne's book. Nabokov recorded dreaming of a yellowish clock with its hands pointing to ten thirty. The next day, he noted (with some delight) coming to a passage in *An Experiment with Time* about a waking precognition experiment in which Dunne pulled books down from a shelf and summoned a mental impression of what he was going to find before opening to a random page. The passage that delighted Nabokov described Dunne's vision of a clock pointed to half past ten before he (Dunne) had opened A. E. W. Mason's *The House of the Arrow* to a random page in the middle of the book, and saw a passage describing a clock pointed to half past ten.[5] Turtles (or clocks) all the way down!

Precognitive dreaming often obeys a recursive logic like this—the precognitive faculty appears to be drawn to things having to do with precognition, time, and anachronistic anomalies. Thus, a funny kind of fractal geometry (self-similarity at all scales) characterizes many pre-cognitive dreams. Moreover, such dreams often remix or mash up the attributes of objects—sort of the way I suggest my 9/11 dream mashed up Islam and the low towers by making the latter mosques. Nabokov doesn't note it, but the early editions of Dunne's book had light yellow ("yellowish") covers, just like the clock in his dream.

Nabokov, it turns out, watched a lot of TV, in various languages. A few days after his hit with the clock, he dreamed he was sitting with the director of a small museum and absentmindedly eating what he thought were pastries arrayed on trays in front of him. He then discovered, to his chagrin, that he had been eating rare soil samples. Three nights later, he sat down to watch a French educational film on television called *Le Pédologue,* which he assumed from the name would be about childhood; instead he found to his surprise that pedology is the science of soils. One of the scenes in the film showed two geologists seated at a table in Senegal, discussing soil samples on wooden trays in front of them. The soils were presented in "appetizing little bags"[6] and shots of edibles—vegetables and fruit collected by the locals—followed the shots of the soil samples.

He recorded another striking hit about two weeks later, when he dreamed he was ascending a hill and realized, to his distress, that the hill was actually an island or an "island-like, hill-like liner"[7] detaching from the mainland and carrying him and other passengers out to sea. A day later, in the evening, he watched an episode of a French TV series called *Cinq colonnes à la une,* in which "an island with 'passengers' . . . broke off the mainland, sailing out into the ocean."[8]

GETTING RESULTS

You don't have to be a famous writer to get the kinds of results Nabokov got—in fact, you can do a lot better. For example, a music teacher in Southern California named Bruce Siegel replicated Dunne's experiment over a total of about seven years and published his results in a book called *Dreaming the Future.*[9] Among the 241 dreams he recorded, he found that a quarter related to some subsequent experience over the next few days. Sometimes the dream foreshadowed an experience within minutes of waking, something I have frequently found in my own experience as well. His book includes many keen insights about how precognitive dreams work and shows their typically mundane, non-extraordinary flavor.

Over the span of two decades, a Hollywood special effects engineer named Andrew Paquette kept a detailed record of his dreams—believe it or not (he says) to disprove the possibility that his dreams could be foretelling future events in his life, something his wife kept insisting was happening. Paquette was super organized about it. He not only wrote down his dreams but also created a coded database so that they could be sorted, indexed, broken down by scene, and studied quantitatively. The project made a convert of him. His 2011 book *Dreamer* describes many of these dreams, foreshadowing both significant upheavals like 9/11 and insignificant ones like a scary scene in the movie *Alien,* and describes the impact of these dreams on his life and spiritual beliefs.[10]

I kept an almost daily dream journal from the mid-1990s onward and only noticed a small handful of puzzling dream correspondences to later events prior to 2012, which is when I first read Dunne's book and began returning to my recent dream records more systematically to look for possible precognitive referents. Taking the J. W. Dunne challenge was quite a revelation to me, as it has been for many readers of *An Experiment with Time*. I generally notice at least one or two and occasionally several precognitive dreams in a single week, and they follow the same pattern as other replicators of Dunne's experiment have discovered: some target life upheavals, family health crises, situations at work and so on, but most are about news stories, singularly interesting articles on the internet, passages in books, or TV or movie scenes, and are often coupled to some minor emotional upheaval. The dreams I described in the previous chapter about "The Apple," *Island of the Blue Dolphins,* and *The Martian* are quite typical.

As I mentioned in the context of astronomer Paul Kalas, a dream journal kept over years or decades can provide priceless evidence of Dunnean precognition even if the original intent was never to document that. Frequently, dreamers with a Jungian orientation record "synchronicities" around their dreams, which in hindsight can be reread as evidence of precognition. Tobi Watari, a highly precognitive collaborator of mine in Denver, kept a detailed dream journal for many years before she ever realized that coincidental events matching her dreams were more than just cosmic jokes or signals that she was on the right track in her spiritual development. In hindsight, learning about precognition from my book *Time Loops* and other books on the subject like *Changed in a Flash* enabled her to make exciting new sense of these experiences.

I'll describe here just a handful of the numerous examples Tobi has shared with me. One morning in 2014, Tobi recorded in detail a dream that she was with a child who had hung a bunch of beat-up antique serving spoons, rusty and tarnished, from a clothesline. She released the tension in the line by cutting it with a knife. Four days later, she brought one of her children to visit a new doctor and was amazed that the doctor had a large mobile in her office made of old tarnished serving spoons, dangling very much as in her dream. "I didn't know what to make of it," she wrote in an email, "I simply documented it as a 'synchronicity.'" Other aspects of the dream related directly to health issues that were discussed with this doctor.

Like many precognitive dreamers, Tobi found that her dreaming mind-brain gravitates to books and movies relating to precognition or time travel, such as the stories of science-fiction writer Ted Chiang and the movie *Arrival,* based on one of Chiang's short stories. In *Arrival,* linguist Louise Banks (Amy Adams) is hired to help the army translate the nonlinear written language of visiting extraterrestrials called heptapods; as she learns to think in the aliens' non-time-bound way, the linguist finds her precognition awakening. Tobi had not heard of this movie until her husband rented it in February 2017, but the day before, she recorded dreaming that she was in a parallel world and realized she had special abilities that her hosts might want to study. "I end up being given a strangely shaped iPad to fill out a survey. As I try to answer questions, finger buttons resembling moleskin patches appear (as for blisters) down the sides." The "moleskin patches" in Tobi's dream were gray rings, and the iPad was just like the iPad Louise Banks uses in the movie to decipher the ring-like logograms of the heptapods, scrolling down the left side of the tablet.

Since Tobi types up and prints out her dreams and keeps them in dated binders, she is able to track precognitive dreams that in many cases span years. One example she discovered and shared with me as I was writing this book had occurred in October 2015. In the dream, she was standing at her bedroom window and invited her husband to look with her:

> I see a single giant skeleton standing directly in front of us, at the back of the yard, silent, filling the sky. There's a giant eagle and another large bird—a condor or vulture. There's a quality to the light and "composition" that seems like Mexican "Day of the Dead" aesthetic. [My husband] says, "I don't see anything," and I feel great apprehension. Only I see this. Then I wake up.

Four years later, in the summer of 2019, a construction company erected a massive crane on a site directly behind Tobi's property. One dark and stormy evening, a possible lightning strike caused the crane to rotate, so that it was suddenly looming directly over their backyard—a tall, ominous, "skeletal" vision, very much like what she had seen in her dream four years earlier. Tobi invited her husband to look at the crane looming over the backyard, but he declined, which slightly frustrated her ("Only I see this"). The following morning, she emailed pictures of the crane to the site's project superintendent, with the subject line "Lightning strike at the Condor." Condor was the name of the town-home complex being built on the site.

Trivial details of the night of the storm add to the specificity of Tobi's dream. She had noted explicitly in her 2015 record that the dream vision seemed to have a "composition" (she had used quotes) that was like the Day of the Dead. For her bedside dream journals, she was now (in 2019) in the habit of using a brand of recycled-paper notebooks called "Decomposition Books" that have widely varied covers. Although skulls and the Day of the Dead are not part of her usual aesthetic, the cover of her current journal on the evening of the crane incident happened to be covered with Day of the Dead–style skulls, and inside was tucked the current issue of one of her favorite magazines, which also, coincidentally, happened to have a skull adorned with flowers on the cover.

In other words, every aspect of this mildly disconcerting experience—a stormy evening resulting in a crane looming over her house from a construction site called Condor, along with details of dream-related materials by her bedside—was foreshadowed in a dream four years beforehand.* This kind of discovery is quite frequent for Tobi, as it is for others who embark on the path described in this book.

---

*Tobi added in an email: "I found out the Condor was planned to go up behind me in December 2016, fourteen months after I had the skeleton/construction crane/Condor dream. (None of the single-family homes it replaced were even up for sale when I had the dream.)"

THE LAW IN THE MIND

I mentioned that C. S. Lewis, author of *The Chronicles of Narnia,* seems to have successfully taken the J. W. Dunne challenge. His posthumously published novel *The Dark Tower* centers on a group of Cambridge academics who interact with a dystopian world—which may be a far-future version of Cambridge or an alternate dimension—via an invention called a chronoscope. Early in the story, the chronoscope's inventor Orfieu serves as the author's stand-in in a debate with a skeptic named MacPhee on the subject of Dunne, precognitive dreams, and the possibility of time travel:

> "And the future?" said MacPhee. "You're not going to say that we 'remember' it too?"
>
> "We wouldn't call it remembering," said Orfieu, "for memory means perception of the past. But that we see the future is perfectly certain. Dunne's book proved that—"
>
> MacPhee gave a roar like a man in pain.
>
> "It's all very well, MacPhee," Orfieu continued, "but the only thing that enables you to jeer at Dunne is the fact that you have refused to carry out the experiments he suggests. If you carried them out you would have got the same results that he got, and I got, and everyone got who took the trouble. Say what you like but the thing is proved. It's as certain as any scientific proof whatever. . . . And there is a reason why we notice it so little. If there is one thing that Dunne has proved up to the hilt it is that there is some law in the mind which actually forbids us to notice it."[11]

Although MacPhee roars "like a man in pain" at the idea of precognitive dreaming—a common reaction by skeptics, who often do appear physically pained at the absurdity of such things—Orfieu wisely observes that there is a kind of "law in the mind" that usually obscures precognition from view and makes it hard to examine and study, and especially hard for certain rigid, literal-minded personalities—the MacPhees of the world—to believe in.

One of the biggest reasons people are liable to overlook their precognitive dreams is that they are seldom literally accurate. Dreams typically show us future experiences obliquely via symbols, puns, and other associative connections. It turns out there are important and interesting reasons why information refluxing from the future must be somewhat indirect, and it is why Freud's work is so relevant to the study of precognition and to precognitive dreamwork. Precognition ultimately belongs to the realm of the unconscious, so illuminating the laws of the unconscious is essential. When we combine the insights of Dunne with the interpretive tools developed by Freud, as we will in part 2, it greatly enhances our understanding of what dreams are, how to identify hidden examples of dream precognition, and how to work with our dreams.

Another obstacle to believing in, let alone studying, precognitive dreams is that unexpected mundaneness of most standout specimens. When faced with evidence from a personal dream journal like Vladimir Nabokov's or Tobi's or mine, the utterly mind-blowing notion that the dreaming brain somehow reaches into our future is clouded over by doubt. Why the heck (pardon my French) would nature give us a way to see the future and use it on a random TV show or Ridley Scott movie, or even a mild upset like a storm at a construction site? A compelling answer to that question emerges when we combine the Dunnean-Freudian approach to dreamwork with contemporary insights from neuroscience about the function of dreams as it relates to memory. Spoiler alert: the seeming mundaneness of most precognitive dreams may actually be symptomatic of the fact that we are in some oblique way precognizing many or even all of the emotionally salient waking experiences ahead, and the dreams we happen to notice are just the tip of an enormous, mostly submerged iceberg.

So C. S. Lewis's law in the mind is the theme of the next, nuts-and-bolts section of this book, where we delve into how precognitive dreams really work, how to identify and interpret them, and the reasons why they often don't seize our attention the way we might expect. There, you will learn several tricks for netting many, many more of these dream-treasures in your journal than Dunne's bare-bones experiment could capture.

PART 2

THE LAW
IN THE MIND

4

The Technicolor Elephant

Freud and the Art of Memory

One of the biggest fallacies sometimes committed in the sciences is claiming (or implying) that a phenomenon that is hard to study with the tools and methods of science therefore doesn't exist. It's especially a problem in psychology and related fields that study human behavior. Questions having to do with meaning—whether meaning in a dream or a novel or a religious text—cannot be subjected to quantitative measurement, tested, and falsified using science's preferred methods. But that doesn't mean experiences expressed in those forms aren't real or that they aren't crucially important in understanding our lives and human behavior more generally. We just need to draw from a much wider range of epistemological tools to make sense of them.

Humans, being meaning-making and meaning-motivated creatures, will always evade and elude scientific scrutiny to some degree, and that is why we have always needed philosophy, history, art and literary criticism, religious studies, and so on—that is, the humanities—to complement and stand in dialogue with the sciences. Yet in a modern world that has elevated the sciences above the humanities—where science gets the big money because it can send satellites into space, build iPhones, and design new drugs—the reality that there is meaning in the world, and that it must be studied in all those other, perhaps less rigorous ways, often gets forgotten or minimized.

Even if some of his ideas and conclusions have been criticized over the years, the great contribution of Freud's approach to the mind and its mysteries was that it drew equally from the then-young study of brain processes and also from fields like philosophy and criticism that study meaning. He stood astride the science-humanities divide, creating a truly interdisciplinary art-slash-science, psychoanalysis, whose relevance cannot easily be dismissed.

Freud's interest in dreams began with his own. In 1895, while he was vacationing at a villa outside Vienna, Freud dreamed he was examining a patient and childhood friend of his, Anna Hammerschlag. In real life, Anna's problems were purely psychological ("hysteria"), but when Freud's dream-self looked inside her mouth, he saw a white patch and scabs on her cheek and palate, as well as a feature that should only have been visible in the nose (the turbinate bones). It was hard to get her to open her mouth—she acted like someone who is shy because of wearing dentures. In the dream, he told Anna, "it's really only your fault,"[1] and summoned a trio of physician friends to have a look—they poked and prodded and pompously mansplained, like stereotypical Victorian doctors—and lastly Freud's dream-self concluded that what caused Anna's oral malady was an injection administered thoughtlessly, with a dirty syringe, by one of those friends, his family pediatrician, Oskar Rie.

In one way or another, the various characters in the dream (Anna and the physician trio) and the overall situation of the dream reminded Freud of medical malpractice issues that were going around in his circle at the time. Another in the physician trio, his real-life best friend Wilhelm Fliess, had recently nearly caused the death of another of Freud's patients through a stupid surgical blunder, and Freud felt a lot of guilt by association. He was also worried he had overlooked something or failed in his treatment of Anna; in real life, Oskar had informed him the day before that Anna had not gotten better as an outcome of her time in Freud's clinic.

It took fourteen pages in his 1899 masterpiece *The Interpretation of Dreams* to unpack all the symbols and associations in the dream. Ultimately Freud concluded that the "latent dream thought" embedded in this tableau was a wish that he be innocent of any failures or malpractice in his treatment of Anna and that Oskar instead be the one at fault for the fact that Anna had not shown sufficient improvement. He gave Anna the pseudonym Irma to protect her identity; Oskar he called Otto.[2]

The dream of "Irma's Injection" is legendary in the annals of psychoanalysis. It is this dream that led Freud to the famous, controversial conclusion that dreams are tableaux staging the fulfillment of wishes that we consciously repress and that they use what he called condensation and displacement—symbols, puns, analogies, and other tropes and tactics that would be familiar to a storyteller—to disguise these wishes. The famous bizarreness of dreams reflected, he thought, the operation of a "censor" forcing unconscious selfish and often sexual thoughts to express themselves in code, like letters between spies. Freud described this transformation process as "dream-work"—the work of the unconscious to suitably distort and disguise its true thoughts.[3] (The more common usage of *dreamwork* is dream interpretation after the fact, and that is how I am using the term in this book.)

Freud's theory was compelling to many in the wider public. Any dreamer can attest to the prevalence of wishes (and sex) in many of their dreams—especially true if we stretch our imagination just a tiny bit (that dirty syringe, for instance). Suddenly it was culturally legitimate to think dreams could be meaningful, and thus to take them seriously as something more than deranged images of the sleeping brain, which had been the prevailing view in educated circles. Freud's work strongly influenced artists and writers. The Surrealists looked to him as a kind of prophet, having revealed the unconscious as an undiscovered country.

But Freud's theory also sparked considerable debate among psychologists and psychiatrists, even in the psychoanalytic community he founded. Where Freud tended to interpret dreams as pointing to unresolved sexual fantasies from childhood, some of his colleagues and protégés were less reductive in their approach. Some saw dreams as expressing ongoing internal conflicts or attempts to negotiate our private desires and social demands. Some, like Jung, felt that dreams' connections to myth and religion were more important than the sexual dimension. More recently, some have argued that dreams are a unique form of expression that surpasses the limitations of language and other forms of communication.[4]

As the behavioral and brain sciences matured over the twentieth century, all these psychoanalytic, meaning-centered views on dreams fell out of favor. Psychoanalytic interpretations were untestable, for one thing—how can anyone scientifically falsify, let alone prove, that a certain dream symbol means what the analyst or the dreamer says it means? As neuroscientists began to understand the biophysiology of dreaming, it became fashionable to assert that, since dreaming corresponds to specific patterns of brain activation, there can be no real meaning or value in dreams other than whatever we project onto them after the fact. They're just deranged images produced by brain when its rational prefrontal cortex goes offline.

In the 1970s, neurologist J. Allen Hobson thought he pounded the final nail in the Freudian coffin with his "activation synthesis" account.[5] This theory was that dreaming represents the cortex's attempt to make sense of neural hyperactivation in the brainstem during REM sleep. This neural activation—the stimulus for dreams—is chaotic and random, he argued; that the resulting narratives make a certain amount of sense upon waking is only a consequence of the awake brain's appetite for meaning, not unlike the way a person might see a face in a rock formation or project some narrative onto an intrinsically meaningless Rorschach inkblot. In the 1980s, Francis Crick, the codiscoverer of DNA, went further, arguing that dreams are just the discharging of mental static, random and meaningless associations, akin to the way you need to empty your computer's trash bin to make room for new files and photos. Finding meaning in our dreams was, for Crick, analogous to finding nutrition in our waste—fundamentally misguided and even potentially harmful.[6]

Evidence gathered over the past few decades has pointed in a somewhat different direction, however: toward dreaming as a kind of offline cognitive processing that plays a role in the formation or consolidation of memories. In laboratory experiments, Harvard sleep researcher Robert Stickgold found that dreams early in the night often contain features similar to a recent waking experience.[7] (Freud and other writers before him had noticed this too. Freud called these obvious referents to recent experience day residues.[8]) Stickgold's finding that dreams play a role in memory and learning added to a growing weight of evidence about the role of sleep in consolidating new memories and in solidifying recently acquired skills. The hippocampus, a brain structure that plays a huge role in making memories, is extremely active while we slumber, and rodent studies have shown that brain areas activated during exploration and learning are reactivated during sleep. In laboratory experiments, people who have learned new material remember it better after sleeping on it than if they don't. And during sleep, complex material is simplified, reduced to the gist.

Stickgold sides with other dream neuroscientists against the popular view that dreams contain hidden meaning cloaked in symbolism. Yet he also admits that only a tiny portion—just 2 percent—of explicit dream events can be shown to faithfully represent some recent waking experience or any real (or realistic) experience at all.[9] While many elements in dreams are recognizable people and situations from our past, they are rearranged, jumbled, recontextualized, and distorted in such a way that the resulting narratives seldom bear an identifiable literal connection to life events. Dreams are, for the most part, bizarre, and Stickgold's account leaves unexplained the lion's share of dream cognition.

HEAD ON A PLATTER

The biggest problem with the reductive, purely neurobiological theories of dreaming of Hobson, Crick, and Stickgold is that they don't match human experience. Many of the claims Freud made for dreams—for instance that they involve clever puns and wordplay and seem concerned with our deepest priorities—are hard to deny, as even superficial involvement with one's dreamlife shows. Ordinary people who have spent time recording their dreams, even outside of one of the standard dream-symbolism frameworks like those of Freud or Jung, see that there is not only an obscure logic to them but also, quite often, a surpassing wit.

I'll never forget the time a good friend who knew of my interest in dreams related an especially disturbing one she had just had. (This was long before my interest in, or even awareness of, dream precognition.) She had dreamed she was at a dinner party being thrown by her older sister, and her sister had the poor taste to appear as just her head displayed on an appetizer tray, with olives stuck into her forehead on toothpicks. My friend felt appalled by this dream and its apparently violent imagery—her sister's head on a platter—so she wanted some insight.

I knew she harbored mixed feelings about her sister's recent accomplishments in life. Her sister had recently gotten married and she and her new husband had purchased a home, two things my friend was nowhere close to doing at that point. So the meaning of this image— or at least, part of the meaning—seemed clear: my friend's sister was *ahead,* and my friend didn't like it.

Her jaw dropped on hearing this—it was so obvious, once you decoded the pun. Freud would certainly have gone much further in his interpretation, pointing out that by putting her sister's head on an appetizer tray (with toothpicks), the dream was also presenting a wish that her sister's accomplishments would be just an appetizer, a prelude or hors d'oeuvre before the main course (my friend's own future accomplishments). He would also likely have pointed out the obvious death wish—something siblings commonly express in dreams, given their natural rivalry. It is a violent image, after all, calling to mind (for me) the story of John the Baptist. If Freud had had my friend on his couch, he would probably have asked her to reflect on that biblical association as well as any others that might come to mind from movies or books in her experience.*

---

*In hindsight, I think it is significant that my friend told me this dream during a conversation at a real party (thrown by a fellow student)—in fact, she told it to me in the kitchen, near the drinks and snacks. The fact that the dream had taken place at a dinner party in the context of a shocking hors d'oeuvre probably signaled its precognitive nature: her dream was really about her amazement and shock, a few days later at a real party, at discovering the meaning of her dream's symbolism.

The wit and brilliance of dreams, viewed through a Freudian lens, is so excessive, so beyond our daily experience of our mundane intelligence, that people unused to recording or observing their dreams have difficulty accepting that their own measly minds could be responsible for creating these tableaux. It may even account for why some people don't remember their dreams at all—such wit simply doesn't fit into who they think they are.

But in fact everyone's dreams, as well as their hypnagogic and hypnopompic images on the edge of sleep, are packed full of these witty puns—some of them perhaps too convoluted and subtle to ever grasp (imagine not only sight gags, like "a head" on a platter, but also touch, taste, and smell gags). It is no wonder that dreams and other visions have historically been assumed to be messages or thoughts from some other or divine source. It's not only, as Freud thought, that we can't believe ourselves capable of the wicked desires our dreams sometimes hint at; it's also that we can't believe our own minds are capable of being so astonishingly creative.

Fortunately, a new synthesis may be at hand, one that offers a kind of reconciliation between the technicolor-dreamcoat Freudian theory and the drab neuroscience ones. Best of all, it also points the way toward a reconciliation of mainstream neuroscientific and psychoanalytic dream approaches with dream precognition, the elephant in the room both camps largely have refused to face until now.

In a major 2013 article in the journal *Behavior and Brain Sciences,* Manchester University psychologist Sue Llewellyn drew the attention of sleep scientists to the strong similarities between dream imagery and the punny and surreal scenes that pre-Gutenberg scholars and orators would use to help them remember speeches and books—the "art of memory."[10] To remember a fact or an idea, an ancient orator would break the idea down into its parts, create a vivid and interesting image to substitute for each part, and then assemble these images together into a weird little tableau or scene. To remember a whole discourse or argument, the mnemonist would place such scenes systematically throughout a familiar or well-memorized environment like a home or public plaza.

Then, when the time came to deliver the speech, another mental stroll through that same building, visiting each vivid image in sequence, enabled retrieving the facts planted along that imagined route. No need to refer to any notes. Renaissance memory wizards memorized whole books this way, and modern memory champions—and clever medical students—use the same principles.[11]

For example, if I wanted to memorize the bones of the ear, I would do the following. Looking up "ear bones" on Wikipedia, I find that there are three of them, collectively called *ossicles,* and that their names are *malleus, incus,* and *stapes.* My first association to the word *malleus* is Mal, the ship captain on the science-fiction series *Firefly* from the early 2000s; my first association to the word *incus* is Inca; and my first association to the word *stapes* is stapler. So to memorize this set of words, I simply picture Mal (the actor Nathan Fillion) dressed in the headdress and robe of an Inca priest at the top of some kind of temple pyramid, performing a human sacrifice using a stapler. It's a ridiculous, absurd image—not to mention possibly ethnographically incorrect (I don't know what Inca priests looked like, and I was not 100 percent sure—until typing Inca into Wikipedia—that they even performed sacrifices; they certainly didn't use staplers) . . . but it doesn't matter. All that matters is that it is an unexpected and absurd image—very much akin to a dream image—and it will stick in my memory without any further effort. I'll always know the bones of the ear now; you will too, probably. (And to remember that they are ossicles, I can stick my Inca-dressed, stapler-holding Mal inside a big icicle, kind of like Han Solo frozen in carbonite.)

Llewellyn showed that the familiar bizarreness of dreams, the abundant research pointing to a role for dreams in memory consolidation, and the known neurobiology of dreaming (such as the hyperactivation of the hippocampus) all converge on the explanation that dreaming is the nightly experience of our brain's rewiring to encode recent experiences in our long-term memory using the same principles I just used to memorize the bones of the ear. When neuronal connections (synapses) are activated, their future activation is facilitated, and according to a principle called Hebbian learning, *neurons that fire together wire together*—meaning when two unlike things are paired through some common association (such as a pun—a word that can mean two or more things), they will tend to be recalled together later, and one of those things will tend to act as a cue for the other.

Essentially, our memory is cross-indexed by puns and other forms of substitution and displacement, the same nonlogical, associative tropes that played such a central role in Freud's method of dream interpretation and the same tropes that ancient orators used for memorization. Mnemonists were essentially doing Freud's "dream-work" while awake, free associating on new material as a way of remembering it. This led Llewellyn to argue that dreaming is essentially the art of memory operating automatically while we sleep.[12] An analogy might be the way a librarian logs a new book, affixing it with a bar code and entering its information into a computer before allowing it to be placed on the shelves. What we are seeing in dreams are those bar codes being stuck on daily events in our lives by the hippocampus (the brain's librarian), enabling them to be quickly and easily found again later via the associative networks in an individual's head.

Apart from positing a different functional role for dreaming, the mnemonic hypothesis is really not too different from Freud's theory. Dreams' surface bizarreness is a function of the individual's unique and idiosyncratic memory associations, which are the product of a lifetime of unique personal experiences, interests, desires, fears, and so on—in other words, a unique history of making meaning (associating the word *malleus* with a character in a TV show I happened to like, versus say a mallet or a mall or an uncle named Mel). The most effective memory associations are so idiosyncratic, so dependent on our personal life experience, that they would never make sense to anybody else, at least without too much explanation to make it worth it—like explaining an inside joke to someone not in on it. They wouldn't make sense because, well, you had to be there. It's why dreams are often best unpacked and interpreted with the help of a therapist—a safe, nonjudging person who knows you pretty intimately. And it's a reason why a friend's or coworker's dream may seem very boring—you really did have to be there for it to make sense or feel important.

This "you had to be there" quality makes it inherently challenging to write about dreams without taxing a reader's patience and credulity. It also makes any laboratory study of the content of dreams very difficult, because even if you confined a group of participants in a room and subjected them to the same waking experiences, they would all encode those experiences differently at night because their personal associations will be different, not to mention the fact that those experiences may be more worth remembering to some than to others. A researcher would not be rewarded with a set of nearly identical dreams from the participants the next morning, and thus may be led to believe that dreams have no meaning or don't relate to waking events in any significant way. I believe that this intrinsic idiosyncrasy of the dreaming brain has been one major reason why dreams have retained their mystery, long after other aspects of human cognition have yielded their secrets to science.

The question, for our purposes, becomes: Could dreams sometimes show us "memories" of our own future? I'm sure you can precognize my answer: there is indeed plenty of evidence—including from Freud's own clinic, and even from his own dreamlife—that dreams reveal a distinctly memory-like function related to future experiences, just as J. W. Dunne claimed and as generations of precognitive dreamworkers have discovered in their own lives. As the White Queen famously said to Alice, "It's a poor sort of memory that only works backwards."

5

Future Towers from Past Bricks

Basics of Dream Precognition

It may seem counterintuitive, but the first key to understanding precognition is to realize that it is an aspect of our memory. My hypothesis, which I spelled out at length in *Time Loops,* is that memory is a continuum that extends not only from our childhood to the present but also into our future as well, even until we die. Because such an idea has no place in our sciences or even our folklore of memory, we will misinterpret our "premories" of things ahead of us in time, attributing them to some other phenomenon or (more likely) chalk them up to the random misfires of the easily deluded brain.

Plenty of evidence suggests precognition is fundamentally memory-like in the way it behaves. For example, as Dunne discerned, it is about our own future and not other people's futures (or about objective events). As most ESP researchers and experiencers have realized, it is facilitated by strong emotion, which is also a well-known hallmark of memory. Future emotional upheavals are more likely to be pre-membered, just as we remember past experiences better if they make an emotional impact on us. And importantly, precognition is highly associative. It's about making connections—nonlogical connections, connections among experiences that happen closely together in time even if they share no other relationship, and connections between future experiences and past ones that resemble them.

We'll see lots of evidence for this associative aspect of precognition throughout the remainder of this book.[1] Dreams seem to reflect the nightly updating of our brain's neural network, and that updating reflects not only recent experiences being encoded associatively in memory (as Sue Llewellyn argued) but also the forming of associations between recent experiences and future experiences. If this is the case, then the interpretation of dreams must look both toward the past, as Freud believed, and toward the future, as Dunne determined with his own self-experiment. In your readerly imagination right now, picture a proper, mustachioed English aviator-engineer (Dunne) shaking hands and joining forces with the grim, cigar-puffing Austrian psychoanalyst, for it is the combined insights of these two figures that provides the foundation for precognitive dreamwork.

Freud probably never heard of Dunne in real life, but Dunne knew Freud's theories well—it was hard not to, at the time Dunne was writing. Unlike Freud, Dunne saw no contradiction between the idea that dreams could represent the disguised fulfillment of our wishes and the idea that dreams can also preview experiences in our future. In fact, it seemed plain to Dunne that dreams may reach into the future for the symbolic materials, what he called "bricks," from which to build some wish-fulfilling scene, as much as they may reach into our past.[2]

Even though Freud rejected the possibility of dreams foretelling the future, a famous, heartbreaking dream from his book *The Interpretation of Dreams* seems like a perfect example of what Dunne was suggesting. Freud reports that one of his patients had been sitting at the bedside of his deathly ill child, and after the child died, Freud's patient went to lay down in an adjacent room. There, the man dreamed that the child was tugging him by the arm, saying, "Father, don't you see I'm burning?" He awoke with a start and rushed into the room with the body to find that, indeed, a candle had fallen over, and the child's sleeve had caught fire and was singeing his arm.[3]

Per his wish-fulfillment theory, Freud argued that this dream enabled the father to prolong his sleep for a few seconds, enjoying the dream image of his beloved child, rather than rise immediately to put out the fire. That's reasonable, as far as it goes. But it leaves unexplained how the man sensed what was happening in the next room, knowing not only that there was a fire but also what was burning. We are compelled to simply accept that the man's super-acute unconscious mind inferred it all, even though he was asleep in another room, behind a door that was mostly closed. Neither the smell of smoke nor the glare of fire were enough to rouse another gentleman who had also dropped off to sleep when he was supposed to be watching over the child's body.

Given the hard-to-ignore evidence for dream precognition, this dream makes much more sense as a Dunne dream. In addition to fulfilling the grieving father's wish of spending a precious moment with his child, the child also served as the dream's messenger of a startling surprise ahead in the man's imminent future in exactly the same way that Lieutenant B. served as the messenger in Dunne's dream about B.'s fatal crash.*

WHAT-IFS

Psychiatrists in the last decades of the nineteenth century had discovered that the unconscious mind appears capable of sensory and mnemonic feats that go beyond what we are aware of consciously. Since Freud's day, invoking these nonparanormal superpowers of the unconscious around uncanny dream correspondences with later experiences has been a common fallback position for skeptics. Even writers who are open and accepting of the possibility of precognition will, when possible, invoke the unconscious mind's superacuity to explain things like warning dreams.

Dream researcher Ann Faraday writes in her bestselling—and still excellent—1974 guide to dream interpretation, *The Dream Game,* that after moving into a new apartment on the seventh floor of her build-

---

*Those who prefer a spiritualist interpretation, of course, will claim that it was the child's spirit getting the attention of his father, just as it could have been Lieutenant B.'s spirit addressing Dunne after his fatal crash. But remember what Dunne discovered in the latter case: the dream-figure of Lieutenant B. was in error about the cause of his crash, and indeed he would have known the real cause (a snapped lift wire), making a spiritualist explanation somewhat strained.

ing, she dreamed of falling off the balcony. Her first rule of dreamwork is to look for a literal, not symbolic, meaning in dreams, and when she examined the balcony guardrails, she discovered that indeed they were dangerously rickety, in need of repair. "This information," she wrote, "had obviously registered at the back of my head the previous day, but I had been too preoccupied to take conscious note of the potentially dangerous situation." Similarly, she writes that when a neighbor dreamed his son fell from a tall ladder, she recommended he take a look at the ladder; as she expected, the neighbor discovered a loose rung. "Once again, the watchdog of the psyche helped prevent a nasty accident."[4]

The problem is, these kinds of explanations are often just as implausible, and more importantly less parsimonious, than the precognitive explanation they are helping dreamers and dream-interpreters avoid invoking. They presuppose a form and degree of mere sensory perception that is itself extraordinary. They also frequently leave details of the dream correspondence unexplained.

Consider a case related by pioneer ESP researcher Louisa Rhine that is similar in most ways to the warning dreams described by Faraday. A woman in Washington State reported waking from a terrible dream in which her infant was crushed by a falling chandelier in its nursery. In the dream, a clock on the baby's dresser read 4:35. Her husband (per the usual male no-nonsense stereotype) assured her it was just a dream and to go back to sleep. But her maternal instincts overruled him, and she went and brought their baby into their bed. Later they were awoken by a crash; they rushed into the nursery and saw that the chandelier had indeed fallen into the crib. Fortunately, because she had obeyed her dream warning, nobody had been hurt. The clock read 4:35, just as in her dream.[5] It would be natural to adopt the subliminal perception interpretation here, assuming the mother had somehow sensed a loose fitting in the light fixture and that this rose to her unconscious in her dream; but how, in that case, did it time the dream so acutely—just an hour or two before the chandelier crashed? More to the point, it would fail to explain how the dream "knew" that the chandelier would fall at exactly 4:35 in the morning.

Always looking firstly to the superacuity of unconscious perception is an apologetic reflex that no doubt springs from centuries of scientific bullying—as though the gatekeepers of Enlightenment reason will look just a little less unfavorably upon a "psychic" explanation if it *only* is applied very judiciously, to the smallest possible number of otherwise inexplicable cases. But in fact, many dreams seem to precisely precognize minute details of events weeks, months, years, even decades in the future and cannot in any way be explained this way. Faraday, as we'll see, very much admitted the possibility of precognitive dreams when superacuity of the unconscious wouldn't work. If unconscious superacuity can at best only account for a fraction of reported precognitive dreams, why presume it accounts for any of them?

A better interpretation—and an explanation that can encompass not only apparent warning dreams but pretty much the entire spectrum of precognitive dream experiences—is that dreams show us our conscious thoughts in response to events and discoveries ahead. Sometimes those thoughts take the form of horrible what-ifs from a future vantage point of having survived some close call. For instance, a natural first thought upon actually detecting a loose balcony railing or a loose rung on a ladder is a mental image of oneself or a loved one falling to their death or to serious injury. (Any parent of a small child, for instance, knows the terrifying mental images that arise whenever the child comes too close to some peril like an electrical socket or a body of water.) These kinds of vivid imaginary what-ifs are likely the real explanation for premonitions of disasters that seem to be narrowly averted in real life—a topic we'll circle back to when we address premonitions in part 4.

By the same token, when an outcome in our future is positive, our thoughts about it or its significance may skew the dream in other ways.

In *The Dream Game,* Faraday describes an amazing time-looping experience during the period she was promoting her first book, *Dream Power,* on U.S. talk shows in 1972. Faraday's partner, scientist and writer John Wren-Lewis, had dreamed he was writing a novel that centered on his/the protagonist's attempt to thwart a rogue scientist who was trying to take over the British government using a spy plane he had invented. In the dream-novel, Wren-Lewis's fictional alter ego enlisted the help of a sympathetic member of the government, modeled on a real-life member of the House of Lords, Lord Snow, but Snow's fictitious name in the dream was Artie Shaw. At the end of the novel—and the dream—the dreamer was successful at denouncing the villainous scientist and was celebrated for his act.

On waking, John felt that the spy plane in the dream somehow represented his insecurity about Ann's success with her book and his wish to keep an eye on her with some kind of magic spy plane. In real life, Lord Snow had once helped him in his career, so that dream association made some sense to him, but his only very vague association with the name Artie Shaw was that a real-life person by that name had been an American bandleader before and during World War II. He knew nothing else about Artie Shaw.

Two weeks later, John was with Ann backstage in the studios of *The Mike Douglas Show* in Philadelphia, where Ann was about to be a guest, and they were shocked to be introduced to whom else but Artie Shaw. Shaw was a last-minute replacement guest for actor Peter Ustinov, who had been scheduled to be the main guest on the show with Ann but had canceled at the last minute. Because Ann carried a folder of dreams with her, she produced John's dream and showed it to the former bandleader, who was stunned at this weird coincidence. He then revealed to John and Ann a private detail that neither of them could have known: he had written a novel under the pseudonym Adam Snow.

The host, Mike Douglas, invited Ann to tell the story of this amazing example of dream ESP during the interview. It prompted discussion among all the guests, and as she puts it in her book, "John was the hero of the hour"[6] . . . just like in his dream novel.

For Faraday, John's spy-plane dream was a manifestation of "the underdog's psychic radar."[7] It would be a funny kind of radar, though, that not only identified a blip closing on your position but also prepresented in glowing green letters the thoughts and emotions you would feel *after* your subsequent close encounter with the object. Yet that is just what dreams often do. John's dream seems not only to have represented his emotional situation—feeling jealous (i.e., the spy plane) and maybe a bit left out by his partner's success—but to have pre-presented the way his feelings would be repaired after he shared his dream with his partner, who in turn shared it with a famous bandleader backstage at *The Mike Douglas Show*. His dream "already knew" that Artie Shaw would come into his life, and even how: as an ally in his effort to defeat or overcome his jealous ego (the rogue scientist in his dream).

Principle #3 of our book is this:

Dreams symbolically show us our future conscious thoughts in response to upheavals and learning experiences.

DREAM MASONRY

I believe there is no more striking, and ironic, example of the principle that dreams symbolically show us our future thoughts in response to upheavals than the very dream that put Freud on the scientific map, his dream about Anna Hammerschlag (Irma), her mouth symptoms, and the dirty injection that somehow made her ill. In 1982, almost half a century after Freud's death, a Brazilian psychoanalyst and cancer surgeon named José Schavelzon noticed that the precise symptoms displayed in dream Irma's mouth matched exactly the progression of oral cancer that Freud himself suffered nearly three decades after his dream, when Freud was in his late sixties.

Freud's doctors discovered a white patch on his palate and cheek, a precancerous condition called leukoplakia brought on by his decades of cigar smoking. It was followed by surgeries and radiation treatments that left big scabs in their aftermath because there was not enough skin to close the incisions inside his mouth properly. As the cancer progressed, a surgeon had to remove part of Freud's jaw and palate, which exposed his nasal cavity to view inside his mouth. It would have exposed precisely the turbinate bones he thought he could see in Irma's mouth in his dream. It became hard for Freud to open his mouth once a denture-like prosthetic was fitted, and he could barely talk for the last decade and a half of his life—again, reminiscent of Anna's/Irma's shy behavior in the dream (like the shyness of someone wearing dentures).

Was the dream a premonition, perhaps even a warning, about the consequences of Freud's smoking? This is how the dream has been interpreted by other writers.[8] In his book *The Secret History of Dreaming*, Robert Moss suggests that a single cancer cell present in Freud's mouth in 1895 could perhaps have sent a kind of warning message to Freud's brain, sparking a perplexing dream about cancer symptoms in the mouth of his patient.[9] Yet if the dream were supposed to warn him, why didn't it just have him looking at those symptoms in his own mouth, for instance in a mirror? How would Freud have ever made a connection between symptoms in Anna Hammerschlag's mouth and his own? Also, an extraordinary body-mind connection could not account for the specificity of the dream's images, which were more about the surgical consequences of Freud's cancer, not merely the presence of malignant cells. There is no way a cancer cell could know about the scabs or the visibility of intranasal features from inside the mouth at any point in time, let alone nearly three decades in the future.

As long as we don't do the easy thing here and just chalk it up to coincidence, this dream presents us with some conundrums, not only for Freud's theory of dreaming—again, Freud rejected any notion that dreams could show us the future—but also for Dunne's. Are we to imagine that Freud's dreaming brain reached twenty-eight years into his future for a brick (his own cancer symptoms) simply to help express his 1895 wish of not committing medical malpractice with Anna? That would be Dunne's formulation, yet it would be a bit like putting the cart before the proverbial horse.

I think Dunne's formulation about dreams reaching into the future for materials to represent some present wish or concern is close, but should really be flipped: dreams represent, or pre-present, a conscious future thought or feeling (or wish, in some cases), but per mnemonic principles, they typically do so using the available bricks (associations) already in memory at the time of the dream. This is Principle #4:

Dreams build future towers out of past bricks.

Those associative bricks can be from recent experience or may go back to childhood. My own precognitive dreams, such as the ones about *Star Trek* and *Island of the Blue Dolphins* in chapter 2, frequently center on future experiences that remind me of something in my childhood. It is this constant use of bricks from the past that causes dream precognition to fly under the radar in psychotherapeutic contexts like Freud's clinic (and even Jung's, as we will see later). It also can be hard to tell when a dream is targeting a future experience simply because so many of our day-to-day experiences and situations tend to repeat. As dreamer Bruce Siegel notes in his book *Dreaming the Future,* "a dream about the future with no verifiable specifics can easily be mistaken for a dream about the past."[10]

An alternative metaphor to brick-built towers would be to think of dreams as effigies of future thoughts, sewn like rag dolls from already-existing, often crazily mismatched materials. Thus, to pull from previously discussed examples, a future discovery about a star that astronomer Paul Kalas had not begun studying (Fomalhaut) would be pre-presented using a star he was intimately familiar with at the time of the dream (Beta Pictoris); the news of Vladimir Nabokov's newfound affluence after the sale of movie rights to his novel would be pre-presented using his rich benefactor (Uncle Vassily) and an entertainment genre (the circus) from his youth in prerevolutionary Russia; and my dream about thoughts of vulnerability in the aftermath of the 9/11 suicide attacks would be pre-presented using my own personal mnemonic associations to suicide and crisis.

Although we are forced to speculate a bit, we know quite a lot about Freud and his life, both in 1895 and 1923, and can thus make some pretty good guesses about his thoughts and wishes at the latter date and about why the figures in his dream in 1895 might have aptly pre-presented those thoughts and wishes in his dream.

It is a safe guess, first of all, that Freud's conscious thoughts in 1923 would have included a self-reproach for not following the urging of his best friend Wilhelm Fliess (one of the trio of physicians in the dream), who in 1895 had been trying get him to quit smoking his cigars for the sake of his health. Just before he had the dream, in fact, Freud had relapsed from a short period of abstinence recommended by Fliess and was specifically worried what his friend would say about his return to smoking. One of Freud's biographers noted that various other maladies of dream Irma and discussed by the physician trio were actually already Freud's own illnesses at the time he had his dream—rheumatism, intestinal issues, and so on[11]—so their inclusion in a bundle with his later cancer makes perfect sense. In the dream, Freud explicitly reproaches Anna/Irma with the very words he might have consciously directed at himself all those years later: "it's really only your fault."[12]

We have already seen how dream figures and objects can swap attributes. In my 9/11 dream, the low gray buildings with corrugated facades like the Twin Towers became mosques, mashing up multiple themes. Freud noted that dreams commonly saddle others with our own unwanted predicaments and give thoughts we don't want to acknowledge having to other people. His theory explicitly framed it in terms of defense mechanisms such as projection and displacement: the unacceptable thought struggling to be expressed is deformed and sent off course by a kind of psychic (in the older sense of the term) force field, a kind of deflection. The mnemonic theory would instead suggest that dream figures tend to be tokens or stand-ins representing some idea or association. A crucial point of the art-of-memory principles on which the dreaming brain operates is that in representing thoughts, it dramatizes them; and in dramatizing, it personalizes. Personalizing an idea brings it down to earth, helps us interact with it, enables us to create a dramatic story with it, and thus facilitates the metabolism of that idea, placing it in memory.* Principle #5 of our book is this:

---

*Similarly, Jung argued that gods in polytheistic societies are really personalizations of basic emotions, motivations, or psychological principles and proclivities belonging to the collective unconscious. In other words, deities are a bit like mental action figures, literal figures of speech and thought, that can be interacted with in myth and dream.

*Peripheral figures in our lives who appear in
our dreams, as well as celebrities, may be stand-ins
for associations about those individuals,
action figures in a symbolic allegory or tableau.*

There are certainly exceptions to this, however—John Wren-Lewis's dream about Artie Shaw would be an example, and we'll see another striking exception in chapter 15.

There is at least one important reason why Anna Hammerschlag, Freud's friend and patient in 1895, may have fit the bill for helping symbolically pre-present thoughts related to his health issues in 1923 and after: she was namesake and godmother to his own daughter Anna, who served as his nurse and close companion after his surgeries and for the final decade and a half of his life. Anna Freud would be born a few months after his dream and in fact was named after Anna Hammerschlag; it was Freud's way of honoring his dream. The twenty-eight-year-old Anna Freud would thus have had powerful associations to the misery he was enduring in 1923 and after, including ordeals related to the monstrous jaw prosthetic he had to wear and that she had to help him insert and remove on a daily basis. His dreaming brain in 1895 might have fastened on the main Anna then available in his life, Anna Hammerschlag, as the closest available brick to help pre-present those later thoughts.*

That dreams could predict the future was a common folkloric belief that, throughout his career, Freud took every opportunity to disclaim and debunk, and he never publicly recanted his dream theory. But I think Freud's conscious thoughts in 1923 around his cancer might well have included puzzled reflections on the uncanny similarity between what was happening in his own body and the symptoms

---

*Also, when bad things happen to good people, even good people may find themselves wishing the bad thing had happened to someone else. We have no proof, but it is very reasonable to think Freud's thoughts in 1923 and later would also have included a vague wish that someone else and not him might suffer the awful cancer and brutal surgeries he was enduring.

Anna Hammerschlag had displayed in the dream that had put him on the map all those years ago. He would have at least noticed the similarity. Did he make any connection that his dream had been a premonition? How could this coincidence not have at least unsettled his outward certainty about dreams never being premonitions? I cannot believe that it didn't. If that's the case, his thoughts may have included a wish that he had been correct that dreams (especially this one fateful dream) are really just wish-fulfillments and never premonitions of future events. Wishing he was right about dreams being just wishes would effectively wish away his cancer as well as put himself above any professional reproach for having possibly misled the world about the meaning of our dreams.[13]

In short, I propose that Freud's anxiety over his smoking in 1895 sparked a kind of temporal short circuit with his health situation in 1923—a condition (cancer) clearly caused by something symbolically like a dirty syringe (cigars). The progression of his cancer, his dependency on his daughter Anna, and perhaps even his belated doubts about his dream theory were pre-presented using another Anna in his life at the time of the dream, one who was, in her own way, associated with all these things, including professional doubts about malpractice and the possible inadequacy of his therapeutic approach.*

Principle #6 is:

_____

A recent situation or experience may spark a dream about a future experience that resembles it somehow (thematic resonance).

_____

The bottom line is that Freud's dream theory was close, but no cigar. He was mistaken about dreams' functional role—they don't simply, or

_____

*We have no way of knowing what specific event or time window Freud's dream might have pre-presented, although a passage in his biography by his friend Ernest Jones is suggestive: an occasion when Freud and Anna (his daughter) needed to summon a doctor to help install his denture prosthetic because he couldn't open his mouth far enough. See chapter 9 of *Time Loops* (Wargo 2018) for more on this.

mainly, dramatize repressed sexual wishes (few psychoanalysts even think that anymore)—but in grasping that dreams operate on associative principles, he correctly identified the way that memory links ideas, events, and emotions. The connective tissue of memory is association, and it works in dreams precisely the way Freud showed: a pun, a metaphor or a metonym (part standing for the whole), displacement onto another item in the same set or series, or some other nonlogical relation based on idiosyncratic past experience. Consequently, Freud's innovative dream-interpretation method, free associating on given dream elements, is an indispensable part of understanding our dreams and revealing the way they metabolize our waking lives, including our future waking lives.

6

The Unusual Suspects
of the Dreamworld

*Applying Free Association
and the Mnemonic Theory*

Most precognitive dreams are not literal replays (or pre-plays) of future experiences. Instead, they relate obliquely, symbolically, and associatively to those experiences. This is why, to create a truly powerful, theoretically informed approach to precognitive dreams, we need to combine Dunne's insights into dream precognition with more recent findings related to dreams' mnemonic function and Freud's method of free association. When we apply these principles and free associate on our dreams, the full smorgasbord of dream precognition will be open to our enjoyment and enlightenment.

Free association is not a difficult, esoteric, or effortful exercise. In fact, it is the easiest thing in the world for the voracious, connection-making brain, yet as adults we typically suppress this inherently playful connection-making in the effort to think more linearly and logically. To free associate just means giving yourself permission to notice and reflect on the first thing or things that come to mind for each noticed and recorded element in your dream. Just note honestly what each character, object, setting, and striking details call to mind. Write those associations down along with your dream, next to the dream description.

An association will often seem random: it may be some recent situation; something somebody said; something that has nagged or troubled you; some scene in a movie or line in a song; or something that provoked frustration, guilt, or desire. Free associate not only on the main figures, situations, and settings, but also on any distortion of reality—an altered locale or geographical feature, altered appearance of a familiar person, and so on. Ask yourself: What is being replaced or distorted or substituted, and what significance does the altered or substituted detail have for you? What is, perhaps, missing in the dream setting that would be there ordinarily or in reality? (We'll see later a number of ways that dream setting can be particularly important—it is a topic deserving a chapter all its own.)

Contrary to what Freud-bashers always assert, free association (when it is done in good faith) is not straining or forcing connections to produce meanings that will lead to a desired conclusion. You do have to play by the rules: only the first thing or two that immediately spring to mind for a noticed dream element are valid connections. If nothing comes to mind, leave it. And you should free associate without any expectation that your associations, by themselves, will add up to something or illuminate the dream's overall meaning, or the future experience it is pre-encoding. The whole point, in fact, is that if the dream relates to some future experience, that experience probably hasn't happened yet, at least when you are writing the dream down. (I have found that whenever I make a guess about what might happen, based on a dream, I am usually spectacularly wrong.) But by including your immediate associations with your dream, you will be more likely to detect such a link later, either when returning to your dream record after the experience has occurred or while the experience is actually happening.

Often simply the act of putting words to an image reveals an association—another reason why writing your dreams down is so important. Here's an example. One morning in 2014, I awoke from a dream that felt like some Eastern European New Wave film from the 1960s.

It was distinctly black and white,* about a couple on vacation, a car at an intersection, and something about a sailboat on a lake—almost more of a vague impression than any narrative I could pin down. I immediately jotted down these images in my notebook, and before setting my notebook aside and getting out of bed, I took a few moments to free associate on the imagery in my dream. All it took was brief reflection to realize that the images and the overall ambience of the dream reminded me of a specific Polish film from the early 1960s, called *Knife in the Water*, that I had seen many years before in a Slavic film festival. So I jotted this association down beside my description of the images. A quick Google search after I got to the office that morning confirmed that this was indeed the film I had been dreaming about.[1]

An hour or two later, I went into the small office kitchen to get a knife to cut and peel my apple. It was a sparsely appointed kitchen, and there was just one knife, a cheap serrated knife. What should I encounter on that day, however, but the sink having backed up—the only time in the three years I had worked there that I could remember that happening—and a single object gleaming at me from under about four inches of gray, filthy water: the serrated knife. It was the only object in the sink. My dream had "come true" in the unexpected and witty fashion that is typical of many or even most Dunne dreams. But I probably would not have noticed the connection had I not taken the time to write down and free associate on the dream initially.

DRAMATIZATION

One of the rules of the ancient art of memory was to make mnemonic images as dramatic as possible, since the emotional charge of an image helps it stick better. Thus, our dreams concoct very dramatic and

---

*The perennial question "Do we dream in color or black and white?" arises from mistakenly comparing dreams to television. Dreams are not stimuli presented to the senses but are imaginative constructs. Color (or distinct absence of color, as in my case) will only be noticed in dreams if and when it is meaningful—that is, carries some significance. Otherwise, colors may be ill-defined.

elaborate dramas to represent even relatively mundane experiences. This is one factor preventing us from detecting dream correspondences to waking-life events: we will imagine that a dramatic dream must be about something similarly dramatic and "big," when in fact the referent could be an upheaval as minor as needing to retrieve a favorite utensil from dirty water and unclog the drain.

Even without regard for precognitive content in dreams, this discrepancy was noted early on by writers about dreams and dreaming. In later editions of his *Interpretation of Dreams,* Freud quoted his friend, psychoanalyst Hanns Sachs, to this effect: "If we look in our consciousness at something that has been told us by a dream about a contemporary (real) situation, we ought not be surprised to find that the monster which we saw under the magnifying glass of analysis turns out to be a tiny infusorian."[2]

Principle #7 is:

_____

The drama quotient in a dream may be wildly out of proportion to the significance of the experience or upheaval that it targets.

_____

This mismatch of scale and importance not only conceals dreams' correspondence to waking events; it also contributes to our natural disbelief that there *is* such a correspondence. Naively, it seems unrealistic that the brain would go to all the trouble of pre-presenting something as stupid and inconsequential as the disappointment of finding a desired utensil in a backed-up sink using something as elaborate as, in my case, a Polish New Wave film about a couple's eventful holiday on the water—as if such an image is, itself, a kind of production requiring actors, a set, props, and so on. But a moment's thought shows how silly that reasoning is: for my brain there was no effort whatsoever in triggering a neuronal pattern associated with my patchy memory of an old Polish movie whose title succinctly expressed, as in a pun, the biggest event in my otherwise boring morning at work. Dreams are easy for the brain, not a production in any sense of the word.

Interestingly, this same apparent mismatch of scale and significance was the mental block for the first modern scholar of the ancient art of memory, the English historian Frances Yates.[3] She had trouble imagining the usefulness of the art as an efficient method of learning because she imagined that creating a vivid mnemonic image was effortful, requiring a lot of additional work. But she didn't practice the art of memory, so it wasn't obvious to her that "creating a mental image" was just the ancients' way of describing free association. The mnemonist uses whatever random, personal associations automatically spring to mind to help them retain and then recall new material (like, for me, the *Firefly* character Mal for the malleus bone of the ear). There's no effort involved whatsoever—such images stick automatically.

My *Knife in the Water* dream is an utterly trivial example, but it shows the principle that dreams represent future thoughts or experiences using material already available in memory. Again, it accounts for why dreams are so full of recognizable stuff from our past even if the thoughts and wishes they encode may really be from our future, in response to things that haven't happened yet. Like the hole in a donut, the experience itself generally is not visible in the dream, at least not directly or literally (although there are occasional exceptions). Without doing a little free association on the dream's core images to fill out that hole, you will be unlikely to notice a connection to a later waking experience, because that missing hole is, itself, the link to the experience.

This is Principle #8 of our book:

It is associations to our dreams and not their manifest content that often reveal the links to later experiences.

YOUR INNER KEYSER SÖZE

The mismatch between the insignificance of most life experiences and the larger-than-life way the precognitive brain tends to pre-present them in dreams acts to cloak most precognition from the gaze even of assiduous dream-recorders. So does the expectation, reinforced by popular books on ESP, that such a "psychic" faculty would mainly be relevant to momentous or tragic events. Was my dream about gray-corduroy mosques on the morning of 9/11 a "premonition"? I suppose you could look at it that way. But to describe my *Knife in the Water* dream as a premonition of finding the sink backed up at work would be comical. The common myths that precognitive dreams center on big traumas and necessarily feel numinous or special are readily put to rest by doing precognitive dreamwork—that is, doing the work of really studying our dreamlife using the principles I have described so far, rather than waiting for that relatively rare animal, the literalistic dream about some tragedy or catastrophe.

Using free association to discover subtly camouflaged dream precognition has an important impact on how we think of the phenomenon. Instead of being a rare occurrence around major emotional upheavals in our lives, it becomes apparent that it may be a nightly thing and we've just never seen it because we don't free associate or, if we do, because we've internalized the Freudian (and Jungian) notion that dreams are in every way, shape, and form about our past, not about our future. When we expand our gallery of precognitive dreams through precognitive dreamwork, it helps us overthrow that law-of-large-numbers argument that is central to the skeptics' gaslighting.

I often think of Bryan Singer's 1994 film noir classic *The Usual Suspects* as a perfect metaphor for precognitive dreamwork—for how our dreams' big productions beguile us and distract us from the minor future upheavals that usually trigger them, as well as how dreams, in typical trickster fashion, often conceal their precognitive nature until after the fact. If you haven't seen it, it's a story about a criminal conspiracy gone wrong, as told to police detective Dave Kujan (Chazz Palminteri) by a two-bit crook with a limp, named Verbal Kint (Kevin Spacey). The convoluted story Verbal tells centers on a legendary, mysterious, very scary Turkish gangster named Keyser Söze, who ends up killing all of Verbal's coconspirators in a fire on a boat. Verbal, seemingly beneath notice, is the only one to escape from the disaster to tell the tale.

In the classic final scene, Verbal finishes telling the story to the detective and gets up and shuffles out of the office, and the detective just sits there with his partner, reflecting on the amazing story this crook has been telling them for the previous two hours. But as he sips his coffee, the detective's eyes fall on random things around his partner's office or clipped to the bulletin board—a mugshot, a corporate logo, a news clipping—and he realizes that each item connects to some part of the elaborate story he has just heard. He drops his coffee mug—it shatters on the floor—as he has the appalling realization that Verbal has been improvising, making up his whole narrative just from random stimuli in the office. Lastly, we see Verbal, limping away from the police station, but he gradually loses his limp and then gets into a dark limousine that has arrived to pick him up—he was Keyser Söze all along.

Spoiler alert: if you haven't seen *The Usual Suspects,* do not—repeat, do not—read the previous paragraph. It's one of the biggest twist endings in film history.

If Verbal Kint is your trickster-like dreaming brain, your near future is like the detective's messy office. Doing precognitive dreamwork is being a detective, paying attention to the "random" flotsam and jetsam of your waking life. Once you get the hang of free associating on your dreams, you'll have these kinds of dumbfounding realizations repeatedly: that the dreams in your journal often seem in hindsight like grossly exaggerated dramatizations—cinematic, in some cases—of mostly objectively minor upheavals and discoveries that follow.

Which brings us to the $64,000 question . . .

HOW MANY OF OUR DREAMS ARE PRECOGNITIVE?

Skeptics with fingers firmly jammed in their ears will say, "Easy. None!" Among those who have bothered to actually study the question, estimates are much higher. After an investigation of his own database of dreams, Bruce Siegel estimated that a quarter of his sample of 241 dreams were clearly precognitive.[4] I am less systematic, but I am also able to identify subsequent correspondences to about a quarter of the dreams I write down. But given all the inherent limitations in recording dreams, interpreting them, comparing them to subsequent and prior events across the span of a whole lifetime, and sharing them with others, there would really be no way to make a firm assessment of how many dreams may relate to future experiences, and certainly no way to make an estimate that would hold water scientifically. We have to appeal to the philosopher's *reason* on this question: if anywhere near a quarter of them can be shown reasonably to be precognitive, then it is reasonable that many more may be precognitive and we just don't detect them as such.

You will seldom see precognition if you aren't looking for it, and until now, few have looked for it. The worst mistake would be to assume that, since precognition is hard to fathom, the brain therefore finds it hard to do. That's a fallacy. If you accept the basic premise that some dreams do relate to future experiences, it raises the reasonable—indeed natural—question: Why would evolution create a brain that reaches into its own future but only manifest that ability occasionally? Might all dreams be precognitive?

It may really be a mistake to speak of precognitive dreams as some distinct set of dreams targeting a future event versus one in the past. Dunne suspected that dreams draw equally on past and future experiences.[5] Again, dreams that seem to be about past experiences, per our cultural assumptions or per some standard dream theory like Freud's, could simply be using past bricks (identifiable items and experiences in memory) to pre-present some future experience that goes unnoticed by the dreamer or dream researcher. Thus, coming to some realistic estimate of the true prevalence of dream precognition is the kind of question that is going to require many precognitive dreamworkers sharing their experiences to help answer.

The bottom line is this: we should stop thinking of precognition as something like the special holiday china our moms kept in a certain cupboard and brought out just once a year. Our brains likely use it every day, every night, possibly even every dream, for all occasions big and small. If the brain ever does it, it probably always does it. Principle #9 of precognitive dreamwork isn't a conclusion so much as a working presumption:

Assume (without ever being able to prove it)
that all your dreams may be precognitive.

Yeah yeah, I know what happens when you assume, but this is something I'm increasingly confident making an ass of myself over. Dreams are guilty of being precognitive until proven innocent. I strongly suspect many if not most of them are guilty of this crime.*

There's nothing disappointing about realizing the objective smallness of the majority of life upheavals that capture the attention of our precognitive brains. Realizing you have had a dream about an event in your future—even something utterly trivial like a sink backing up—brings the same amazement Chazz Palminteri's character feels when he drops his coffee mug. Your brain has been pulling an amazing trick, reaching into its future—reaching into the place that science for three centuries has said was the most forbidden place of all—for cinematic stories to beguile your dreaming self.

As it starts to really sink in that your brain is doing this, and doing it constantly, you begin to see that the insignificant, puny, two-bit personality you thought you were is really something secret and huge. Hopefully not a murderous underworld boss, but something similarly legendary, powerful, and defiant of the laws our society holds dear—the

---

*For instance, I can't imagine a way to test it, but I would imagine that the vast majority of Americans probably dreamed somehow of the 9/11 terror attacks on the night of September 10, 2001. The hundreds or thousands who actually reported their premonitory dreams of the event would have been just a fraction of those who noticed such dreams and didn't report them, which would itself have been a tiny fraction of those who had dreams associatively linked to the themes of the day but without ever noticing the link . . . and that would have been a tiny fraction of those who had such dreams but didn't remember them at all, and so on.

laws of causation itself. You've been a very, very bad person. You've harbored a trickster in your head, one that walked with a limp and made itself seem pitifully small; but when you realize what it really accomplishes on a nightly basis, you see that that trickster was literally a kind of time traveler, a Time Lord, and you never knew it.

Time to stand tall, lose the limp, and get into your Time Lord limo.

PART 3

GIFTS IN THE
LANDSCAPE

7

Rules of the Grail Kingdom

Dream Space and Dream Time

In Richard Wagner's opera *Parsifal,* the Grail Kingdom is depicted as a land out of time. When the knight Gurnemanz leads the young would-be hero of the opera's title into this realm, elaborate stage mechanisms create the illusion that the characters have been transported from the forest into the castle of the Grail King without moving. "I hardly walk," Parsifal says, "yet seem t'have gone quite far." Gurnemanz replies, "You see, my son, that here time turns to space."[1]

Wagner's weird opera, which infused the soaring Germanic myths about the Holy Grail with elements of Eastern philosophy drawn from the composer's interest in Buddhism, has always seemed strangely prophetic. First performed in 1882, the opera anticipated Einstein's scientifically and culturally transformative discoveries over two decades later about the interconvertability of time and space.

Through a series of thought experiments involving trains with lanterns on parallel tracks, Einstein—who was working by day at a patent office in Bern, Switzerland—divined that if an object accelerated to speeds approaching that of light, its length would appear (to an outside observer) to shorten; it would essentially angle into the fourth dimension, time, becoming increasingly perpendicular to the three dimensions of space. He later figured out that gravity is just the acceleration of objects in space as it curves into that fourth dimension.

Around massive objects like black holes, where space is curved to its utmost, space turns into time. Consequently, as mentioned earlier, Einstein's math teacher Hermann Minkowski realized that his student had really discovered spacetime, a block universe in which the future already exists and the past still exists. From any particular point along an object's worldline, there is theoretically a whole range of vantage points from which it is already in the past. This also goes for you right now, reading these words.

This has serious implications for things like free will, and philosophers bent on preserving human freedom at all costs have never liked the block universe. In 1922, the philosopher Henri Bergson publicly debated Einstein in Paris about this question. Bergson thought time was its own thing, *durée* (duration), irreducible to any other category. Einstein, who was happy treating time as a dimension like space, is often said to have won the debate, but people have never really settled the issue. It is particularly troubling to the French, for some reason. In the middle of the century, the existentialist philosopher Jean-Paul Sartre, who held a more Bergsonian view, publicly conflicted with his countryman, the anthropologist Claude Levi-Strauss, who held a more static, structuralist view. The anthropologist wrote a classic book, *The Savage Mind,* partly as a kind of rebuttal to Sartre's dialectical view of history: people everywhere, he argued, not just in Europe, turn time into space.

Levi-Strauss seems to be right that the spatialization of time is not just some Western conceit. Humans everywhere seem to have a hard time understanding temporal relationships—that is, causality—so to understand those relationships, we model them physically and spatially. One oft-cited example is the Dreamtime of the native peoples of Australia. The mythic past and present merge in the landscape, and the history of a lineage or clan is fixed in the landscape's concrete objects and features; in some sense it is history de-abstracted from space.[2] But it is really true for all humans, and for all kinds of abstractions such as death and negation, as well as complex causal relationships: we manipulate difficult concepts metaphorically using concrete objects, bodies, people, and their physical interactions.

It turns out that there are interesting neurobiological reasons for our overriding preference to think in terms of space, the body, and the landscape, and they are hugely important for dreams, memory, and the portion of our memory that is from the future (our premory).

THE INNER DREAMTIME

The hippocampus, the brain's librarian and archivist, happens to be where our neural place representations, our maps of space, are found.[3] A growing body of research shows that autobiographical memory, or memory for our life experiences (called episodic memory), is significantly a matter of tying our experiences to these spatial maps. So-called place cells in the hippocampus used for navigation may also be the neural substrate helping to organize our life experiences.

Even if they lacked a neurobiology to link it to, mnemonists have always grasped that our memories are structured spatially. People with powerful memories know intuitively how to tie new experiences to familiar places, turning them into stories unfolding in a kind of whimsical mental geography. The classical arts of memory formalized this by situating images for material that needed to be remembered in imaginary memory palaces and stringing long texts and arguments together into narratives—stories or journeys—that unfold in or among those mental spaces. The art of memory simply utilizes and amplifies the way the mind naturally keys memories to the details of setting and circumstance.[4]

For nonliterate societies, the places of the physical world become a sort of lived-in memory space. I stayed for a few months in a remote village in Papua New Guinea, surrounded by rainforest. To my eyes, the forest was dense and beautiful but without variety. Space had no meaning, let alone time. But my local companions and guides would often stop and point at some bent root, some certain small rise or gulley, and laugh, remembering something funny so-and-so had said in that spot or remembering a particular pig they had killed there. The jungle was, for them, a familiar landscape of memory. Our urban and suburban environments work the same way, even if we're not as conscious of it. So do the virtual spaces we inhabit. In school, you probably had the experience of trying to hunt down some fact in a textbook, remembering that it was in the lower left corner of some page. It's the same thing. (This kind of book "orienteering" may be lost with e-books.)

As an extension of this principle, songs, poetry, and myth, with their schematic storylines, are excellent mnemonic devices and serve as cultural hard drives for nonliterate societies to archive their histories. Myth, like memory, works on art-of-memory principles and can preserve amazingly old historical events such as climate catastrophes. Oral myths of the Klamath people, for instance, appear to preserve a record of the eruption that formed Oregon's Crater Lake 8,000 years ago.[5] Storytelling is really the creation of an effective memory architecture to encode information, a spatial-metaphoric journey through a sequence of events such as a quest. The power of story is something we all intuitively understand from our experience with the entertainment industry. Like Gurnemanz and Parsifal zooming from the forest to the castle in only a couple steps, a well-scripted film is not only memorable but feels like you accelerate through it in no time at all; a badly written one, by the same token, can feel excruciatingly long, like trudging through molasses, and is distinctly unmemorable. (Anyone who has studied filmmaking or attended amateur film competitions knows that a five-minute student film—at least, one that is by another student—can feel like it is an hour long.)

Dreams, including precognitive dreams, obey the same principles that govern good stories.

IMAGINAL CAPACITY

One feature our dreaming brains share with Hollywood is amazing special effects. And one of the coolest features of our inner special-effects studio is its ability to create a totally immersive virtual reality. Just as dreams personify ideas and abstractions and thereby allow us to interact with them physically, they also create a spatial environment within which to have those symbolic interactions.

A precognitive dream (or, rather, one containing precognitive material) typically compiles or gathers together free associations to future experiences or thoughts and then places those associations in a setting. The setting might be unfamiliar, but frequently it is a familiar location like an office, school, home, or town, or more typically it will be like a familiar setting but with distinct features or characteristics that don't exist in reality, or it will mash up different locations into some composite. Those deviations from reality are often significant terms in the dream rebus and are worth free associating on (for instance, the associations I had to the real location of the "mosques" in my 9/11 dream). But whether the space is familiar or unfamiliar, most if not all REM dreams "take place" somewhere—you will be hard pressed to find a dream that isn't situated in some kind of (at least vague) location. And true to the memory-palace principle used by ancient mnemonists, a typical dream may be divided into a few separate scenes in slightly different locations within that unified setting.

We have seen already that interesting media stories, films, and pictures are often precognized in dreams. When this happens, the dream will typically place you within the dramatized scene, rather than just looking at it. In the age of social media, I find that many of my "trivial" precognitive dreams relate to pictures or stories encountered on the internet the next day, but the dream will inevitably place me within the scene or some semblance of the scene, interacting with its figures and objects. Even if the precognized experience is passive, dreams generally put us in the thick of the action. (I'll describe an example of this in chapter 17—a lucid dream in which I was physically interacting with prehistoric creatures seen in a magazine the following day.) Elizabeth Krohn's dreams about air disasters (chapter 2) are also examples. In some of her dreams, she felt she was in the scene, interacting with the people on the flight,[6] even if the dream was (I suggest) actually about the news report and her reactions to it.

The symbolic space the dream uses to pre-present an experience is probably never random, even though it may seem that way. If it is not the actual location of the future experience dreamed about, it may be associated with the experience somehow or may be narratively consistent with some key association or symbol used by the dream, as seemed to be the case with my dream on the morning of 9/11.

The ability to recall dreams is correlated with the ability to imagine visually while awake, such as when mentally rehearsing actions or generating inner visual representations when reading or listening to another person speak.[7] Conjuring and manipulating these images is simply what we call using our imaginations. Imaginal aptitude falls on a spectrum— some people readily conjure vivid mental images, some not at all, and many (probably most people) fall somewhere in between. (For instance, despite considering myself fairly imaginative, my mental pictures per se are mostly pretty dim and unstable, gray-on-black cartoons.) It may also be that mental imagery can take multiple sensory and even conceptual forms besides vision. In any case, facility with conjuring and manipulating mental imagery can be cultivated—for instance, shamanic training involves learning to create and stabilize vivid internal images[8] as does training in various magical or occult practices. But when sleeping, we probably all do it.

For premodern mnemonists, memory and imagination were a single thing.[9] Dreams, by encoding memories via interactive scenes unfolding in space and time, seem to show us this secret identity. I strongly suspect that the kinds of immersive mental images many people are aware of spontaneously conjuring when reading or listening to a story are the real targets of many precognitive dreams, such as J. W. Dunne's dream about the volcano eruption (really, about reading the news story) or his friend's fatal crash (really, about reading a letter or bulletin informing him of the crash).

Given the spatial immersiveness and narrative structure of dream experiences, we may naively assume that they unfold in something like real time, but this is probably not the case. The few images in my *Knife in the Water* dream could have been a brief flicker of cortical activity lasting a few seconds. This is important, because it helps us not be thrown by the prevalence of precognitive dreams about what seem like trivialities. When we realize we may spend a few hours each night dreaming and that any given dream we actually remember may represent just a small fraction of that cortical activation, then it becomes easier to imagine how we could potentially be (pre)metabolizing many if not all waking experiences that make some impact on us—perhaps both of prior days and subsequent days—in the course of a night. The ones we catch and remember are just a small, seemingly random selection. (It is also the case that dreamworthy moments that seem trivial at the time assume greater significance further ahead in our future, for reasons we cannot yet know—a topic we will return to later.)

THE DREAM WINDOW

One of the many mysteries of neuroscience is determining how the brain represents time. Neurons called time cells, which fire at distinct temporal intervals, have been discovered in several brain areas and seem to help reckon sequences of events over short time frames (seconds and minutes). But how the brain keeps track of sequences of experiences over the course of days, weeks, months, years, and decades has eluded researchers.[10] There is no objective temporal yardstick to hang our lives on, and time cells could hardly be expected to keep some mental beat over months and years and decades.

One possible answer comes from the study of people with synesthesia—that is, those who perceive sounds as colors, and so on. Synesthetes sometimes report having vivid mental maps of time, calendrical maps.[11] It may be that we all reckon time this way but are generally less aware of it. I am not a synesthete, for example, but I am still dimly aware of representing the year spatially as a disk, and of pictorial-spatial representations of various swathes of my life as neighborhoods and curving roads. Ultimately, we may have a coherent sense of our autobiography because events that occurred in temporal proximity are bound together in our memory, perhaps being placed together on idiosyncratic mental calendrical maps and landscapes. And in the same way geologists cross-correlate events using relative references such as carbon-14, tree rings, and other dating methods, it makes sense that the brain would create coherence in our autobiographical chronology by binding or linking together experiences that happen in temporal proximity. Dreams could be the key to this, by bundling experiences that are closely proximate in time, even if (or especially if) those events do not share any other kind of logical association. Consistent with such a hypothesis, very often precognitive dreams contain references to multiple, otherwise unrelated experiences that happen closely together during waking life.

Here's an example. In early 2017, I dreamed about a gang of young hoodlums rushing toward a certain house across a valley from my mother's home in Morrison, Colorado. I was observing this somehow in the rearview mirror of my car, from a very specific spot off to one side in my mother's driveway, and a voice in the dream made a comment about how someone was going to regret crying wolf (sounding a false alarm). A couple evenings later, I received an email from my mom with night-vision videos of three young mountain lions prowling among trees and converging on the carcass of a newly killed deer behind the very house I'd dreamed about. I'd never dreamed about that house before, and had never had a reason to (I didn't even know the people living there), so I realized my dream was likely precognitive of this email and video—simply replacing mountain lions with young hoodlums. (The animals did distinctly remind me of a gang of cocky adolescents prowling their 'hood.)

But here's the thing: less than an hour after getting that email and viewing the mountain lion video, I stupidly decided to take out the trash in the middle of a rainstorm that had (unknown to me) turned into a typical mid-Atlantic ice storm, and I humiliatingly fell down an entire flight of ice-slick steps in front of my building. In my fright, I found myself calling for help as I tumbled and couldn't find anything to hold on to. When I caught my breath and regained my composure at the bottom of the steps, I realized nothing was broken but my pride: I was embarrassed that I had "cried wolf"—that is, sounded an alarm for no reason. The upstairs neighbors came out and asked if I was all right, and I said I was, and that was that. When I returned to my computer, I looked at my dream record to refresh my memory, and I realized that the specific spot on my mother's driveway where I had been looking in the rearview mirror at the hoodlums across the valley in my dream was exactly where I had actually slipped and fallen and sprained my wrist several months earlier when visiting my mother—my only other fall in recent memory.

Thus, my dream had mashed up associations to multiple interesting or upsetting experiences during a single eventful evening, including a video of mountain lions and a slip and fall, but those events in the dream were totally unrelated . . . except that they occurred within, as I said, about an hour of each other. The dream had glommed them together into a composite tableau. It also made significant use of a spatial location: the dream setting was meaningfully related to one of the events it encoded and thus became a significant term in the dream rebus.

This temporal-window effect is so prevalent in my own dreams and dreams of others I have studied that I have come to believe it is a central principle in precognitive dreamwork. Principle #10:

Dreams often encode experiences within a single temporal window of waking time, although not necessarily to just one emotionally salient occurrence during that window.

The window is sometimes as wide as a few hours, in my experience, but exactly how wide it may be remains an open question. I have yet to record a dream that seemed to mnemonically encode experiences happening across a whole day in waking life, but that doesn't mean such dreams don't exist. "More research needed," as they say. It is another aspect of the phenomenon that armies of dreamworkers can now help answer with their own dream journals.

This counterintuitive temporal-window effect is just one of many reasons the mnemonic hypothesis formulated by Sue Llewellyn is so compelling. Again, the operative principle in the neuroscience of memory and learning is that neurons that fire together wire together.

It makes a lot of sense that experience X, which happens during the same time period as experience Y, might be bound with Y associatively by being literally wired together with it in a dream; that way the experiences will be forever linked in our long-term memory. I'll always remember that I got that one mountain lion video from my mom on the night of the big ice storm in 2017, and vice versa.

Incidentally, this is also one reason why mnemonists always pay attention to the setting and to the haphazard circumstances where they first learn a new fact. Counterintuitively, paying attention to seemingly unrelated details like the noises outside the classroom, the funny outfit the instructor was wearing, or the peculiar smell of the student sitting next to you will help you remember the otherwise boring facts of a lecture.

UNKNOWN UNKNOWNS

Associative binding of experiences in memory to create an internal chronology would also help explain why most precognitive dreams are only identified as such in hindsight. Even if premory is just an aspect of memory and obeys most of the same principles, the stand-out exception is that only with memory for things past can we engage in what psychologists call source monitoring. We can often tell more or less how we know things from past experience because we can situate them, at least roughly, in relation to other biographical details. We can't do this with experiences refluxing from our future, because they lack any context. We don't know yet where or how they fit into our lives, so it may be natural for the conscious mind to assume that they don't fit at all.[12]

Again, it is natural and inviting to think of precognition as a kind of radar or sonar scanning for perils in the water ahead. A metaphor that Dunne used for precognitive dreaming is a flashlight we point ahead of us on a dark path. But it makes more sense that our brains are constantly receiving messages sent back in time from our future self and are continually sifting and scanning those messages for possible associations to present concerns and longstanding priorities without knowing where that information comes from, let alone how far away it is in time. Items that match our current concerns or preoccupations will be taken and elaborated as dreams or premonitions or other conscious "psi" experiences, but we are likely only to recognize their precognitive character after the future event transpires and we recognize its source. And even then, we will only notice it, by and large, if we are paying close attention.

That matching or resonance with current concerns may be important in determining the timing of a dream in relation to its future referent. For instance, it is possible Freud dreamed about the oral symptoms in the mouth of his patient Anna Hammerschlag when he did because of a confluence of events in his life in 1895 that pre-minded him of his situation all those years later, in 1923—including his relapse to smoking his cigars after his friend Wilhelm Fliess had told him to quit. Again, his thoughts about his smoking may have been the short circuit or thematic resonance between these two distant points in his life, precipitating the dream.

Incidentally, there is no reason to assume that that single dream of Freud's was the only one in his life about his cancer and surgeries. Multiple dreams may point to the same experience via multiple symbolic or associative avenues, so it would be expected that some of Freud's later dreams, especially closer to 1923, may have also related to the same experiences. We'll never know, of course. But dreamers frequently report multiple precognitive dreams targeting the same later upheaval in their lives, especially major experiences like health crises and life milestones. We'll return to this, and to dream daisy-chains, in chapter 17.

Because of our inability to engage in source monitoring with information refluxing from our future, we should think of precognition less like shining a flashlight ahead of us than like sorting through a pile of mail where, in almost all cases, the return address is missing or unreadable. This produces a problem of definition, because if we don't know where a piece of mail comes from, or whether it is junk, do we call it information or noise? Its origin, its "sender," only becomes apparent after the fact ("It was from me all along!"). Meanwhile, unknowingly, we will have taken the necessary actions to bring us to the point from which that fact can be apprehended—a theme I foresee we will be returning to later when we delve into the thorny question of fate.

CALENDRICAL RESONANCE

The idea that dreams bind time using space and co-locate proximate events on some kind of mental map or physical geography of time helps explain another of the most uncanny and pervasive features of precognitive dreaming: the fact that even if we don't yet know where or when our dreams come from, our dreams often seem to "know" precisely what time it is and especially what date it is.

I mentioned a sort of inverse-square law possibly governing how likely it is to notice a dream connection to an event, with precognitive dreams most likely to be fulfilled or realized within a day or two of the dream and tapering off after that. A thematic resonance strong enough to spark a short circuit between temporally distant experiences may skew this, as we have seen, but the other big exception is dreams exactly a year or multiple years prior to the experience they precognize. Probably because of those mental calendars, times of the year and even specific dates resonate with each other in our biography. As your dream journal grows in size to comprise years of dreams, it becomes possible to detect that highly salient or important experiences were sometimes captured precognitively exactly a year, two years, or more in the past— sometimes even decades.

A reader of my previous book named Janet shared several precognitive dreams she had recorded in a dated journal that proved to be calendrically resonant with surprising events involving her own or her family's health. Some of the dreams were several years or even a decade or more in advance of the events precognized, but they were always exactly on the same date of the year. One of the remarkable dreams Janet shared was from February 2001, when she dreamed of visiting the health clinic at a specific university far from where she actually lived, because her hands "felt stuck" and she was worried she had multiple sclerosis. In reality, she had never been to that university, let alone that clinic, nor did she have any personal associations yet to multiple sclerosis (although her hands did feel numb when she woke up that morning). On exactly the same date, fully fifteen years later, she received news that her niece, who had just enrolled at the very university she had dreamed about, had just been diagnosed with multiple sclerosis.

Depending on how focused you are on things like dates and anniversaries, calendrical resonances may or may not be exact. My dream journals contain several examples of dreams that later appeared precognitive of a significant experience (or bundles of proximate experiences) one year or multiple years later, and sometimes it is exact, but not always. For instance, I precognized uncannily specific details of the births of both of my children exactly a year before, in both cases. Most of my calendrically resonant dreams, however, are off by a day or two in either direction.*

My collaborator Tobi (whom I discussed in chapter 3) frequently records calendrically resonant precognitive dreams, and usually she can count on them being exact, although there are exceptions. In late March and early April of 2017, for instance, Tobi recorded a series of dreams that, in hindsight, related to specific events and experiences three years later during the stressful initial weeks of the COVID-19 pandemic in the United States. On March 19, 2017, she dreamed about her late grandmother, who had been in an assisted living facility before dying of cardiopulmonary issues, with repeated reference to the number 4,477; in another part of the dream, a physician friend complained of exhaustion and overwork from having to repeatedly work weekends. Two days short of three years later, on March 17, 2020, at a point when

---

*In the afterword to *Time Loops* (Wargo 2018), I described a dream in 1999 that clearly pointed to a single afternoon eighteen years ahead in my future, minus two days. True to the dream-window principle, this very profound-seeming dream captured multiple unrelated experiences and thoughts within a couple hours of each other on that afternoon, including highly specific associations to the near-completion of my book, regret and embarrassment about a chapter I had to cut after I discovered I had made a mistake, as well as an equally specific worry about my health. The dream compiled these associations into a Jung-style initiatory journey through an imaginary structure on the campus where I had in 1999 been attending school.

the mysterious virus was principally claiming the lives of older people with underlying heart and lung conditions, Tobi printed out a CNN front page with the bold headline "Health Officials Warn U.S. Is at a Tipping Point." The highly anxiety-provoking stories and graphics on the page reflected all of the themes from her dream: stressed and overworked doctors, escalating deaths from the virus, and most importantly, a graph showing 4,477 cases tallied at that point in the United States.

But most of Tobi's calendrical resonances are exact. A couple weeks after the above dream, on April 7, 2017, Tobi awoke with a snippet of a song and the lyric, "I ain't done nothing since I woke up today" in her head. She recognized this as being from the John Prine song "Angel from Montgomery."[13] Prine was not an artist she knew that well, so she looked up the song out of curiosity and was surprised to find that images in its first verse, which she hadn't known, had dominated her dream: an old woman, an uncanny "child grown old," an old house, and lightning.* Three years later to the day, on April 7, 2020, John Prine became the first celebrity fatality of COVID-19—a loss widely reported in the media. ("Angel from Montgomery" had been played in his honor at the Grammy Awards two months before his death.)†

Principle #11 of our book is:

Dreams sometimes pre-present significant experiences exactly (or almost exactly) a year or multiple years in the future (calendrical resonance).

To discover and perhaps to trigger calendrical resonance in your dreams, it is essential to consistently date your dreams and their associated notes in your journal.

---

*"Angel from Montgomery" by John Prine begins, "I am an old woman named after my mother / My old man is another child that's grown old / If dreams were lightning, thunder were desire / This old house would have burnt down a long time ago . . ."

†Tobi had sent me a corpus of her dream records containing this John Prine–related dream (with a handwritten annotation about the lyrics of the song, added after looking them up) on April 27, 2019. I was thus in a position to independently confirm this striking calendrical resonance upon Prine's death.

FLIPPING THE UNCONSCIOUS

Freud thought the landscape of our biographies was shaped, even deformed, by a sort of dark matter consisting of the traumas in our past and of the forbidden wishes that linger in the unconscious. He saw our life stories as a series of swerves to avoid reminders of this hidden material constantly calling to us from our past, like revenants of souls never properly put to rest. Given what we've seen so far, I believe we can flip Freud's idea to arrive at an even more powerful and exciting way of understanding the unconscious: as conscious thought—or if you prefer, cognition—obliquely displaced in time from our future.

The spatial metaphors we inevitably use to imagine mental processes keep us from seeing this. In one way or another, psychologists have imagined the unconscious as coexisting in time with conscious thought, either unseen or separated somehow by a metaphorical barrier such as Freud's censor. In imagining the entirety of mental activity, Freud pictured the unconscious as the submerged majority of an iceberg; Jung thought of it as ever deeper strata in the earth, buried below the structures visible on the surface. But if the unconscious is really precognition, then a better place to metaphorically situate the unconscious would be *ahead of us,* in front of us. What defines an unconscious thought, in my view, is not that some other, hidden part of you right now is thinking it, but that your behavior, especially your dreams, is being influenced by a conscious thought that you haven't had *yet.* (Spoiler alert: this idea may help rescue our cherished free will from the snapping jaws of fate in a block universe, as we'll see in part 4.)

Think of your Long Self as a landscape through which you walk, down a path that (for the time being at least, until we develop time travel) you walk in a single direction. What we are learning is that even if you cannot go back and physically revisit your past, your life landscape is full of grottoes, the mouths of subterranean passages that until now you had never noticed or just regarded as pretty or scary features in the landscape. They are the openings of a subterranean cave system that interconnects your past and future. The echoing voices issuing from those grottoes, or the glowing eyes that peek out from them and frighten you, are symbolic representations of your own thoughts at different points in your life, including your future. Stop hurrying past these dark places and instead pay attention, take notes. Precognitive dreamwork is not only being a detective like Chazz Palminteri in *The Usual Suspects*; it is also being a ranger or a naturalist of your soul.

It is a little bit Einsteinian, or Minkowskian, this block landscape. It is also like the Grail Kingdom in the medieval myths that fascinated Wagner, a land ever-pregnant with possibilities and responsive to the quality of the one who occupies or traverses it. As we become aware and in tune with our precognition and learn to ask the right questions of this mysterious Grail in our lives, what may have seemed a Waste Land revivifies, comes alive with hidden possibility. It often produces gifts that feel like miracles.

8
Library Angels and Scarab Beetles

Synchronicity, Retrocausation,
and the Tesseract Brain

On the night of August 9, 2013, I recorded in my dream diary, "Hypnagogic vision of an old but crisp/unread paperback from the 70s about some esoteric science-fictioney topic, with a dark blue or black, orange, and red starburst cover." The concentric colorful radiating circles suggested an explosion of light or perhaps consciousness. The next morning I went to my bookshelf to pull out an old pulp collection by Alfred Bester called *Starburst,* thinking it might be what I was remembering in my vision, but the cover showed a moon of Mars and a rocket, nothing like what I'd seen.

The very next day, on August 10, I was in an unfamiliar city, Providence, Rhode Island, on a trip with my wife's family, and as I always do in new towns, I beelined to the used bookstores. Perusing the occult section of Paper Nautilus bookstore on South Angell Street, my eye fell on the black spine of an old paperback book, *The Roots of Coincidence,* by Arthur Koestler, and I slid it out. I was astonished and delighted to find that it had nearly the exact cover I had seen upon drifting to sleep two nights earlier. The colors were slightly more dark and muted, and there was a tiny infinity symbol in the center of the starburst that I had not seen in my dream, but otherwise it was exactly the same concentric design in the lower half of an otherwise black cover, the same familiar 1970s paperback size and feel and smell and typography, yet crisp and still unread. It was about precisely the somewhat science-fictional themes that were then obsessing me: ESP and coincidences.

Although I knew Koestler as a journalist on political topics, I was at that point totally unaware that the study of ESP had dominated his interests during the last decades of his life. Finding his book was quite a reward, probably the most striking instance in my life of the "library angel"—the weird way that books manifest in our lives exactly when we need them. Appropriately, this happened in a bookstore on South Angell Street, in a city called Providence. Doubly appropriately, it was Koestler himself who coined the term *library angel* . . . although alas not in *The Roots of Coincidence*. (That would have made my little precognitive episode perfect.)

Koestler's book proved to be a crucial touchstone for me in my thinking and writing about coincidences and miraculous encounters in my life's path, because much of the book is devoted to consideration of Jung's popular theory of synchronicity.

When people who are open to the miraculous in their lives experience an uncanny coincidence between a dream and a later event or a later reading experience, more often than not they will describe it in terms of the "acausal connecting principle"[1] that the Swiss psychoanalyst described in his writings in the early 1950s. Although he was no stranger to paranormal experiences, Jung was only a grudging believer in precognition, at least in the way I am using the term.[2] He argued that coincidences between a dream and a later event cannot be explained through the linear conception of cause and effect at all; instead, he thought, we should collapse the time dimension (turning time into space, again) and see that archetypes of the collective unconscious exert a kind of stage-managing power over events and experiences. A synchronicity is when two or more events meaningfully fall together in time (as he put it) in defiance of the usual causal rules.[3]

Jung's most famous example of this has become a staple in New Age and inspirational writing. One day, he was listening to a young, highly rationalistic female patient tell him her dream in which someone gave her a valuable piece of gold jewelry in the shape of an Egyptian scarab beetle. Just then, he heard a tapping at his window, turned, and saw a European relative of the Egyptian scarab, a rose chafer, which seemed to be trying to get into his office. He opened the window and handed the wriggling insect to his patient, saying, "Here is your scarab"[4]—an impressively coincidental moment that had the effect of "puncturing a hole" in the rationalism the woman had displayed until that moment and that, he felt, had kept her therapy from making headway.[5]

Because the scarab beetle was an ancient Egyptian symbol of rebirth, it seemed significant to Jung that the arrival of such a beetle at his window was the occasion for a breakthrough in his patient's therapy. Consequently, he framed this event as the meaningful alignment of an archetype with a therapeutically significant moment for his patient, an alignment that could not be chalked up to mere chance and could have no standard causal explanation.

Where astrology had been an antique idiom for describing such meaningful alignments, Jung's more sciencey sounding theory of synchronicity was meant to fill the gaps in that old (and for scientists, discredited) mode of thinking and to integrate human experience with physics in a novel way. He was inspired by the weird statistical laws governing the behavior of atoms and electrons that were being described by physicists, such as his friend and patient Wolfgang Pauli, in the middle decades of the century. Discoveries in this new realm seemed to open the door to a new way of thinking about the mysterious correspondences between inner and outer worlds, between psyche and cosmos, that he had observed both in his clinic and in his own life.

Jung's intuition that new discoveries in physics might help illuminate meaningful coincidences was probably right—he was ahead of his time. But being ahead of your time can have drawbacks, and in Jung's case it kept his theory from having much explanatory traction. Pauli himself was disappointed in his friend's 1952 monograph, *Synchronicity: An Acausal Connecting Principle.*[6] And Koestler, despite great admiration for Jung in general, described the theory put forth in that text as a "non-starter," laying out a pretty devastating critique of it in *The Roots of Coincidence.*[7] It is not enough to say that meaningful events are acausal or that they simply fall together in time, as Jung had asserted; some picture of how meaning—or an archetype—interacts with the physical world is still needed.*

Consequently, while Jung's concept has been extremely popular among the wider public, and most importantly has given us a very handy term to describe meaningful coincidences, synchronicity has been regarded by most scientists, and even most parapsychologists, as the "then a miracle occurs" in the middle of the equation.† It is a black box or placeholder for some future theory of how human (and animal) affairs might be shaped in a way that goes beyond mechanistic physics as then understood. *Retrocausation,* which was not yet a term widely used in physics, let alone in the wider world at the time Jung was writing, now provides us with the rudiments of such a theory.

Here's a warning from your future: the following short section contains the much-feared and much-loathed word *quantum.* I always think of the late Phil Hartman and his SNL character Unfrozen Caveman Lawyer—despite his legal acumen and suave courtroom delivery, things of the modern world like cell phones and fax machines frightened and confused him. The word *quantum* frightens and confuses most people (me included), so if you are among the physics-fearful, you have my permission—it won't cause some paradox or a warp in the fabric of this book—if you skim over this section.

---

*Koestler also showed that *Synchronicity* wasn't very original—the Austrian biologist Paul Kammerer had already offered a theory of seriality that sounded very much like Jung's concept, over three decades before Jung wrote his monograph.

†In a famous cartoon by Sidney Harris, a professor standing in front of a chalkboard dryly recommends to his colleague that he should "be more specific" at a point in a long equation where the colleague has simply written "here a miracle occurs."

WEAVING A WORLD

Physicists up until Jung's time remained obedient to the Enlightenment presumption that causes cannot "travel" backward in time—or if they did, there would be no way of detecting such a thing and no way it would make a difference. But it was always a presumption, and it is not really supported by evidence. Even in the equations that had been formulated to describe electromagnetism, there is no natural directionality to the interactions of particles; the equations look the same going both directions. If you looked at a video of atoms interacting, you could play it backward and you wouldn't be able to tell which was correct. It is only in the macroworld of objects, people, planets, and so on, the world governed by entropy, that causation appears to unfold in a single direction. The second law of thermodynamics describes the increasing disorder in the universe at macroscales and is often seen as equivalent to the one-way arrow of time.

More and more physicists over the past few decades, sensitive to the nondirectionality that seems to rule at the micro or quantum level, have begun to question the no-teleology rule. Recall that the tiny particles making up the matter and energy of the physical universe are really like worms or strings snaking through the block universe of Minkowski spacetime. Their interactions, which look to us a bit like tiny balls colliding on a billiard table, are from a four-dimensional perspective more like threads intertwining; the twists and turns where they wrap around each other are what we see as collisions, interactions, and "measurements" (in the physicists' preferred idiom). Each interaction changes information associated with those threads—their trajectory through the block universe (position and momentum) as well as qualities like "spin" that influence that trajectory. According to some recent theories, a portion of the information particles carry with them actually might propagate backward rather than forward across their world lines. For instance, an experiment at the University of Rochester in 2009 found that photons in a laser beam could be amplified *in their past* when interacted with a certain way during a subsequent measurement—true backward causation, in other words.[8]

The Israeli-American physicist Yakir Aharonov and some of his students are now arguing that the famous uncertainty principle—the extent to which the outcome of an interaction is random and unpredictable—may actually be a measure of the portion of future influence on a particle's behavior.[9] In other words, the notorious randomness of quantum mechanics—those statistical laws that captured Jung's imagination—may be where retrocausation was hiding all along. And it would mean Einstein was right: God doesn't play dice.*

If the new physics of retrocausation is correct, past and future cocreate the pattern of reality built up from the threads of the material world. The world is really woven like a tapestry on a four-dimensional loom. It makes little sense to think of a tapestry as caused by one side only; its physical structure arises from tension in all its threads between its left and right, top and bottom, and (in this case) past and future. That metaphorical tension is information traveling in both directions through the thread of a particle in time—and by extension, in both directions through larger objects made of particles (such as humans). It may be no accident that the oldest idiom in our language for fate, the interplay of future and past in human life, is related to the warp and weft of woven threads, the threads of life—a theme we'll wind back to.

We are not ordinarily aware of that "from the future" component of causation, because its influences wash out on a large scale due to the second law of thermodynamics (entropy). But there appear to be exceptions. When you isolate groups of particles like atoms from their surrounding thermodynamic environment and entangle them—a trick you can perform in the quantum world that causes particles to share information without actually communicating—you can scale up the spooky properties of the quantum realm and potentially capitalize on it.

This is what a quantum computer is: a matrix of entangled atoms kept isolated as much as possible from the external environment. You can use this matrix of atomic bits (or qubits—quantum bits) to perform

_____

*Elsewhere I argue that twentieth-century quantum physics, with its uncertainty principle and its "many worlds," is physics' hysterical symptom to avoid the cognitive dissonance of facing up to retrocausation (Wargo 2018).

calculations—hence it is called a computer—but there are potentially even more amazing possibilities. Computations using such a device may defy or ignore temporal order, for one thing, which suggests that quantum computers are really little islands of eternity amid the ocean of entropy that surrounds them. Theoretically at least, you could harness this causal nondirectionality to produce an output before an input with such a device. It is a principle that could one day be used to create a "precognitive circuit," useful in things like safety devices. Imagine how handy it would be to have an airbag that deployed a second in advance of a collision. My 2029 self-driving Tesla Model Q has one (I bought it on a trip through a wormhole, something we'll learn about in part 4). Or indeed, such a circuit could even perhaps carry messages from future users to past users, a kind of "chronophone." (Such messages would be somewhat garbled and unclear, however—we will delve into why when we get to those wormholes.)

The implications go beyond computers and cars. There is currently a kind of gold rush among biologists to find evidence of quantum computing in living systems. It was discovered a little over a decade ago (as of this writing) that plants are quantum computers: a spooky phenomenon known as quantum tunneling (electrons passing through barriers when they behave as waves) allows for the efficient translation of solar into chemical energy during photosynthesis.[10] And there is special interest in identifying quantum processes in the brain. Cognition has long been noted to have weirdly quantum-like properties even apart from paranormal phenomena psychologists won't even consider, like ESP.[11] Given the mounting evidence for sense-defying (if not even causality-defying) quantum behavior in many life processes, it is appearing increasingly likely that the similarity between the brain and a quantum computer will turn out to be more than accidental.[12]

Here's the part that especially interests me and is especially relevant to precognition and precognitive dreams: it so happens that the current best candidate for neuronal quantum computation is one of the molecular structures responsible for the memory processes described in chapter 4. Microtubules are tiny tubular lattices that constantly shape and reshape neurons as they form new connections with each other during learning. They have been shown to conduct electricity like superconductors, hinting at their quantum-computational properties. For this reason, microtubules are especially exciting to researchers seeking a physical explanation for consciousness—one of the current holy grails in neuroscience.[13]

Personally, I'm not very interested in efforts to reduce consciousness to physical processes in the brain (even quantum ones). I can't imagine scientists and philosophers and mystics and ordinary people in the street ever agreeing on what consciousness even means, first of all, and my mystical side seriously doubts I will ever read a satisfying physical explanation for it. My friend Jeffrey Kripal at Rice University has been an active promoter of the so-called filter thesis, for instance—the idea that the brain acts as a kind of reducing valve for consciousness, or even a receiver for it somewhat in the manner of a radio.[14] That's one interesting way of thinking about the problem. Panpsychism, the idea that consciousness is basic in the universe and pervasive in all matter (not just brains), is another idea gaining popularity among philosophers and even some physicists.[15] It could even be that philosopher David Chalmers's famous "hard problem" of consciousness really arises from the limits of concepts and categories needed for solving it.

Whatever consciousness is, I am comfortable distinguishing between that and the ever-changing contents of our (or an animal's) awareness—most or all of the things we may be conscious *of.* Our memories, our motivations, our emotions, our sensory experiences (such as pain and pleasure) moment to moment, as well as our patterns of personality and habits of behavior, are much less thinkable without the brain and nervous system. They are features of the organism, bound inextricably with the body and its well-being, and they correlate in very predictable ways with brain activity. I am happy thinking of precognition as a brain-based function too—but (and it's a big but) we're talking about a brain that doesn't look much at all like a standard computing device.

Even after more than a century, neuroscience is still in its adolescence. How neurons function together as parts of computer-like neuronal circuits is increasingly well understood using various imaging tools that can capture brain cells and their ever-changing synaptic connections. The ability to see or infer what is happening at the really micro level within neurons remains limited, though. A future neurobiology of precognition may well supplement the current, computational understanding of interactions between neurons with a theory of how molecular quantum computers inside the brain's 86 billion neurons and 150 trillion synapses might tap into eternity. My money right now is on those microtubules. Since they play a role in reshaping synaptic connections (known as plasticity), if they are indeed little eternity islands it would explain how memory and learning could be shaped not only by an individual's past experiences but also by his or her future experiences. Phenomena now called psychic and disregarded by mainstream psychologists and skeptics could well have a place in an overhauled and reimagined future science of mind-brain.

The findings of parapsychologists like Daryl Bem, Dean Radin, and Julia Mossbridge—of behavioral and emotional pre-sponses to imminent stimuli—could be the best existing laboratory evidence, even if it is indirect, for such temporal shenanigans going on inside our nervous systems. But dreams and synchronicities are daily reminders that, however it exactly works, we are indeed precognitive creatures. Somehow, information is carried in both directions across our timelines, and experiences in our future help shape our thoughts and motivations now, albeit largely outside of conscious awareness. Because we have no idea it is happening, and until recently had no scientific idiom in which to even talk about it, it gets either overlooked or misinterpreted or chalked up to some external (or even divine) intervention.

FLIPPING JUNG

The physics of retrocausation are still poorly understood, and they are only part of the story—a very small part, for those of you who skipped that last section (welcome back, by the way!). The bottom line is, it is crucial not to just throw out the time dimension because it confuses us and we have trouble seeing how causes could run backward. In special circumstances, including very possibly in the brain, they can. Information refluxes from the future, even directs our actions subtly, and the voracious, meaning-making mind tries to make some sense of this informational reflux from the Not Yet as best it can.[16]

Retrocausation and the theory of precognition it makes possible enable us to look at miraculous experiences like synchronicities in a whole new way. Generations of readers have seen Jung's scarab story, for instance, as a meaningful alignment of physical events (the arrival of the beetle at his office window) with hearing his patient tell her story about a dream she had, involving a scarab. If we view it this way, as a coincidence between hearing his patient tell her dream during the session and the simultaneous arrival of the beetle, then indeed it appears uncannily coincidental. But centering the narrative on Jung's experience ignores the patient's dream itself, which occurred the night before. She dreamed of being handed a beetle (or a symbol of one, in the form of jewelry) hours before a very similar situation actually happened in her therapist's office. It was thus, quite simply, a Dunne dream—his patient's Dunne dream—one in which that therapist, the man who would eventually write about the incident, happened to play an important (if disguised) role.

To fully understand what was happening, we need to reinflate that flattened time dimension and restore the dream, and especially the patient who had it, to their rightful place at the heart of this story. Because of information revealed in 2014 by a curator at the C. G. Jung Institute in Zurich named Vicente de Moura, we now know a good deal about the patient, including her name: Henriette Madeleine "Maggy" Quarles van Ufford.[17] This wealthy, highly educated, artistic young woman from Holland had moved to Switzerland with her two younger sisters in 1918, partly so one of those sisters could enter treatment with Jung and partly also to escape the stultifying aristocratic atmosphere of their home. Maggy entered treatment with Jung about a year later, and like many psychotherapy patients, she felt strong transference feelings for her doctor—that is, a kind of intellectual and erotic attraction.

Jung's feelings for her, it turns out, were similar (known in psychoanalytic writings as countertransference).

More to the point, we also now know Maggy was a "precog" at other times in her therapy—producing dreams and even physical symptoms that would elicit not only her doctor's approval but also some fascinating and rewarding explanation of ancient mythology or Eastern religion.[18] Producing such explanations was what Jung was good at, and connecting their dreams and symptoms to these archetypes was what rewarded many of the spiritually seeking patients in his clinic. Thus, being handed a relative of the scarab beetle along with an explanation of the scarab's symbolism in Egyptian religion was undoubtedly (as Jung indicates) a highly significant moment in Maggy's life. It makes perfect sense that her precognitive brain would have seized on this mini-miracle a few hours ahead on her life's path to fashion a little jewel of a dream.

LION AND EGG

Like Freud with his wish-fulfillment theory of dreams, Jung with his synchronicity theory was also close, but no cigar. Because there was no mechanism in physics yet able to explain how meaningfully coincidental events could be caused, it was easier (even if ultimately unsatisfying) to say they weren't caused at all. However, by putting a handy and appealing label on something that Enlightenment science had made no conceptual place for, Jung did something extremely valuable: he made it permissible for his generation and subsequent generations to record causally baffling events without necessarily making any psychic or paranormal claim. His "non-starter" theory thus facilitated the amassing of a considerable data set that strikingly supports Dunnean precognition—a data set that has successfully flown under the radar of the rabid skeptics who ordinarily pounce on things paranormal, shame the claimants, and intimidate experiencers into silence with their law of large numbers.

Open many memoirs by Jungian analysts or patients and you will find many arguably precognitive experiences, often centered on dreams, yet framed as archetypal encounters meaningful in terms of the person's journey of individuation. These narratives often implicitly follow the template laid down by Jung in his narrative about Maggy and the scarab. In addition to some remarkable interaction, for instance with an animal, they may involve reading a text that seemingly both explains and confirms that prior interaction. Some reading or learning experience that puts a framing on the coincidence between the dream and the interaction may often be what elevates the interaction to being precognition worthy.

Consider for instance a story told by Barbara Dean, a book editor living in a heavily wooded area of northern California in the 1980s. In January 1986, Dean dreamed she was in a zoo watching a mountain lion about to give birth. "I was watching with my brother and a friend. We looked right into the cat's vagina, and we could see the folds of its uterus contract, struggling to give forth. The new life hadn't quite been born when the dream ended." A few weeks later, while working at her desk, she was stunned to watch a real mountain lion walk through her backyard—the first and only time in fifteen years living in that house that she had seen such an animal. Because she had dreamed about it, the sighting took on a numinous quality for her.

> So when the mountain lion walked in front of my woodpile a month later, I was . . . aware of a certain feeling of nonsurprise, as if some secret part of me had, in fact, been awaiting such a visit since the night of my dream. I had no doubt that this cat had come for me. For me to be at my desk on a Sunday morning and to be looking out the window at the precise moment when a shy, seldom-seen, nocturnal predator appeared was too much of a coincidence.
>
> The synchronicity of having lived here for fifteen years without seeing a mountain lion—and then to dream of a big cat and to see one within six weeks brought my inner and outer worlds together with a force that literally left me tingling for hours. . . .
>
> This, I understood, is the experience of living in a world in which inside and outside are one. . . . Experiencing this feeling from the inside, as I did, courtesy of the mountain lion, is to know what it

means to live in perfect accord with nature: as if all life, inner and outer, is engaged in a single revelation.*[19]

It was quite a reward for Dean—as she said, it left her tingling for hours. But note that the reward came significantly from the fact that her dream had presaged and prepared her for this moment. And crucially, her dream had also prompted her to read about lions and their archetypal symbolism, specifically in a book by Laurens van der Post, an explorer and friend of Jung's. She quotes van der Post:

> The lion, not only in the imagination of first man, but even in our day, is not the king of the beasts for nothing. It is so chosen because, of all forms of animal life, it is the most many-sided, the most highly differentiated. It is powerful. It is swift. It is strong. It can see as well by night as by day. . . . It is very intelligent, and it doesn't abuse this formidable combination of powers. It has a sense of proportion, and does not kill except for food. . . . Above all, the lion is fundamentally the cat that walks alone. In other words, the lion is the individual; it is the symbol of the instinctive and royal individual self.[20]

Dean writes that it was this passage that helped her understand her dream as being about her own "royal, individual self" that was, as the dream showed, in the process of being born. The logic here is very similar to that of the scarab incident: a dream precedes an animal encounter, which assumes greater significance and value because of a learning experience (in Dean's case, a reading experience) that frames that encounter's meaning for the dreamer. Dean would not have been so amazed by the appearance of a mountain lion at her woodpile had she not recently dreamed about such an animal and, as a result, read a book by Laurens van der Post on the meaning and significance of lions. As in Jung and Maggy's case, the notion of precognition or seeing the

---

*Thanks to Michael Jawer for first alerting me to Dean's story.

future doesn't seem to have crossed Dean's mind; she saw it instead as the archetypal cosmos sending her a message.

I mentioned earlier that it would be a weird radar that shows us how we will feel after our encounter with the blip on the screen. It is also a funny radar that actually acts as a tractor beam for that blip on the screen. But as we have seen, dreams have a way of eliciting their own fulfillment. I think of precognition as being less akin to radar and something more like dowsing, the ancient divination practice that typically utilizes bent rods, sticks, or pendulums to locate hidden objects or water. Precognitive dreams orient us toward rewards in our life, those gifts in the landscape, subtly helping us reveal and uncover them even though dreams may not represent those gifts literally or clearly.

The dreaming brain is a coincidence detector and a coincidence creator. With its voracious appetite for association, it orients us toward confluences of events and experiences that meaningfully rhyme or resonate with each other, or are connected through some idiosyncratic personal association. Objectively, this confluence may truly be random (there are such things), or one may lead to the other sequentially, like reading about a rare animal and then seeing one, or vice versa. Such convergences act as bait for the precognitive brain. Dreaming about them beforehand is what intensifies and elevates their significance and makes them miraculous.

Principle #12 is this:

Synchronicity is what it feels like when we precognitively orient toward rewarding miracles, gifts in the landscape of our life, and are unaware that our actions played some role in leading us to (and even creating) those miracles.

BIGGER ON THE INSIDE

Among many who take psychic phenomena seriously, reducing them to functions of the brain is seen these days as a narrow materialism. I'm often taunted on the playground of paranormal studies for my heretical beliefs on this question, because unlike some of my friends and colleagues, I don't think we can minimize the brain or its materiality . . . but as I hinted earlier, we are probably picturing different things by that word *brain*. My study of precognition and synchronicity over the past ten years has led me to imagine this organ as a kind of higher-dimensional cathedral, an "interior space" whose vastness extends in four dimensions, not just three, and extends ahead of us in time, not just behind.

Objects that are bigger on the inside than on the outside are a common trope in time-travel stories. Dr. Who's TARDIS—a giant time machine whose exterior is a London police call booth—is the best-known example. I believe we need to include the brain itself in this auspicious sci-fi lineage. Whether or not it produces consciousness, it is at least a vessel, a "ship" for consciousness; we travel through time with and in this ship, including into the future. We sail the seas of a life that is somehow all contained inside it, even though it is merely a material object little bigger than a grapefruit.

The designers of Christopher Nolan's 2014 film *Interstellar* came close to picturing what I have in mind by the brain. Near the end of the film, astronaut "Coop" (Matthew McConaughey) is able to communicate with his younger self (as well as his daughter) decades in the past using a tesseract, a higher-dimensional portal created by our descendants thousands or millions of years in the future. Visually, it is depicted as a kind of M. C. Escher library, extending in every direction to infinity. Despite being practically infinite on the inside, it has a very humble and innocuous exterior—the bookcase in Coop's home on Earth. Older Coop communicates with his younger self by pushing books from behind the bookcase to get his attention (titles like Edward Abbot's *Flatland,* which introduced Victorians to the idea of higher dimensions two decades before Einstein's relativity theory[21]).

If the brain capitalizes on molecular quantum computers (trillions or hundreds of trillions of them) to communicate with itself through time, then we should think of it as something like Coop's tesseract bookshelf—an information tunnel extending across our whole life. The future experiences and thoughts that dreams show us are not only already present in the block universe but are, impossibly, already present in our brains. Maybe not perfectly, however—because those dream messages are limited to whatever "books" (life experiences) happen to be on our bookshelf at any given point, our messages to our younger self are necessarily oblique and easily misunderstood. Since we prefer to think spatially about things, not temporally, when we dream of strange books and animals that subsequently manifest in our physical reality, it never occurs to us that those dreams were us, announcing these encounters from our slightly more informed future, and drawing us toward those encounters.

So in other words, I see the material brain as a higher-dimensional object, literally our portion of eternity, a timeless Indra's Net amid the thermodynamic flux, the arrow of time and entropy that surrounds it. It could even be something like that external material world turned inside out. That, if anything, is the central mystery: those inner and outer worlds, whose interconnection Barbara Dean marveled at when a mountain lion prowled past her woodpile, are really in a deeply mysterious way the same, viewed under a different aspect.

Dean's encounter with the mountain lion left her, as she said, tingling for hours. It doesn't lessen the electricity and excitement of synchronicities to see these experiences as products of our own vast tesseract mind-brains rather than as the machinations of transpersonal archetypes. The "confirmations" of my own "The Apple" and *Island of the Blue Dolphins* dreams, for instance, were thrilling at the same time that they threw my old understandings of causality into upheaval. They punctured a hole in my previous beliefs about the world, just as Jung says his gesture with the scarab did to Maggy Quarles van Ufford. They were also profoundly important in my personal journey of individuation—becoming who I am. But best of all, realizing these were my own mind-brain in action and then seeking out these experiences through precognitive dreamwork has empowered me to have these kinds of experiences on a weekly basis, not just once in a lifetime.

9

Beyond Archetypes

The Fractal Geometry of Prophecy

On the last page of J. R. R. Tolkien's *The Hobbit,* Bilbo Baggins is entertaining the wizard Gandalf and one of his Dwarvish friends in his cozy hobbit hole, some years after their adventure to reclaim an ancient Dwarvish kingdom from the dragon Smaug. When his guests tell him that the rivers of the reclaimed kingdom far away in the East now run with gold, Bilbo notes with some amusement that "the prophecies of the old songs have turned out to be true, after a fashion." At this point, Gandalf sagely chides his small, inherently skeptical host for thinking this is just a coincidence. "Surely you don't disbelieve the prophecies, because you had a hand in bringing them about yourself?"[1]

An awkward—but really, sublime—circularity lies at the heart of reality, and precognitive dreamwork reveals this circularity in spades. Jung would not have noticed and caught the beetle at his window and handed it to his patient Maggy Quarles van Ufford had she not been telling him her dream about being handed a piece of scarab jewelry. Isn't that paradoxical (I hear you asking)? Not at all—and it's a common mistake, made even by the keenest scientific thinkers when writing about things like time travel and the causally circular situations it gives rise to.*

---

*For instance, in his book *Parallel Worlds,* famous physicist Michio Kaku calls tautological results of time travel "paradoxes" when they are not (Kaku 2005).

A tautology is not the same thing as going back in time and killing your grandfather or your younger self. In fact, it is the opposite—and as we will see later, the universe has no problem with such circular causal relationships, even if they give headaches to pedantic professor-logicians.

We've already seen several other, much more mundane examples of dream precognition's tautological logic. I would not have rewatched "The Apple" had it not been for my dream, which connected to a picture I saw the next morning that reminded me of that *Star Trek* episode. And I would not have looked up *Island of the Blue Dolphins* online and randomly read the chapter where Karana and Rontu are trapped in a spooky cave with a bone flute had I not similarly associated another picture drawn from an envelope with that book's cover. The scarab episode is no different, even if it seems to involve a more dignified and ancient piece of cultural stuff—that is, an "archetype."

I suspect that the worrisome circularity of precognitive explanations—dreams coming true partly as a result of our own actions—lies behind Jung's preference to collapse the time dimension altogether in framing these episodes as somehow outside the realm of physical causation, products of an archetypal world of meaning. It may be that we all share this mental block against tautology, and it is probably a significant reason why that River Lethe largely washes precognitive dream experiences out of our memory or even awareness . . . or at least why we prefer to imagine some external principle or agency orchestrating these coincidences on our behalf, rather than imagine that the secret agent producing these miracles in our lives is our own Long Self. One of the most ancient archetypes of gnosis, as a matter of fact, is the serpent (or dragon) biting its own tail. Fear of this tautological serpent is one of the biggest hindrances to becoming a conscious precog. One must learn instead to accept and embrace the self-fulfilling, chicken-and-egg logic that everyday common sense has taught us since childhood to avoid.

Quantum physicists will now tell you that a kind of causal circularity or "bootstrapping" appears to be the rule at the smallest scales in nature. Particles arise from nothing in the so-called quantum foam and seem in some ways to be self-caused. The physicist John Wheeler argued that the universe itself may be a gigantic time loop with superintelligent observers at the end of cosmic history looking back at the Big Bang and retro-causing it through their observations.[2] Humbler versions of this same chicken-and-egg logic are to be expected, and would actually be the norm, in a world that includes precognitive beings who act on the basis of their precognitive dreams and visions—even if (or especially if) they are unaware that this is what they are doing.

Another way of putting it is that we often—and technically, always—have a hand in bringing about the fulfillment of the future obliquely glimpsed in our dreams. This is not accidental—it's a rule. It's also Principle #13, which is in some ways a corollary of the previous one:

In one way or another, dreams lead us
to the future that they prophesy.

Our dreams create time loops in our lives.

What's wrong with just calling these time loops synchronicities and leaving it at that? As simply a handy label for meaningful coincidence, there's nothing wrong with the term. But there is a vast gain in understanding when we trace out the multiple loopy, knotty threads of causation in a miraculous event that appeared at first to have no possible causal explanation. When we apply the X-ray illumination of the time-loops theory to an otherwise opaque synchronistic occurrence, a kind of inner, fractal-geometric structure becomes visible—you could call it the fractal geometry of prophecy. Maggy's dream about the scarab and Dean's dream about the mountain lion giving birth can help illustrate what I mean.

The most important principle to remember is Principle #3, that dreams show us our future thoughts in response to significant moments in our lives, not events per se. In Maggy's case, her dreaming brain seems to have pre-sensed not only that scarabs are meaningful but also that being handed a live specimen, along with her doctor's exciting explanation of its symbolism, would be of immense value—"golden . . . costly"—in her life.[3] Consequently, instead of dreaming literally about her doctor handing her a wriggling insect, Maggy dreamed of some-one (Jung unfortunately does not say who it was) gifting her with a valuable piece of jewelry in the shape of that insect's highly symbolic Egyptian cousin. In other words, the dream seems to have pre-presented the whole scene in Jung's office along with her thoughts and feelings in reaction to it, the immense value of the moment to her.

Similarly, Barbara Dean's dream about a mountain lion giving birth pre-presented not only the real appearance of a (nonbirthing) mountain lion at her woodpile but also the role that encounter would play in her life as a kind of certification of her own individuation or rebirth. Circularly (or loopily), it would play that role because she had already dreamed of it and had read a passage in Laurens van der Post explicating the symbol-ism of lions. Here again, her later interpretation of the encounter's signifi-cance for her life seems to have been pre-presented *in* the dream.

Principle #14 of our book is:

A dream may pre-present the dreamer's later thoughts about the dream, or its value to the dreamer, in a kind of fractal fashion.

Those future thoughts may include reflections on the dream that are more equivocal, of course. For example, I argued in *Time Loops* that the bureaucratic-nightmare portion of Dunne's dream about the volcano about to blow may have pre-presented confused thoughts he would have after reading about the Mount Pelée eruption, having already dreamed of it: "If I precognized this, why didn't/couldn't I prevent it?"[4] These kinds of confused and guilty thoughts in the aftermath of a dreamed-of disaster are central to the topic of premonitions, and we will come back to them in part 4.

CONNECTING WITH PRECOGNITION

Jung left a number of interesting—I think, crucial—details out of his bare-bones narrative about the scarab incident, facts that greatly help illuminate it. The most important is this: Maggy was in love with Jung, probably the same way patients are often in love with their therapists. His own feelings for her were powerfully reciprocal—a detail he revealed in an essay on the so-called countertransference that he never published during his lifetime.[5] Although Jung is widely believed to have had affairs with some of his patients and former patients, no evidence has come to light that he acted on his feelings for Maggy besides divulging his feelings to her. But I argue in *Time Loops* that this emotional context—a thwarted or inhibited sexual frisson—had everything to do with the psychic abilities Maggy seemed to display during her time as Jung's patient.

In addition to the scarab incident, on at least two other occasions Maggy precognized occurrences in her therapy. In one case, she had a dream that strikingly matched a passage in a book on paranormal phenomena that Jung had read just before one of their sessions. When she told him her dream, he told her about the passage.[6] In another, even stranger case, she exhibited a series of psychosomatic symptoms and associated visions (such as an elephant coming out of her genitals) that uncannily matched symbols in a book Jung was reading concurrently on kundalini yoga.[7] I think these episodes (and who knows, there could have been others) amounted to a kind of precognitive seduction by Maggy, via her doctor's reading habits. These dreams and symptoms certainly succeeded in fascinating him.

Frustrated or inhibited connection or communication has long been observed to correlate with psychic phenomena, so it makes sense that the professional boundaries that are ordinarily observed in the psychotherapy clinic might elicit them in spades. Freud noticed it with his patients too, interpreting uncannily coincidental things patients said on his couch as "thought transference."[8] And this sort of thing seemed to happen with some of Jung's other patients besides Maggy.

Jung describes in his *Synchronicity* monograph, for instance, that in 1918—a year or two before he began treating Maggy—he became fascinated by a particular ancient Orphic text that described the god Phanes and his title Ericepaeus, noting that he misread and misremembered the name as Eric*a*paeus. (Nerd problems.) At this point, a patient he had not seen for a month and who lived in a town fifty miles distant—and who knew nothing of his Orphic studies—came to her session with a recent dream in which "an unknown man handed her a piece of paper, and on it was written a 'Latin' hymn to a god called Eric*i*paeus."[9] Although she knew a little Latin from her schooling, she did not know the classics, and the name was meaningless to her. Jung was no doubt happy to enlighten her.

Jung imagined that this patient must have clairvoyantly read the same Latin text he did, but that her reading of it was skewed by his own misspelling of the name—a far more convoluted explanation (involving both clairvoyance and telepathy) than simply seeing that her dream was a precognitive dream about his undoubtedly fascinating, probably singularly validating exposition of Orphic texts during their session. (Note how the Dunnean precognition theory allows us to cut out unnecessary psychic middlemen like telepathy. Parsimony—or simplicity—is always a desirable quality in scientific theories.)

Like many in his cultural milieu, Jung was fascinated by world mythology and religious symbols, and his patients produced such material for him in their dreams to please him. They mirrored his interests back to him, the same way Freud's patients produced dreams that reflected the Oedipus complex and other Freudian notions. I argue that they sometimes did this mirroring precognitively, and that seems to be what happened not only with the woman who dreamed of "Ericipaeus" but also what happened with Maggy on that day in or around 1920 when she brought Jung her dream about a scarab. In fact, it is a very common occurrence in Jungian psychotherapy, and it is only Jung's own resistance to the idea of dream precognition that keeps writer-analysts in his lineage from seeing these stories as Dunne dreams rather than as objective evidence of a collective unconscious.

Analyst and author Donald Kalsched offers a vivid example of this seeing/unseeing in his book *Trauma and the Soul*. A stockbroker named Richard who almost never remembered his dreams and whose therapy had bogged down in a kind of oppressive dullness finally produced a fascinating dream of encountering a hooded child on a beach while dolphins jumped in the water near them. Shortly afterward, Kalsched encountered precisely such a mythological motif in one of Jung's essays, and despite his better analytic judgment, told Richard about it. "I excitedly spilled out to him my youthful enthusiasm for the uncanny parallels between his dream and the ancient mythological material."[10] The patient was struck by his doctor's excitement—it is the deepest desire of many patients that their doctors find them interesting—and it was a major turning point in the previously stalled therapy. Naturally, Kalsched saw it as confirmation of the Jungian ideas he was then undergoing training in. "That a contemporary patient, a businessman and stockbroker that was completely unaware of these ancient symbolic parallels, should dream of a recovered hooded child in connection with leaping dolphins is about as dramatic an example of what Jung meant by the archaic and typical (archetypal) components of the deep unconscious as could ever be imagined."[11]

I disagree. It makes much more sense that Richard was unconsciously dowsing for this rewarding connection with his doctor, via the doctor's own interest in ancient mythology (a trait shared by most Jungian analysts). In other words, it was a precognitive dream about his doctor's excited story about Jung's essay. When we see these uncanny dreams simply as archetypal, we miss the dimension of interhuman connection by focusing too much on the symbol. The analyst's own interests—in this case, mythological interests—play a central role in these narratives.

Here's another fact that Jung left out of his narrative of the scarab incident but that is highly relevant to that story and to Maggy's "seduction": Jung had an especially deep personal interest in scarab beetles. He had seen a scarab in the first of his own visions he called his confrontation with the unconscious[12] several years earlier. Interestingly, this was after having encountered some real Egyptian scarab artifacts in his former mentor Freud's office.[13] He had become a bit of an expert on these ancient insectoid symbols of transformation over the subsequent years. Like Richard with his doctor, Maggy's precognitive unconscious was dowsing for this mythological information in the landscape of her future when she had her dream and told it to Jung.

In short, Maggy had her scarab dream not because ancient Egyptian symbols—or any culture's particular symbolism—are permanent features in the collective unconscious or are somehow written into the fabric of reality as the language spoken by objective events, but because scarabs would be the focus of her doctor's rewarding exegesis on this insect species the next day (elicited, loopily, by her telling him her dream). A cultural symbol got dragged into the vortex of her time loop because Jung himself was interested in such things and he was poised to dispense his wisdom on the subject. Such time loops coming to closure during his sessions with Maggy naturally contributed to Jung's belief in the higher organizing power of ancient myths and archetypes, just as an uncannily similar occurrence did for Donald Kalsched. In both cases, nonrecognition of precognition produced a kind of echo-chamber effect.*

These are not stories about archetypes, in other words. Nor are they stories about psychically reaching across space into ancient texts or other minds. They are stories about real people with irreducible and complex histories and desires, reaching into their own futures with their dreams, dowsing for acknowledgment and validation (or something more) from another person—in these cases, an admired or even beloved doctor. In Maggy's case, her precognitive seduction with her dreams and symptoms earned her not only Jung's intellectual as well as erotic fascination, but also immortalized her (if not by name) in the most famous paragraph of one of his most famous books. They were still friends three decades later when Jung wrote that book. He even wrote to Maggy when writing it, for her recollections of the experience.[14]

I have come to think of precognition as a kind of social orienting function, drawing us toward the reward of meaningful human connection and making that connection in the same stroke. The psychiatrist Bernard Beitman (working within the synchronicity idiom) calls it

---

*The Jung scholar Richard Noll argues that the collective unconscious is nothing more than the books on Jung's own bookshelf and those of his well-read, spiritually-seeking patients (Noll 1994, 1997.)

connecting with coincidence.[15] Insofar as we are willing and courageous enough to share our dreams and are open to the role of something like magic in our lives, other people frequently complete our time loops for us, in many cases by providing some sort of verification of what we've seen or heard in a dream. These are meaningful moments, powerful experiences of connection. Recall for instance John Wren-Lewis's dream about the spy plane and Lord Snow in chapter 5: it was like he had dowsed for the reward of shock and amazement from a complete (but famous) stranger, and this led to a redemptive moment of communion backstage at a popular talk show.

I can't help but suspect that this precognitive social orienting function may have played an important part in human social evolution, one that future paranthropologists will study and characterize.* It can bind and unite people, create a kind of communion of fellow travelers on this life's journey. It could also be an important, largely unexplored mechanism underlying many paranormal and spiritual phenomena, including mediumship.[16] Clients of mediums frequently have an experience similar to what Jung might have felt in that session with Maggy, or with his client who dreamed a hymn to "Ericipaeus": that the psychic produces interesting but perhaps not unbelievable information, but buried amid all that, there is something extremely specific that they could not possibly have known, that is impossible to chalk up to coincidence. One imagines that encounters with shamans and witches might have been like this in cultures that made a place for those social roles. One hypothesis I find particularly compelling is that misrecognized precognition, experienced as synchronicity, is the motor of religious belief and conversion: a text or a symbol may be much more compelling if we come to it with a sense of familiarity, perhaps having already encountered it in a dream.[17] The roundabout ways our future communicates to us while asleep and awake are involved in the divine or our experience of the divine.

Paranthropology is the title of a journal aimed at legitimizing the social-scientific study of paranormal phenomena.

To fully capitalize on this orienting function, to connect with pre-cognition, share your dreams when you can, at least with people you trust. And be forthcoming with your own stories when others share their dreams with you.

Which brings us to Principle #15:

A precognitive dream may be unimportant in itself;
what matters, what it is really about, is what it leads you to
do in your life, or the connection it helps you make.

That connection that arrives in the future, via your own actions and especially the actions of others, is (in a sense) the real meaning of the dream.

ANIMA WOMEN

Pulling human psychology out of the swamp of sex and selfishness that dominated Freud's attention and into the more noble and misty reaches of religion and myth is one of the appeals of Jung's writings. But when we ignore humans' baser motives completely, our eyes fixed on those noble archetypes, we may miss something crucial. Skipping over the real, messy human stories at the heart of synchronistic experiences prevents us from seeing the precognition that powers them and also leads us to miss other less obvious instances of precognition. The remarkable but sadly misframed dreamlife of Jung's friend, the physicist Wolfgang Pauli, offers an especially striking object lesson in the pitfalls of assuming dreams only have archetypal meaning.

Between 1952 and 1954, Pauli experienced a series of dreams about a Chinese woman who seemed to hold some secret or secrets in store for him—"psychophysical secrets ranging from sexuality to subtle ESP phenomena"—and whose movements seemed to convey something important about the physical structure of reality.[18] In one dream, this exotic, alluring woman led the dreamer down a trapdoor into an auditorium, where she then danced rhythmically, went back up into the open air, and came down again, dissolving the barrier between upper and lower worlds. In another dream, Pauli and this mystery woman observed some experiments that supposedly created twin objects that were reflections of one another, but they shared the secret between them that the objects were just mirror images, and this secret filled them with apprehension. In another dream, the Chinese woman had a child that "the people" refused to acknowledge.[19]

Jung insisted these dreams were about Pauli's anima, his feminine archetype. Men are generally out of touch with their feelings, and alluring mysterious women appear in men's dreams to awaken men to their sensitivity, according to Jungian thinking. The anima also represents a man's creative side, his muse. Yet events in 1957 revealed a different, much more concrete reality to Pauli's dreams. In that year, a charismatic and brilliant Chinese-American physicist at Columbia University named Chien Shiung Wu designed and conducted an experiment showing that the symmetry (or parity) that governs gravity, electromagnetism, and strong nuclear interactions does not hold with the weak nuclear force, which governs the decay of particles. A slight asymmetry governs the quantum world, in other words. This came as a serious blow to Pauli, who had harbored a deep-seated belief (or even need) that the physical world be completely symmetrical on all scales. Wu's discovery, and the revision of physical law it required, upset Pauli greatly and even prompted the hot-tempered and impulsive physicist to behave badly at a Princeton seminar where one of Wu's collaborators, Chen Ning Yang, was presenting their work.

Pauli was indeed out of touch with his feelings, but clearly that fact didn't exhaust the meaning of his dreams. As Robert Moss puts it in his book *The Secret History of Dreaming,* "the 'Chinese woman' in [Pauli's] dreams was more than a Jungian anima figure from his personal unconscious. She had a physical body and a name, and she was now known as one of the world's greatest experimental physicists."[20] And true to his dream about her "baby" being unacknowledged, she was not acknowledged by the Nobel Prize committee for her landmark contribution. The 1957 Nobel Prize in Physics went solely to the two young male physicists, Yang and his colleague Tsung-Dao Lee, who had invited Wu to perform the experiment. "Clearly Pauli had previewed an event three years before it took place,"[21] Moss writes. Pauli seems to have done this a lot, and this case exemplifies a principle that is seen commonly in dream precognition (and is Principle #16 of our book):

Precognition often orients us to experiences that challenge our prior beliefs or worldviews.

Maggy Quarles van Ufford's transformative experience in Jung's office, her life-changing Dunne dream, would be another example of this, as would Barbara Dean's transformative sighting of the mountain lion in her backyard.

Jung's acknowledgment of dream precognition in the sense I am using the term was, as Moss notes, "grudging and very limited."[22] He admitted that prophetic dreams sometimes occurred, but since they seemed so rare, unreliable, and unpredictable, he felt that looking for them was not worthwhile. Talk about a self-fulfilling prophecy! They were clearly staring him in the face, but he preferred to give them other interpretations. "We can only speculate how many messages about the future that Jung—and Pauli, to the extent that he conformed to Jung's approach—may have missed by taking this line," Moss writes.[23] And we can only speculate how many more precognitive dreams Maggy Quarles van Ufford had that were never noticed or registered, for the same reason.*

Jung's writings are deservedly popular among those who contest the extreme reductionisms of materialist science, but archetypal readings of human affairs can sometimes be equally reductive—offensively so, in some cases—even if the reductionism is in an idealist direction rather than materialist one. Reducing women to archetypal anima figures in the lives and dreams of powerful, brilliant men, for instance,

---

*Sometime after the scarab incident, Maggy married and took the surname Reichstein. For more details on Maggy and her precognitive experiences, see my book *Time Loops* (Wargo 2018).

was symptomatic of the same sexism—no doubt partly a product of his times—that led Jung to overlook and diminish the intellectual and artistic talents, as well as precognitive abilities, of his female clients.[24]

In a letter to a younger analyst protégé who was having an affair with Maggy, probably several years after the scarab incident and other episodes described above, Jung called her "the ideal anima woman . . . it is her vocation."[25] *Anima woman* is Jungian code for an intellectual and erotic muse for a man. Readers inspired by the scarab story should keep that quote in the back of their minds, along with the ethically dubious detail that Jung said this is in a letter to his patient's lover. As much as he liked and respected Maggy in many ways, Jung basically saw her role in life as being an excitement for men.

JUST A LITTLE FELLOW

Part of what defines the stout and skeptical Bilbo Baggins is his puny size in relation to the bloated archetype Smaug sprawling on his pile of stolen gold. Along with the fear of tautology that deflects us hobbits from seeing how we fulfill our own dream-prophecies through our dream-inspired actions goes an assumption that little old me couldn't produce "big" magical effects in the world. We habitually think of ourselves as unimportant bystanders to the universe and our fates. It is a presumption reinforced especially by materialist psychology, with its denials of anything transcendent about us. But it is also reinforced by metaphysical belief systems that reduce human experience to the interplay of preexisting cultural or archetypal symbols. As long as we uncritically take Jung's word for it that some external Platonic mechanism does the heavy lifting of creating the miracles in our lives, we are unlikely to realize that we're the ones creating those miracles ourselves, and we thus may not learn how to invite them into our lives with greater regularity, let alone learn much from them.

It is why, even though Freud was subject to his own blindness about precognition, I find his warts-and-all sensibility about the unconscious more helpful than Jung's more noble and pristine archetypal view.

Dreams are about our real lives in their rich, random, sometimes trivial and sometimes inexplicable glory—the messy, truly irreducible Chazz-Palminteri-dropping-his-mug stuff. If we focus on archetypes, as Jung did with Maggy Quarles van Ufford's and Wolfgang Pauli's dreams, we are liable to overlook the scene of ourselves sharing an uncanny and thrilling moment with a doctor we secretly or not-so-secretly desire, or being inspired by a fascinating passage in a book, or excitedly watching a silly old TV show that reconnects us with our childhood. When we realize that we ourselves are the orchestrators of the synchronicities in our lives and that we are our own library angels, it empowers us to intensify that "real magic," revivifying our life landscape.[26]

PART 4

THE LAW IN THE COSMOS (ON FATE AND FREE WILL)

10
"But I Survived"
Understanding Premonitions

There was a screech of brakes, and then a terrible crunch of metal on metal and shattered glass. Steve bolted up in bed, his heart racing. It was a little after midnight, and somebody outside needed help.

Steve lived near a busy intersection in downtown Seattle. He ran out his front door and into the street and looked around. Nothing. There were no smashed cars. There was no evidence of any accident at all.

"I was dumbfounded," he told me in an email. "It didn't feel like a dream. It was much more specific. . . . Still, I put myself back to bed and told myself it was probably a dream, however unique it felt."

Steve went to work the next day and forgot about his strange awakening in the middle of the night. He came home that evening, went through his usual routine, and went to sleep about 11:00 p.m.

An hour or two later, it happened again. He was jolted awake by the same violent screech of brakes, the same impact of metal on metal. It was like a bizarre replay of the previous night. "I distinctly remember being confused: *Is this last night? Why is this repeating? What's going on?*"

Sitting in bed, trying to process what had happened, Steve heard someone outside on the street shouting, "Oh my god! Somebody get help!"

At this point, he was rocked by a wave of adrenaline. "All at once, I realized this was in fact a different night than the previous one. And this time the accident was real." He ran outside, and his eyes were greeted by a horrific sight. A car had been broadsided by another vehicle going through the intersection. It had rolled several times and landed in his neighbor's yard.

"I learned later that a young man in the car died," he said.

Premonitions of death and disaster, like what Steve experienced twenty-four hours before the fatal accident on his street in 2009, are probably very much in the minority of precognitive dreams. Yet they are some of the most commonly reported, since the gravity of the events surrounding them may counterbalance the doubt and embarrassment that ordinarily shrouds the topic in silence. And despite their rarity, they are the most distressing and perplexing variety of precognitive dream, both for the dreamers themselves and for those who wonder what this "super ability" of our brains could possibly mean, for instance about the role of free will versus fate in our lives.

Could you have a dream that warned you about something like a terrorist attack that you could then prevent? Is that paradoxical? What about dreaming of a fatal accident like the one Steve dreamed about before it happened? Could he have warned someone, had he realized his dream the night before was a premonition? Is the dreamer responsible somehow for failing to act on a premonition? Is there some way to identify for sure when a dream is a premonition versus when it is . . . just a dream?

Is there even such a thing as "just a dream"?

Answering these complex questions is crucial to precognitive dreamwork, and it is what we will try to address over the next few chapters.

FATAL ATTRACTION

It has often been supposed that there is something about catastrophic events, and human trauma or crisis more generally, that attracts the precognitive brain. Premonitions of death don't only happen in dreams. A man named Oscar sent me several waking premonitions he experienced as a teen in the 1950s in Kansas City. The most striking occurred in 1958:

I was riding in a car with my friend Tom. It was about 5:00 p.m., and we were driving down Prospect Avenue in Kansas City. We were laughing at a joke he just told and it was so funny. At an instant something intense told me there was a problem and I stopped laughing and told him something was wrong. Neither of us knew what it was and began to search the car. After quite a while of fruitless searching I told him to turn on the radio and maybe there was something there. As the tube radio warmed up there was a broadcast just starting announcing the auto accident involving some acquaintances who went to our high school, and one had been killed.

These kinds of intimations, visions, or dreams about tragedy were among the first psychical experiences studied in the 1880s by the Society for Psychical Research (SPR). Its cofounder, psychologist Frederick W. H. Myers, theorized that extreme trauma rippled through a subliminal psychic aether from mind to mind. It was Myers who first coined the term *telepathy* to describe the way thoughts could be transmitted between minds, especially between friends and loved ones, when one individual was in crisis.[1]

A prominent American member of Myers's SPR was the journalist and novelist Mark Twain. All through his life, he had experienced premonitions, instances of what he interpreted as telepathy (or what he called mental telegraphy), and baffling, seemingly impossible coincidences of the sort that Jung would later call synchronicity. Books on ESP commonly feature premonitions of the rich and famous, and one of Twain's dreams has become a modern staple—although it happened long before he had adopted his journalistic nom de plume, when he was just a twenty-three-year-old Mississippi River steamboat pilot-in-training named Samuel Clemens.

In 1858, Samuel secured a job for his younger brother Henry, aged nineteen, aboard the steamboat *Pennsylvania*. One afternoon when the young men were ashore, staying with their older sister's family in St. Louis, Samuel awoke from a nap in which he had had a startling dream of Henry's dead body, a bouquet of white roses and a single red rose on his chest, laid out in a metal coffin that was propped on two chairs. In the dream, Henry was wearing one of Samuel's suits.

When he dictated this recollection to his stenographer late in his life, for the purposes of his autobiography, he said he was so convinced by the dream that he rose and hurried to attend his brother's wake, only gradually realizing as he did so that had been just a dream. His niece related the story somewhat differently and somewhat more realistically: Samuel came out of the room where he had been napping and told the family (Henry included) about his vivid—he might have used the word *numinous*—dream and how disturbed he was by it. His family members thought it was silly he was taking a dream so seriously, she said.[2]

A few days after the dream, the brothers shipped out to New Orleans, where Samuel was made to stay ashore after a fight with the boat's pilot. The *Pennsylvania,* with Henry aboard, made its run back north. Then Samuel received horrible news that a boiler explosion on the boat had killed many of the crew and passengers near Memphis. Samuel hurried to Memphis, where he sat with his severely burned brother, who died that night from an overdose of morphine. The next morning, Samuel visited the room where many of the dead were laid out in coffins, and he was astonished to see Henry laid out in one of his own suits that his brother had borrowed (without his knowledge) when they were in St. Louis.

All of the other bodies were in white pine caskets, but the nurses, impressed by Henry's stoicism with his terrible burns, had pitched in to buy him a metal one. While Samuel was standing over the casket, a nurse entered and placed a bouquet of white flowers, with a single red rose in it, on Henry's chest. Later at the wake at their sister's home, he found the casket resting across two chairs, also as in his dream.

Dreams about air and sea disasters and natural disasters claiming many lives are an especially common genre of premonition stories. Earlier I mentioned the air-calamity dreams of Elizabeth Krohn and the famous Mount Pelée eruption dream of J. W. Dunne. These are also the type of dream that has garnered the most attention from researchers on dream precognition, since it is sometimes possible to find multiple individuals claiming to have had premonitions of the same event.

In the weeks leading up to the sinking of the *Titanic* on the night of April 14–15, 1912, for instance, many people—including several due to travel on the ship—had dreams about some kind of terrible disaster in the water. For instance, ten days before he planned to sail on the "unsinkable" ship, a businessman named J. Connon Middleton dreamed the Titanic was floating keel-upward, with its passengers swimming in the water around it. He had the same dream the following night, and it sent him into a depression. His pride would not allow him to cancel his booking just because of some dreams, but fortunately his American business associates suggested coming on a later voyage, which saved his life. A researcher named Ian Stevenson compiled and wrote about several cases like this for a parapsychology journal in the 1960s.[3]

After a horrific mudslide in 1966 that killed 144 people (mostly children) in a school in the coal-mining town of Aberfan, Wales, a psychiatrist named John Barker collected letters from sixty people around Britain who reported having had dreams or other premonitions seemingly related to mudslides or sudden burial in the days and weeks before the disaster. Eryl Mai Jones, a ten-year-old girl who died in the school, told her parents of a dream she had had the night before she perished, that something black had come down around the school and buried it. These dreams, like those about the *Titanic,* have been the subject of attention by later ESP researchers as well as skeptics attempting to debunk the subject of premonitions.[4]

And of course, I'm hardly the only person to have dreamed of something plausibly connected to 9/11 in the days or weeks beforehand. In his book *Dreamer,* Andrew Paquette describes several memorable and numinous dreams that seemed to prefigure the events in New York.[5] An art teacher in England named David Mandell, who already had a history of predicting terror attacks and other disasters in his dreams, painted watercolors of a series of dreams that vividly pre-presented 9/11, including a dream of the twin towers falling into each other exactly five years to the day before 9/11 (calendrical resonance). A few months later he dreamed of planes hitting the buildings.[6] A quick internet search turns up page after page of reports of people's vivid dreams and visions seemingly presaging the events of that day, not to mention artworks that seem to depict the destruction of the towers from the weeks, months, and years leading up to the event.

THINGS FALL APART

As part of their mandate from their government funders, the California ESP researchers whose work led to the Star Gate remote-viewing project tried to get to the bottom of how psi worked. One thing the researchers and operational remote viewers discovered was that hot or explosive events resulted in particularly accurate psychic hits. Psychics were always most accurate when the target involved an explosion, a nuclear reactor, a fire, a plane crash, or some similarly entropic event—that is, something moving rapidly from a state of order to a state of disorder. Dale Graff, who directed the Star Gate program, writes in his memoir *River Dreams* that "energetic incidents are great beacons in psi space."[7] He also notes that in a large database of psi experiences collected by pioneer ESP researcher Louisa Rhine in the middle years of the century, half were premonitions of fire.

Sometimes, remote viewers seemed to see explosive events before they occurred.* Edwin May, who led the research arm of the project during Star Gate's last decade, theorized that the connection to fire and other rapid entropy gradients may be fundamental to the way psi works as a form of a precognition.[8] This idea makes a certain sense, if you think of entropy in its relation to time. Again, many physicists consider the arrow of time to be nothing but a function of entropy. Things lose order as escaping heat, according to the second law of thermodynamics, and this is what we perceive as events marching in temporal sequence. Thus, it seems reasonable that if certain events can be seen remotely in spacetime, maybe it has to do with the extremity of their entropy—things moving

---

*For instance, in his memoir, *Reading the Enemy's Mind*, remote viewer Paul Smith describes viewing the 1987 missile attack on the USS *Stark* two days before it occurred (Smith 2005).

especially rapidly from order to disorder, as in a fire or explosion. Even the ultimate transition from order to disorder—the death of a person—might count as highly entropic in this sense. Such events might be like a thermodynamic cliff in the spacetime landscape up ahead.

There are a couple of serious problems with this at-first-compelling hypothesis. As Graff notes in his book, simply a picture of a fire, a picture suggesting an entropic event like an explosion, or a picture of an entropic event that occurred in the past may be just as fascinating to the precognitive unconscious as a real event and may just as readily be seen by psychics. Again, dreams seem to show us our own future emotional reactions to learning experiences rather than events out there in some future objective reality, as Dunne discovered. And recall Krohn's dreams about air disasters: even if the events her dreams precognized were in some (but not all) cases entropic, there was nothing fiery or explosive about the pictures themselves; yet it was these pictures and the accompanying news reports that she seemed to be seeing in her dreams. Such cases call into question any notion that it is some entropic signal that travels directly from a future calamity to a psychic receiver or antenna in our heads (or what May calls a psychic retina[9]).

The entropy theory, like the unconscious-superacuity assumption discussed in chapter 5, also cannot account for the specificity of the information in disaster premonition dreams. Why for instance did my 9/11 dream make the gray-facade buildings mosques? There was nothing intrinsically Islamic about the collisions of the planes with the towers (or Pentagon) or the collapse of the buildings. Rather, Islam was part of the media chatter, the discourse around the events; Islam almost instantaneously became a cultural obsession, since it was presumed at that point that Al-Qaeda had been responsible. As in many other cases of precognition (assuming that was precognition), I was more likely presponding to thoughts about an entropic event I was soon to learn about via the media, not detecting some ripple through the psychic aether directly from the explosions of the planes colliding with their targets.

Humans are wired to take an interest in entropy—that much is true. Graff notes that fire is fascinating to humans: "Fire resonates with something in us that we fear or fear we cannot control."[10] And it happens that all our senses are attuned to energetic, chaotic, and sudden stimuli, as well as anything explosive that could be threatening. But for Graff, the real carrier of the psychic signal is not entropy but strong emotion. After a decade of working with my own and others' precognitive dreams, I agree with Graff that it is our future strong emotion upon learning a piece of striking or upsetting or disturbing news that carries the psychic signal, not entropy as such. It obviates the need for any transmission of information outside the head. As we've already seen in the previous chapters, frequently what our dreams show us is not literally that future stimulus at all but our thoughts and emotions in response to it. Those thoughts are very often existential thoughts—that is, thoughts of survival.

MIXED EMOTIONS

One case from my own dream journal powerfully persuaded me that dreams often pre-present thoughts about survival in response to learning about a disaster. On a July morning in 2014, I dreamed that my wife and I were visiting a pyramidal stone temple in Mexico. Standing on part of it, the rocks were unsteady under our feet, and a woman who worked there ushered us into another room where we would be safe. The scene shifted, and I found myself facing a tall, triangular, treeless space or "absence" on the bank of an otherwise densely forested river, where I knew a huge temple pyramid had once stood but had long ago collapsed. Its collapse had left behind this big triangular gap in the forest.

My wife and I had been camping in Rocky Mountain National Park in Colorado on the morning I had this dream. That afternoon, we left the park and drove down Route 34 between Estes Park and Fort Collins, and I rubbernecked at the evidence of a flood that had destroyed numerous homes in Big Thompson Canyon about a year earlier. The destruction was still very visible, and the most striking evidence of it was an enormous pinkish triangular cut or gash that extended surprisingly high up a hillside on the opposite side of the river where the flooding below had caused much of the hill to give way, carrying a jumble of huge boulders and dirt and trees with it into the water. Even after a year, the rubble still sat in the river, a huge pile of naked pink granite with bare pine tree trunks jutting out like matchsticks. As we drove slowly past, I had an unsettling thought: any animal on that hill would have perished as the ground fell out underneath them.

It was only later that afternoon, when checking my notebook at our next campsite, that I recalled my previous night's dream and saw the connection. The notably triangular shape of the cut in the hillside was the same size and shape of the pyramidal temple. The dream, by making this triangular "absence" a three-dimensional presence in the form of a temple pyramid, enabled us to get on it (in the first part of the dream) and feel it slipping away under our feet.* This was precisely the disturbing thought that seeing the evidence of the landslide had provoked in me: anxiety over mortality amid an uncontrollable natural disaster, the earth giving way under my (or an animal's) feet. This thought, a precarious sense of survival, was the real salience being indicated by the dream, I believe.

In this case, a highly sudden and entropic event had in fact occurred, but that was a whole year in the past. And it makes no more sense to think of this as "retrocognition" of a past event than it would to think of my "The Apple" dream as a product of cryptomnesia (memories of the *Star Trek* episode from my childhood)—because why in that case would I have had the dream right before seeing the real damage?† The simplest explanation is that my dreaming brain was feeling its future. The emotionally distressing thought of dying in a landslide refluxed

---

*Freud argued that the unconscious can only represent the absence of something by showing the thing and placing it somehow under a sign of erasure (Freud 1984b). Consistent with this principle, my dream showed the absence of a triangular piece of mountain in two ways: the triangular gap in the trees and the pyramidal temple.

†Retrocognition is promoted by some ESP writers to account for impossibly knowing about some event in the past. It is sometimes invoked to explain feats of psychic archaeology, for instance. Besides lacking a coherent theory of how events remain encoded in the objective landscape, the notion of retrocognition ignores the fact that the psychic is rewarded in her future by new knowledge of the past; it is this future discovery and reaction that is being pre-sensed or felt, not some direct connection to a past event. Retrocognition is simply precognition, in other words.

backward in time a few hours, along with the implicit rewarding thought "but I survived."

Although Myers and many subsequent writers on psychic phenomena assumed that fear or grief were the main strong emotions bringing us premonitions of future upheavals, as often as not the dominant emotions may actually be rewarding: excitement, in many cases, and more importantly a sense of relief at having survived or withstood something. A sense of safety following upon a feeling of danger or threat is often the real focus of dream premonitions, not the danger itself. For example, Valerie, the Englishwoman who dreamed of the burglary of her parents' home two days before burglars stole her parents' car, also shared with me the following account of a dream from when she was in grade school:

When I was about ten I had a terrifying, vivid dream that my whole school had been evacuated to the main hall because there was some kind of terrible disaster outside. The sense of dread in the dream stayed with me for weeks after. I was having something of a religious Bible-reading phase at this point and decided I had had a dream about the impending Apocalypse/Judgment Day. However, months passed and nothing happened . . . until about nine months later, there was a huge electrical storm, the school electricity generator was struck by lightning and some of the classrooms flooded. The whole school was evacuated to the main hall. As I sat there, looking around, I realized this was the scene I had dreamed of so long before.

The dream focused on the situation of taking refuge after a threatening situation, rather than the threat per se (the entropic flood).*

---

*An audience member at a talk I gave about precognition approached me afterward and related a similar, even more striking story. He said he had dreamed vividly of the inside of an unfamiliar restaurant—just that, nothing else. Some days or weeks later, he said, he and a number of others were evacuated from a building because of a bomb threat. The police told them to leave the area, so he and a few companions drove some distance away and found a diner to get a meal. When he walked into this restaurant, he was stunned to find that it was the setting of his dream.

Strictly speaking, you might even think of a news story or news photograph about a disaster as a kind of refuge too: if you are able to view pictures of a disaster—for instance, watching the World Trade Center towers collapse on CNN, or looking at a picture on Twitter of a plane about to crash—then it probably isn't happening to you. It is important to remember—even though we might prefer to deny it—that there is an animal, instinctual side of us that interprets calamities befalling other people as signals of our own survival. "Luck," as Aristotle said, "is when the guy next to you gets hit with the arrow."[11] Consequently, underneath our shock and grief at such events, there is inevitably the realization "But I'm alive. It's not happening to me."

Something similar may be said of trauma more generally. If you are able to be traumatized by something, it means you have, at least physically, survived the ordeal. This precarious relief at our own survival—coupled with extreme guilt in many cases—is exactly the kind of mixed emotion that acts as a magnet to the precognitive brain.

A perfect example would be Samuel Clemens's dream about his brother's death. Note that he did not dream about the boiler explosion itself—which the entropy theory would predict[12]—nor did he dream of Henry's suffering and death either. The dream was specifically about what he saw the morning after Henry died: his brother, wearing his borrowed suit, laid out in a casket. Mingled with the obvious terrible grief, Samuel's emotions would also have included guilt. Henry had only been working on that steamboat because Samuel invited him and got him the job. Even more importantly, he would have had an overpowering sense of *it could (or should) have been me.* Remember that it was only a fight with the *Pennsylvania*'s pilot that forced Samuel to stay ashore during its fatal run north to Memphis. The fact that Henry was wearing one of Samuel's suits would only have intensified the awful irony of the situation and that sense of surviving a close call.

Principle #17 of our book is:

The thought "but I survived" is a very common target of precognition.

And it is yet another reason why Freud and his legacy are so valuable for helping us think about precognition. It often and maybe even always operates on a very base, selfish level that we like to keep buried from conscious awareness. As long as we remain in denial about this amoral, instinctual, "lizard brain" part of ourselves that values our purely organismic survival over even the well-being of our siblings (let alone strangers on TV), we may miss important clues to our precognitive functioning. In many cases this survival focus cannot help us avert disaster or tragedy, especially those befalling other people, for reasons we will explore more fully in the next chapter. However, the exceptions sometimes prove the rule and reveal something crucial about the way precognition works to promote our survival.

The annals of dream precognition are full of stories of people saving their own lives or the lives of others because of a dream. For instance, in his book *Dreaming True,* Robert Moss tells a story from his scary days as a war correspondent in Cambodia. A photojournalist friend had talked him into joining an expedition outside of Phnom Penh, but the night beforehand Moss dreamed of being killed in an explosion. He declined to go on the adventure, and his friend never returned from it.[13] I believe the key part of stories like this is that subsequent discovery about surviving a close call. In many cases, the "I survived" signal must be carried by a counterfactual hinted at or directly signaled by tragic or threatening news, perhaps befalling someone else. In Moss's case, he was not dreaming about some alternative future timeline where he himself was killed with his friend, even if that's the way he naturally interpreted it. He was dreaming about his future thought, *It could have been me,* that he would have after his friend never returned. Aristotelian luck, in other words. Acting on his dream—bringing about the prophecy through his actions—is what led to the completion of Moss's time loop.

Oddly enough, this survival focus can also help us understand the lion's share of precognitive dreams that are much more trivial, like dreams about backed-up sinks and other minor disappointments. The common pattern in many, if not even most, precognition-worthy experiences is that they are upheavals withstood. Having to deal with a backed-up sink is pretty minor, but it is still a surprise and a challenge in your day, yet ultimately it could always be worse. We're generally still standing after such occurrences. The situation is resolved, one way or another; we're still alive, and life goes on. We may find ourselves a little wiser and also a little more humble than we were before.

Principle #18 of our book is:

Experiences that cause some chagrin because they are somewhat embarrassing or humiliating are a common target for precognitive dreams.

(Another example of this would be my dream about the "hoodlums," related to my calling for help during a fall on the stairs, in chapter 7.)

And note that this same logic would also apply to transformative dream-related experiences like those described when we discussed synchronicity. Giving up some prior belief in favor of an expanded worldview that includes miraculous coincidences (or better, dream precognition) is like a death and rebirth, something that is scary and humbling at the same time that it is exciting or even paradigm-altering.

11

Four-Dimensional Billiards

*Time Travel and Meaning in a
Self-Consistent Universe*

People who dream of a disaster that comes true often, in one way or another, become gripped by the following thought: since they had dreamed of the tragedy, they should have been able to avert or prevent it somehow . . . yet they didn't. Thus, people who have precognitive dreams about disasters may feel guilt and engage in self-blame. For years, Elizabeth Krohn experienced her dreams about impending disasters like air crashes as a curse, not a gift. Even if she "saw" a disaster or its aftermath clearly and even in some cases could get a rough sense of the airline or the location of the event, there was never enough information to warn anyone.[1]

The frustration that there is no premonition infrastructure to help avert dreamed-of disasters has inspired researchers to create premonition registries. After the disaster in Aberfan, Wales, a psychiatrist named John Barker tried to pool the efforts of various psychics to predict and perhaps avert such tragedies in the future.[2] Thus far, such efforts have never quite panned out. When you think of the imprecision of even the most vivid premonitory dreams, along with the skepticism of the bulk of society (including authorities responsible for public safety such as the police, military, and so on that might be in a position to intervene) toward ESP, the challenges facing something like Barker's Premonitions Bureau become apparent. Even if dreamers were able to call or email some kind of central premonition registry, what would any authority really be able to do about a premonition of a plane crash or terror attack? Yet that is no help to all the dreamers who feel guilty that they somehow might have done something and couldn't, or didn't, because they didn't realize until too late that a troubling dream had really been a premonition.

When dreamed-of disasters hit closer to home, the emotional toll on the dreamer may be even greater. Steve, who dreamed of a car crash near his home in Seattle twenty-four hours before a real fatal crash occurred there, was profoundly affected by the incident. His feelings included, he wrote to me, "a feeling that I could've prevented it but didn't." All he could do was write a letter to the city about poor visibility of the signs approaching his intersection. That was a meaningful act that made his neighborhood safer and may well have saved future lives, but it still couldn't bring back the young life that had been cut short by the crash.

When a dream involves the death of a loved one, it may exponentially compound an individual's sense of guilt on top of their loss. I have had the heartbreaking experience of hearing a precognition-experiencer lament that she had had a dire premonition that she thought was about a friend, even warning that person, only to find that the specific dreamed-of calamity took the life of a close family member. Like anything else in life, prescience has its pitfalls.

The guilt and confusion surrounding premonitions is, I believe, one of the most important mental health consequences of precognitive dreaming, and the misinterpretations and false explanations that surround the topic of precognition and prophecy in popular books on the subject only exacerbate the problem. It is important for precognitive dreamers to understand that their feelings of guilt arise from the quite natural but (I believe) quite false assumption that premonitions show us "possible futures" that are subject to our freely willed actions to fulfill or prevent. It is an assumption that even some parapsychologists have unfortunately perpetuated, through assurances that some or all premonitory dreams represent probabilistic outcomes that might or might not come to pass, not events that are set in stone and unalterable.

For instance, there are those dreams that seem like warnings but don't come true completely—like a vivid dream about a fatal accident that then seems to be narrowly averted in real life. These examples, on the surface, appear to support the ESP-as-radar notion. Louisa Rhine cites several examples of "foreseen calamities prevented" in her book *Hidden Channels of the Mind,*[3] and her daughter Sally Rhine Feather highlights a particular striking case from her mother's files in her book (with Michael Schmicker) *The Gift.* A Los Angeles trolley conductor dreamed vividly of a catastrophic accident at a specific intersection on his route, caused by a bright red truck making an illegal turn while obscured from view by another trolley; in the dream, he crashed into the truck, killing two male passengers and severely wounding a woman, who "looked at him with the largest blue eyes he had ever seen and shouted at him, 'You could have avoided this!'" The next day, he came to the same intersection in his dream and, as he started to pull through it, began to feel queasy and slammed on the brakes instead. The bright red truck from his dream zoomed past, from behind another trolley, and he saw in the truck the three passengers he had seen in the dream— two men and a woman with big blue eyes who gave him an A-OK sign with her thumb and forefinger as she passed by.[4]

Even if precognition guides us on an unconscious level (and orients us toward survival and positive outcomes), given the principles I have been describing throughout this book, it likely does not literally represent alternative outcomes in some probabilistic future. Instead, our precognitive dreams represent our future thoughts and mental images in response to events or to learning about events. Those thoughts may include vividly imagined calamitous what-if scenarios in response to close calls and near misses. Rhine herself notes this possibility: "Perhaps the part of the dream that showed the tragic end in each of these events was an imaginative elaboration of foreseen settings."[5] There is no guarantee the trolley driver would have hit the truck; his instincts—on high alert because of the dream—may indeed have avoided an accident, but what he dreamed of the night before was likely a mental image of near-catastrophe sparked by his close encounter with the truck (and the blue-eyed woman who caught his attention), not an actual representation of some alternative history, some alternative timeline where things turned out differently.

While the natural idea of precognition as a radar scanning for possibilities is superficially believable when talking about imminent events—the fall of a chandelier in an hour, say (the other Rhine example from chapter 5)—it strains plausibility when thinking of premonitions of events that lie further ahead in one's future, not to mention complex scenarios involving multiple variables like a situation at an intersection involving illegal turns, multiple vehicles blocking each other's points of view, and so on. In a butterfly-effect universe, it is impossible to imagine that a very specific situation or set of circumstances like what the trolley driver experienced even a day ahead, let alone years or decades ahead, could be foretold through a kind of psychic radar scanning for variables and possibilities in the dark water of the future and which would be contingent in some way on our actions during the interim.

The annals of precognitive dreaming are filled with strikingly precise prophecies and premonitions that span months, years, and decades of a person's life. A dream like Freud's, which I argue was about the consequences of cancer and surgeries twenty-eight years in his future, would be unthinkable in a world where premonitions showed us some probabilistic future subject to alteration through our actions. Any little deviation in his life story on the basis of his dream—such as quitting smoking, or not spending all that time writing his book *The Interpretation of Dreams*—could have led to a different outcome. The same with Vladimir Nabokov and his dream about "Harry and Kuvyrkin" restoring his lost fortune, which came true when Harris-Kubrick Pictures sent him a check for $150,000 for the screen rights to *Lolita* a full forty-three years after he had his dream. Tobi's crane dream depicting an evening four years in her future (chapter 3) or Paul Kalas's dream about his astronomical discovery nine years later (from the introduction) are also examples. These kinds of long-range precognitive dreams are so common that I cannot believe they are just exceptional, dismissible as coincidence or the law of large numbers. We'll see some even more mind-boggling examples later (yes, I'm still holding out on you—chapter 15 might particularly shatter your reality).

Grasping that precognitive dreams show us our future thoughts about our own survival and withstanding of inevitable upheavals, changes to our worldviews, and even tragedies not only helps explain the discrepancies between dream premonitions and the tragic or (quite often) less-than-tragic events they are pre-presenting (such as that near collision in Rhine's story) but also illuminates why many or most genuinely tragic premonitions are not actionable in the way we imagine they would be if they were really radar-like warnings. Indeed, you may even find that your confused thoughts about your failure to act are already included in a premonition. Had you not failed to act and felt guilty about it, you would not have had the premonition in the first place.

Oddly enough, it is by understanding a bit about the physics of time travel and the laws that prevent paradox in a universe that includes time travelers and time-traveling information that we may understand better why we should never blame ourselves for missing the true significance of a "dream warning" from our future. Speaking of, here's another warning from your future, addressed to the physics-fearful: the following section contains the word *wormholes*. I'm sorry to say, this time you cannot avert the dread fate of reading it. So just relax, don your time-traveler goggles, and give in to its pull (or suck, depending on how you think of this book). Fortunately, you will be ejected at the other end of the section a little wiser (yet weirdly, also a little younger) than when you went in. You will survive.

EIGHT BALL IN THE CORNER POCKET

Einstein's theories about relativity—the ones that inspired his teacher Hermann Minkowski to conceive of a block universe and that gave Dunne permission to speculate about how consciousness might come unstuck in time at night—allow time travel. There are various methods including spinning the whole universe really fast, which is a bit extreme, but there are also simpler ways. If you radically bend the fabric of spacetime, you can create a shortcut called a wormhole—very much a "wrinkle in time," if you remember Madeleine L'Engle's novel from your childhood.[6] Some astronomers have suggested the universe could be riddled with such portals or shortcuts, which are often visualized as something like coffee-mug handles extending between distant regions.

Einstein and his colleague Nathan Rosen published a paper on these objects in 1935—they are sometimes called Einstein-Rosen bridges—but they were given the more colorful name wormholes by the physicist John Wheeler in 1957. It was not until the 1980s, however, that wormholes really began to capture the public's and physicists' imaginations. This may be partly to do with the growing popularity of sci-fi TV and movies featuring faster-than-light travel, such as *Star Trek* and *Star Wars*, but it is also thanks partly to Carl Sagan. When the astronomer and science popularizer was writing his science-fiction novel *Contact*, he needed a scientifically legitimate way to get his heroine, Eleanor Arroway (played by Jodie Foster in the movie), to the Vega star system and back within her lifetime, so he called upon black-hole expert Kip Thorne at Caltech. Black holes and wormholes are similar—some think they may even be essentially the same (at the other end of black holes may be white holes, where all the in-falling matter is ejected, but so far those remain theoretical). Thorne obligingly roughed out the wormhole equations that would allow Arroway's journey.

Despite the exciting promise of wormholes as an answer to how to traverse interstellar distances faster than light's snail's pace, there was the inevitable concern about what such shortcuts through spacetime might mean for causality, since wormholes through space meant, inevitably, wormholes through time. Wormholes could theoretically carry objects and people from the future to the past, which effectively means that the future could influence or cause the past. As I mentioned in that section you skipped in chapter 8, a growing number of physicists have no problem with that premise, at least on the microlevel of subatomic particles and the special situation of a quantum computer performing calculations that defy causal order. But when you start talking about physical objects and people traveling into their own past and mucking about, beads of sweat begin to appear on some physicists' (and even some sci-fi writers') brows. "Don't hand the time traveler a weapon" is the unspoken rule when we think about this possibility.

I'm referring of course to the famous grandfather paradox, that strange fantasy of going back in time and killing one's patriarchs, thus preventing oneself from ever having been born. Killing one's grandfather or (like the Greek tragic hero Oedipus) one's father, really boils down to a fantasy of *self*-negation, so when physicists model this problem, it is more convenient for simplicity's sake to cut out the patriarchal middlemen and ask about the neurotic possibility of self-inhibition or (more extremely) suicide in time-traveling objects. What happens to a billiard ball, say, if you shoot it through a wormhole at its slightly younger self, trying to deflect it off course?

A physicist at the Russian Space Institute in Moscow named Igor Novikov worked out the math that would govern a trans-temporal, suicidal (or at least self-inhibiting) billiards game (a sort of cross between billiards and Russian roulette), and he discovered something remarkably reassuring: physical law would actually prevent the billiard ball from inhibiting its past self. In fact, a *principle of self-consistency* would govern a wormhole-riddled universe. Even if an object could enter a wormhole at some time point B and emerge earlier, at some time point A, it could never actually interfere with its own entry into the wormhole at that later time point B.[7] Two of Thorne's students checked and found that Novikov was right: a time-traveling billiard ball cannot take the place of its younger self.[8] (According to physicist Nick Herbert, it is analogous to the exclusion principle discovered by Wolfgang Pauli, which prevents any two electrons from occupying the same states simultaneously—a principle that ultimately makes the world built of tiny probabilistic particles solid.[9])

More recently, the physicist Seth Lloyd designed and actually conducted such an experiment using a photon and what he called a quantum gun—essentially shooting the photon a few billionths of a second back in time to interfere with its past self. He discovered he couldn't. "No matter how hard the time-traveler tries, she finds her grandfather is a tough guy to kill."[10] This does not mean that time travel is impossible. Quite the contrary. It means that the time-traveling object encounters and interacts with its earlier self in precisely such a way that its later entry into the wormhole is facilitated rather than impeded. In other words, all possible paths of a billiard ball entering a wormhole would, upon exiting the wormhole earlier, nudge itself into the mouth of the wormhole later, thus completing the causal tautology, or what physicists call the *closed-timelike curve.*

These days, quantum physicists like Lloyd use the idiom of *postselection,* a kind of informational-causal Darwinism that ensures that the only information that survives its journey into the past is information that does not foreclose its origins in the future. It's not like there's a Causality Police stepping in now and again to prevent grandfather paradoxes from occurring, or that time travelers need to step gingerly in the past to avoid disturbing things (a common trope in time-travel stories)—although they may in fact find that funny paranormal experiences impede them in ways they hadn't expected. Guns might misfire at a crucial moment, for instance. (There's nothing keeping you from *trying* to kill your grandfather.) But mainly, it is that time travelers from the future who survive their journey into the past are the ones whose actions somehow lead to the identical future from which they will have been sent back.

Time loops, in other words.

When we are talking about precognition, or time-traveling information, it means that all prophecies would have to be self-fulfilling—exactly what we discovered along with Bilbo Baggins when addressing synchronicity in chapter 9. Paradox is prevented by the very nature of the rules that allow information to reflux into the past in the first place. Importantly, those rules include limitations on making that refluxing information *meaningful,* as opposed to noise. These self-consistency rules produce uncanny coincidental occurrences in our lives, because our unfrozen caveman (or hobbit) brains don't realize what's going on.

PHYSICS + FREUD

Novikov's self-consistency principle fits so well with what we have seen about the Freudian law in the mind governing precognitive dreaming (and, more generally, memory) that I believe it is no accident. Our tesseract brains not only capitalize on the retrocausal possibilities of the Minkowski block universe; they also obey the laws governing time travel, and the associative way memory and premory work reflect those laws in action. (Who knows—wild speculation alert—it could even be that memory evolved as a byproduct of precognition rather than the other way around. That would account for memory's essentially indirect, associative character.)

As we've seen, a typical precognitive dream is an oblique and indirect associative halo around some future experience or train of thought. Its exact relationship to that experience or train of thought *only* becomes clear in hindsight. There are apparent exceptions, such as more obvious premonitions that may even be almost "video-quality" in their transmission backward of some future scene. (I believe this may be exactly what some sleep-paralysis episodes and so-called out-of-body experiences are—we'll come back to this.) But even in those cases, what you might call the metadata of the transmission is always lacking: the when and where, as well as how the event fits into the ordinary course of life—in other words, the meaning. One way or another, the information that arrives from the future is incomplete or distorted enough that it cannot consciously be used to foreclose the inciting experience, even if it might cushion or prepare us for that experience on an unconscious level.

Novikov's self-consistency principle is reflected in Christopher Nolan's film *Interstellar*. The tesseract only allows Coop to send his younger self a message obliquely, using the books on his bookshelf. Younger Coop fails to understand the message: a warning not to go on a mission to a distant black hole (via a wormhole). Freud's dream in which he tells his friend Anna Hammerschlag (Irma) that her condition is her own fault after examining strange smoking-related symptoms in her mouth was a real-life version of Coop's situation and, I suspect, a perfect demonstration of Novikov's self-consistency principle at work.

Again, some writers have considered Freud's dream a kind of warning from his future self—"Quit smoking!"—a message that he didn't pay attention to, to his detriment. You can certainly look at it this way, even if Freud wasn't consciously sending himself such a message. Although it didn't exactly use books on his bookshelf, the message from Freud's future did use familiar people, places, and objects in Freud's life at the time he had the dream. But per Novikov's self-consistency rule, Freud could never have correctly interpreted (and thus heeded) such a warning any more than Coop could have heeded the warning he was sending himself with the books. Had the dream showed Freud clearly the consequences of his smoking, for instance by having him look in his own mouth in a mirror, he might have quit smoking and thus averted cancer, but then he would not have had the dream. That truly would have been an "impossible dream" from the standpoint of a self-consistent universe. A dream message about his thoughts around his cancer could only show those thoughts in an oblique, indirect way, in part by giving his condition to another person who had many associations to his future circumstances (i.e., his patient Anna, after whom his daughter—his nurse in his infirmity—would be named).

The mechanisms that control the back-flow of information across our "brain line" are probably not as picturesque as spacetime-bending wormholes. As I suggested in chapter 8, they likely will turn out to have something to do with quantum computation controlling brain plasticity, the constantly updated strengths of synaptic connections. But the principles will have to be similar: our future conscious thoughts interfere with us in the present and deflect us *just the right way* so we end up having those future thoughts at just the right time, creating time loops in our lives. Those time loops naturally involve our survival, because if they didn't, *that* would be the paradox.

It is inviting to imagine some kind of higher, tricksterish intelligence choosing to show us our future in this distorted way to edify or enlighten us—the synchronicity idiom encourages that externalized view of dreams' causation—but the reality, I suspect, is more like this: information "wants" to flow into the past within quantum computers like brains, but it is constrained in its flow just like rainwater is constrained to flow in specific channels and twisty rivulets down a hill. It doesn't just go anywhere willy-nilly; it follows paths of least resistance. Information from our future follows sinuous, roundabout, but resistance-free paths determined by the self-consistency rules Novikov divined mathematically: paths that don't produce paradox but that do lead to the persistence—that is, survival—of the individual sending that message back in time. The laws that govern dream distortion show us those deviated, circuitous paths to meaning.

Banish from your mind, once and for all, the notion that dreams show us possible or probable futures. They bear information from what will be, not what might be—but that information is distorted in all kinds of weird ways. Let's make that Principle #19:

Dreams obliquely and symbolically pre-present actual experiences rather than literalistically pre-presenting future possibilities.

TESLA THOUGHTS

Again, we should not do what most popular books on ESP imply we can do, which is think of precognition as a kind of radar. Even on those rare occasions when it brings us a foreshadowing of death and disaster, it is more like that precognitive circuit in my 2029 Tesla, deploying a protective airbag a second before an (inevitable) collision. The precognitive circuit didn't see the oncoming car and calculate the probabilities of impact—the conventional computer that drives the car, along with its cameras and GPS and other standard safety features, did that. The precognitive circuit in the quantum computer controlling the airbags does something else entirely: pre-act to the breaking of the circuit (a collision) roughly a second ahead of time. It's an entirely different trick than data-driven inferential prediction. (It also makes the Model Q really expensive. See, writing about time loops and precognition made me fantastically wealthy by 2029.)

Even without precognition, we already have a radar that works quite well. Our ordinary conscious thought processes constitute a radar-like system that scans for possible and avoidable future outcomes and warns us of dangers. That 3:00 a.m. wide-awake worrying about health catastrophes, financial ruin, and accidents happening to your kids? That's you scanning the future and rewiring yourself to pay attention and make the best possible decisions based on available information and even remotely plausible threats. Precognitive dreams, visions, and so on are different and serve a different function. They are better thought of as airbags pre-deploying to cushion us from upheavals. They are previews of us already having withstood some challenge to our ego or (much, much more rarely) to our physical well-being or that of our families. The way they mislead us via indirection can be thought of as a way to prevent paradox in a universe of freely willed precognitive beings (ourselves), but in the time-loops universe this is no different from saying that these oblique and distorted dreams are part of the carrot that motivates us to take the course of action that leads to that survival. Remember, the threads of your life woven on time's loom are pulled tight from both past and future. Our precognitive dreams are really summonses from our future surviving, successful self. They are as much symptoms of our persistence in the block universe as the cause of that persistence.

Survival doesn't mean surviving unscathed, of course—and success doesn't mean we've sailed past all difficulty. Some tragic outcomes cannot be averted, because they are like enormous, unavoidable icebergs in the water of our fate. Consequently, bad things happen to good precogs, just as they happen to everyone. When people dream about such events, it is only because those events did—er, will—happen in the block universe, not because they might happen or might not. Dream premonitions are showing us important thoughts about those events, including confused and guilty thoughts, and thoughts about what it means that the bad thing happened—for instance, a family member died, as in Samuel Clemens's dream about his brother Henry—and that I, the dreamer, am still here.

Those kinds of deeply baffling existential thoughts about being and nonbeing can take much life work to digest. I strongly suspect that premonitions are a preemptive aspect or component of that working-through process. The Freudian-Dunnean unconscious also happens to be Jean-Paul Sartrean. It's all, in the end, about being here and imagining what it's like to not be here. It's about death and mortality—the one thing the unconscious cannot symbolize, according to Freud, and I think this may be one of his greatest insights. His fascinating essay "Negation" was about how the unconscious cannot directly represent nonbeing and absence, and thus finds clever ways of using tangible, present objects and situations to show a thing under threat or erasure.[11] This difficulty symbolizing the traumatic taking-away of something valuable is the great catch-22 Freud saw the unconscious as built upon, and it is captured with the single, often reductively misunderstood word *castration* (it's not only, or not mainly, about the phallus). It's also a principle in all dreamwork, precognitive or otherwise, and is Principle #20 of our book:

Dreams cannot directly represent nonbeing,
but they nevertheless are often about nonbeing,
our thoughts about loss or the possibility of loss.

The equivocal nature of the kinds of experiences that seem to be the focus of many precognitive dreams—not just tragedies but also mildly embarrassing or humbling experiences like plumbing mishaps, or exciting synchronicities that force a broadening of our worldview—suggests that we are guided toward withstanding, and growing (even a tiny bit) as a result. Note that this Goldilocks logic would make perfect evolutionary sense as well as Jungian or New Age sense. The primrose path of comfort and contentment, avoiding all stresses and obstacles, would place no pressure on an organism to adapt and survive. If precognition has arisen and been sustained through natural selection, it would have to do with surviving and withstanding inevitable challenges, not steering us clear of challenges entirely. The latter would carry us right back to that paradox of having a premonition of an event that we avoided entirely and thus never knew about.

So to reiterate, dreams that come true (or mostly come true) are side effects or byproducts of a largely unconscious behavioral orientation or polarity toward our own persistence in the block universe. Those updatings of our neural network in advance of upheavals perhaps prepare us, cushion us like a predeployed airbag, for surprises that, on an unconscious level, are not completely surprises after all. They are not warnings about possible futures we could somehow avert if we were only somehow more on the ball. This is why precogs should feel absolved of guilt for failing to correctly interpret or act on their premonitions, as if there were some other timeline where they might have known better and could have taken another course of action that prevented a tragedy.

Principle #21 I already gave a spoiler for, but here it is again:

It is not your fault if you have a premonition that comes true.

Again, we will often find, when we actually do the work of closely interpreting our dream premonitions, that the inevitability of a dreamed-of outcome—as well as our hindsight regret about our failure to prevent that outcome—is already prewritten into the dream. Dreams are weird that way.

12

The Wyrd of Doctor WTF

The Real Superpowers of the Unconscious

The reality in our lives of mental time travel as precognition offers a totally new way of looking at the basic question Freud posed most clearly for modern times: Why do we know ourselves so poorly? What accounts for the vastness of our *un*conscious? If our future is constantly refluxing back and shaping us and we are getting glimpses of it, shouldn't we know ourselves *better*? Those laws governing wormholes in a self-consistent universe seem to give us the answer: we misrecognize our own future experiences and thoughts and wishes in our dreams, and thus take oblique and maybe even neurotic, self-destructive paths in our lives, precisely to the extent that we cannot recognize ourselves in them and still remain self-consistent.

That may seem strange and surreal to you, a modern twenty-first-century person, but I don't think it would seem strange to an unfrozen caveman, or to an ancient Greek. The ancients intuitively understood the circular and fractal laws of fate. Classical tragedies like Sophocles's *Oedipus Rex* were thought experiments about how we fulfill our fate precisely by trying to escape it. Oedipus accidentally killed his father and married his mother in the effort to evade an oracle's prophecy that he would do both of those terrible things.

Oedipus was a kind of premodern time traveler, since marrying your mother is kind of equivalent to traveling back in time.[1] You might call him Doctor WTF. Because he was married to his mother but didn't know it, he was like a shopping cart, going in circles (and bringing ruin on Thebes) when he thought he was moving forward in life and avoiding the dark prophecies of the oracles. Symbolically enough, Doctor WTF walked with a limp. It's even implied by his name: Oedipus means "swollen foot."

The word the Anglo-Saxon poets of Dark Age England used for fate highlights this ironic, circling, swerving logic; they called it *wyrd*— a word related to a lot of other w-r words still existing in our language that connote twisting and turning (*worm, wrap, writhe, wreath, wring,* and so on—even *word,* which, as *writers* know, is made of bendy-twisty marks on paper or stone). Wyrd, or *weird,* is the bending force in our lives that, among other things, causes dark prophecies to be fulfilled not only despite but actually *because of* our best efforts at preventing them. It also *warps* our mind and induces a kind of compulsion around more appealing-sounding prophecies, as it did to Shakespeare's Macbeth after hearing the Weird Sisters' prophecy that he would become king.

When we realize that the Minkowski block universe, in its resolute self-consistency, imposes a wyrd-like law upon us (a "law in the cosmos," you might call it), then all those antique myths about prophecy and the ironic insistency of fate start to appear less like the superstitions of benighted folk in the Back When and start to seem remarkably, well, prescient. And not only prescient, but based on real-life experience with prescience. Divination was an important part of Greek culture, for instance; it was even the basis of their medicine. Sick patients went to temples and caves to have healing dreams in the presence of priests who could interpret their dreams' signs. They were not strangers to this stuff, as we now are.

As intrinsically precognitive beings who think of ourselves as freely willed, the logic of wyrd is our ruler. We can't go anywhere that would prevent ourselves from existing, prevent ourselves from getting to the experiences and realizations ahead of us that will turn out to have retro-influenced our lives now, and this imposes a kind of blindness on us. That blindness may keep us from going insane, reducing the level of prophecy to a manageable level. It is why our dreamlife only shows us the future as through a glass, darkly. It is also why the world seems so tricksterish to those who are really paying attention. That we are interfered with by an intelligence that is somehow within us but also Other is the human intuition that Freud theorized in such a radical new way. His focus was on how this Other inside could make us ill; the flip side is that it really does serve as our guide, especially when we let ourselves be led by our unreason. Research shows that "psi" is an unconscious, un-willed function or group of functions.[2] The laboratory experiments by Daryl Bem, Dean Radin, and many others strongly support something like presentiment (future-feeling) operating outside of conscious awareness, and it could be a pervasive feature or even a basic underlying principle of our psychology.

WYRDAR

For people without prior experience getting in touch with their psychic side, dreams are the easiest and most reliable avenues to explore, and thus this book has focused on them. But rewards and upheavals on the road ahead can and regularly do influence us while we are awake—and in many of the same ways Freud identified as waking manifestations of the unconscious: via uncanny out-of-the-blue feelings, via misperceptions of speech or texts, via slips of the tongue or pen, via songs that get stuck in our head—the lyrics of "earworms," I find, sometimes relate to something that will happen later that day—and just generally via "random" thoughts and obsessions that end up corresponding to some imminent unpredictable encounter or experience.

Freud reports a few such experiences in *The Psychopathology of Everyday Life,* the book he wrote after *The Interpretation of Dreams.* For instance, he writes that he had a sudden fantasy, while walking along a Vienna street, about a couple who had rejected his services for their daughter months earlier—the fantasy was that they would now seek him out since he had just been named Professor, but that he would reject *them,* as they had rejected him. Just then he heard himself addressed, "Good day to you, Professor!" It was the very couple he had just been thinking of. Unwilling to countenance anything causally untoward like psychic foresight, Freud came up with a handy but convoluted psychoanalytic explanation: he supposed that he had looked up to the street ahead just before his fantasy and unconsciously recognized the couple's approach but blotted it out of his conscious awareness through "negative hallucination,"[3] so that his mind could prepare his little wish-scene. But given everything we've seen so far in this book, it is far more parsimonious to think Freud was simply feeling his future and that his presentiment took the form of a seemingly random fantasy: being addressed as "Professor" in public by patients who had previously disrespected him.

Readers of my previous book and my blog have sent me many compelling examples of this kind of waking presentiment, sometimes around unsettling imminent learning experiences. Oscar, the man in Kansas City with the premonition about learning of the death of someone from his high school in a car accident (chapter 10), also related another similar experience from his teen years. He told me he used to stay up late on weekends building ham radio equipment. One Friday night in 1957, around midnight, he was suddenly gripped by an inexplicable worry that something was terribly wrong—he assumed it was something electrical:

> I was building a short-wave receiver using vacuum tubes which required potentials around 250 volts. Suddenly, a terrific mental alert hit, indicating a major problem. I checked and double checked my wiring. All was OK. So I began to check around the big ham equipment that had 1500 volt potential but found nothing. I spent a good hour more looking around the room for anything, even checking books in the wall library. So, still alerted and really concerned something bad was about, I went outside and searched, walking around the house. Finally about 4:00 a.m. I decided whatever it was could get me if it wanted and I went to bed in the radio room. Next morning there was a news broadcast of a brutal murder of a lady I knew, from her working at a local drugstore, and lived about a block away from our house.

Valerie, who dreamed about her parents' burglary (see introduction), reported another, more consequential "premonition" that may have averted a robbery. She described to me in an email that she was studying at college for her finals, in a relaxed, focused flow state—not at all stressed—when she was gripped by a sudden urge to call her mother. "This was odd," she said, "since I was not in a procrastinating mood that day. Also, when I looked at the time, it was not yet lunchtime, so I knew my mum would be at work in her office." She went with her spontaneous feeling, however, and rang her mother's mobile phone. Her mother answered, but seemed distracted—finally saying, "Listen, can I call you back in a minute?" Valerie told me she was "p—ed off" at her mother's brusque cessation of the phone call.

A few minutes later, Valerie told me, her mother called her back, wanting to know why she had rung just when she did. She explained that she had in fact been on her lunch hour (it was an hour earlier than Valerie supposed) and that she had been out walking with a coworker on a quiet secluded street when a strange man—who had evidently been watching them from behind a wall—approached them and started behaving suspiciously. She thought he was about to attack them . . . but just then, her phone rang in her bag (Valerie's call). This startled the stranger, who quickly hurried off.

Julia Mossbridge, a neuroscientist who has done pioneering work studying presentiment in the laboratory, relates an even more high-stakes example of a catastrophe-averting presentimental hunch. In her book *The Premonition Code* (cowritten with Theresa Cheung), she describes how one day she had found herself getting inexplicably angry at her thirteen-year-old son for (she thought) leaving the garage door open after riding his bike home from school. When she repeatedly told him to close the door and he repeatedly denied leaving it open, she stormed out to the garage to check for herself—only to find that her son had in fact closed the door.

Perplexed at her assumption of her son's carelessness and at her own anger, Mossbridge went back inside. On the way, she discovered that their electrical meter was on fire. Right on the other side of the wall, she knew, was her sick partner's oxygen tank. Had she not seen the fire and put it out, it could have caused a deadly explosion. Mossbridge adds that she has noted many instances in her life when, as she puts it, "the future has leaked some information into my present consciousness."[4]

Experiences like Valerie's or Mossbridge's might seem at first to contradict my argument that precognition isn't a form of radar. Couldn't Valerie's sudden urge to call her mum and Mossbridge's inexplicable need to check the garage door be seen as radar-like warnings? Yes and no. Neither received any kind of mental impression showing them what was wrong (at least, nothing accurate; what Mossbridge imagined about the garage door was incorrect). Yet following through on their sudden urges (and inaccurate assumptions, in Mossbridge's case) produced courses of action that saved the day. That's not radar—it's something far wyrder. Call it *wyrdar*, perhaps.

In *Time Loops*, I noted that precognition is a bit of a misnomer, since it implies thinking (cognition). I use the term because it is the most common and familiar term for future influence, but really we should define it as *behavior oriented toward forthcoming rewards*.[5] It needn't involve conscious thought at all. It might manifest as an urge, a hunch, or a gut feeling without any kind of mental representation attached.

Waking premonitory experiences quite often produce positive effects in our lives, indirectly and unconsciously, via our behavior and via intentions that are unclear or that we are likely to misinterpret at the time. People who are highly intuitive may be especially good at acting on the kind of strange, senseless impulse that ends up saving a life or preventing some lesser mishap—perhaps by not censoring their reason, which will tend to get bogged down in finding rational causes for feelings and hunches rather than simply acting on those feelings. Intuition, I think, is just presentiment by another name, and being an intuitive person is just not getting in the way of this presentiment by overthinking our motives. Indeed, the kind of intuitive, spontaneous behavior displayed by Valerie or Mossbridge may be the most direct, important, and immediate, not to mention potentially survival-relevant, manifestation of the precognitive unconscious.

Even though the Star Gate remote-viewing program shut its doors in 1995, the military continues to study psychic abilities, and the kind of intuitive nudge that may have saved Valerie's mum from a mugging and Mossbridge's household from a deadly explosion is explicitly what some of the research focuses on. The Navy, for instance, actively studies people who have so-called Spidey sense, like a squad leader who instinctively guides her platoon down the right path in enemy territory because she senses danger down the left.[6] Such people figure prominently in battlefield folklore, and those who study ESP take these stories seriously. Long before he became a remote viewer, the most storied Star Gate psychic, Joe McMoneagle, attributed his survival in Vietnam to a precognitive inner voice steering him and his comrades away from danger.[7]

Psychical and ESP researchers have generally adopted some intuitive model of information transfer across space to explain Spidey-sense-type abilities, using for instance the metaphor of some psychic antenna.* But if psi is really precognition, then nothing necessarily needs to be sensed or detected from outside the body or even outside the nervous system; it would be the nervous system's connection to itself across time that matters. Thus, a soldier with Spidey sense might not actually be receiving some kind of waves coming from the IED down the left path and then leading her squad down the right path. Her brain might instead be pre-sponding to the ambivalent future reward of having taken the right path and then hearing the explosion and screams of some other less fortunate squad that took the left. Conscious presentiments like Valerie's or Julia Mossbridge's would work on the same counterintuitive yet also more explicable principle I described in the context of premonitions: they are the reflux of our future conscious emotions and thoughts about survival—conscious what-ifs coupled with relief in the aftermath of a

---

*Telecommunications metaphors have always governed assumptions about psychic abilities. The telegraph dominated the thinking of Frederic Myers with his theory of telepathy in the last two decades of the nineteenth century. In the early years of ESP research in the 1930s and 1940s, radio was an obvious metaphor. And remote-viewing researchers of the 1970s naturally likened the practice to tuning in on a TV signal.

narrowly averted disaster. By the weird logic of time loops, our thoughts about survival bootstrap us toward that survival. Those thoughts are like billiard balls from our future, deflecting us just past the margin of danger, and in a manner that is beyond sense and reason and literality.

A variant of this same logic could be operative in dowsing, one of the most ancient forms of divination. The efficacy of dowsing is hotly debated, with skeptics insisting it is bunk—they point to experiments showing it doesn't work better than the random chance of guessing.[8] Yet people all over the world, even some modern water companies, swear by it. Despite the skeptics (and a handful of small, biased experiments), there's every reason to believe that the believers are probably right—it's just our mental images that are wrong. It is easiest to imagine that a dowser holding bent rods or sticks over the ground is detecting energies from the earth indicating buried water or lost object, but the reality may be that their precognitive brain is keying in on subtle presentimental tug toward a location where they will imminently feel the reward of finding what they are looking for. Such a temporal causal/retrocausal explanation will seldom occur to our space-bound way of thinking, but it fits with everything we have seen about wyrdar, not to mention the time-looping types of precognitive experience that captivated Jung in his clinic and that he called synchronicity. It would explain why researchers feel drawn to just the right book in a strange bookshop or to just the right quote in an article on the internet. The library angel is really book dowsing. And the Spidey sense that saves a platoon could be called survival dowsing.

People who express strong intuitive ability often seem to do so in the context of some automatized and highly enjoyable or thrilling motor skill, such as piloting a plane, practicing martial arts, or mountain climbing, but also through performative arts like music or stage magic, as well as through painting or sculpture or creative writing.[9] Whether you are a race-car driver, a surgeon, a soldier, or a poet, self-consciousness that might include an awareness of making choices is usually the last thing you want—especially when you are in the zone, or a state of flow like Valerie says she was in with her studies when she unthinkingly acted on the strange urge to call her mother.

But really, this may apply to all skill performance. Anyone who knows how to navigate rush-hour traffic skillfully, be super witty on a date, or swiftly change a baby's diaper while talking on the phone knows that we are most effective when we don't think about what we are doing but just do it.

The general principle is this: the brain seems to be an organ that reaches forward across its timeline, pulling conscious thoughts and insights from the "more informed" future. Animals may be so good at living, so miraculously effective at moving through their environment, because of this relation to a future self that knows just a little bit more than the present self does. The brain (and I suspect, smaller cellular units or cells themselves) *thinks across its history,* not just in the instant. It means your conscious thought processes right now, along with a fan of many other conscious moments, are the unconscious of you a few seconds ago, a few minutes ago, a few hours ago, and even a few weeks or years ago.

Stated differently, your future consciousness is the unconscious of your present moment, quietly animating and informing your thoughts and actions, maybe causing a slip of the tongue or (if you are sleeping) a dream, or giving you some intuition or hunch of where to go and how to proceed, or perhaps generating a precognitive vision of something you will encounter tomorrow, or creating some other kind of uncanny synchronicity. It is the same intuition that is guiding us toward success and pulling our strings when we make a painting, drive a race car, or perform a flawless martial-arts move. The unconscious is consciousness displaced in time. Who knows—wild speculation alert again—but maybe consciousness is what it feels like for thoughts, actions, and outcomes to be perpetually out of sync. Go forth with your notebooks, precogs, and help answer this question!

I argued in *Time Loops* that some of the neuroses that occupied Freud in his clinical work may arise from our misrecognition of the precognitive nature of the unconscious. We may be less psychologically victimized by the twisting and tricksterish power of prophecy when we understand that the quiet voice speaking to us in our dreams and intuition is really ourselves, addressing ourselves confusedly and obliquely from different vantage points in our life's long story, even if we can never fully understand its messages. The unconscious is really the landscape we traverse across our life, the road we walk down. Wyrd is the curvature of that life-landscape, the topography that directs our footsteps. That familiar-looking but slightly more experienced traveler up ahead is you.

13

What's Expected of Us in a Block Universe

New Myths for Precogs

Thanks to myths like Oedipus, the ancients instinctively understood the block universe and the ironic rules that follow from such a cosmology. By resurrecting that ancient time traveler, Freud almost restored that mythic framework for the age of Einstein and Minkowski. Unfortunately, he fixated on the "loving your mother" part of Sophocles's tragedy and ignored the much more interesting and pertinent issues related to informational time travel—prophecy—which as a modern, scientific person, he simply didn't and couldn't believe in. It was his tragic flaw, you might say.

Because we've lost touch with the ancient myths, today's precogs may find themselves without guidance in navigating the complexities of the precognitive life. Jung's writings on synchronicity—perhaps the closest thing to a secular unifying framework for miraculous experiences—at least encourage us to pay attention to dreams and coincidences. But by reducing these experiences to the interplay of archetypes, that framework also downplays our own role in creating rewarding meaningful coincidences, and it provides only very limited interpretive tools for exploring dream precognition. (Synchronicity giveth; synchronicity taketh away.) Parapsychologists' scientifically framed writings on

ESP, on the other hand, alert us to precognitive possibilities, but often with the assumption that this is a statistically significant but nevertheless minor effect in our lives, and never with a coherent theory of how precognition really operates. They also promise that our dream premonitions only show us possible futures, and we saw the unexpected pitfalls of that way of thinking.

Fortunately, science fiction is providing us with some new myths, and they have been extremely valuable for precognitive dreamers and dreamworkers. I already mentioned the movie *Arrival,* based on Ted Chiang's "Story of Your Life."[1] It is about a linguist named Louise Banks (Amy Adams) whose precognition awakens from studying a nonlinear alien language. Chiang's 1998 story is tantalizingly sketchy about the mindset of the extraterrestrial heptapods and their purpose in visiting earth, but Denis Villeneuve's film depicts them as ancient, wise, and selfless—one of the two heptapods Louise interacts with sacrifices its life to save her from a bomb even though it knows in advance what will happen. Their language is a gift to earth, which not only brings peace among nations (via Louise's precognitively informed actions) but also prepares for humans' reciprocity in the block universe. In 3,000 years, the surviving heptapod tells Louise, humans will offer their species some needed aid, just as they have helped us now.

Arrival is a gripping and moving story, and it has proved to be an important life-touchstone for precogs. I mentioned my collaborator Tobi's dream the night before seeing *Arrival,* in which she was in a parallel world being studied by cosmic researchers, using an iPad displaying circular symbols just like the iPad Louise uses in the movie. She later discovered from her dream journal that she'd precognized the movie in several other dreams as well, in addition to other stories by Ted Chiang that she later went on to read.* And Elizabeth Krohn, the Houston woman who dreams about plane crashes and other disasters that she

---

*I was similarly excited and moved by *Arrival,* and discovered that I too may have been precognizing it. On the afternoon before going to see the movie, I spontaneously became interested in Zen brushstroke circles and hunted down a lecture on the subject by Daisetz Suzuki. Heptapod B as depicted in the movie consists of very similar circles.

is powerless to prevent, took important inspiration from *Arrival* and its positive portrayal of precognition. The movie helped her do what Louise does in the film: accept as a gift what originally seemed like a curse, due to her inability to change the outcomes she was foreseeing.[2]

Precogs get it. Doubt still reigns, though, among the wider public not yet acquainted with their precognitive powers and the real presence of the future.

THE AGE OF THE PREDICTOR

People in a modern, individualistic Western society have a mental block against the block universe. Even those who are open-minded in general to ESP at some point balk, and I could see you doing it too earlier, that tightening in your abdomen. "Doesn't everything you're saying about precognition go against free will?" (you muttered). "If future events are fixed, then doesn't that consign us to the most dismal kind of determinism, something like the Predestination doctrine of the Calvinists? Why embark on the precognitive dreamwork path if all it does is show us things that are set in stone, and we can't change them?"

Another short story by Ted Chiang, "What's Expected of Us," is a brilliant thought experiment about the exact anxiety precognition skeptics feel when they sniff Calvinism in the air of the block universe. Originally published in *Nature* in 2005 and reprinted in Chiang's 2019 collection *Exhalation,* "What's Expected of Us" describes a kind of toy, called a Predictor, with a light, a button, and a precognitive circuit (or "negative time delay") linking them. The light goes off one second *before* the button is pressed, and cannot be fooled no matter how hard the user tries. Users treat it like a game, trying to beat or outwit the light, but find they cannot. The device becomes super popular and people play with it addictively, but roughly a third of users succumb to a kind of hopelessness and immobility called akinetic mutism, because of what the device has taught them about the nonexistence of free will, the futility of trying to change their fate. "Like a legion of Bartleby the Scriveners, they no longer engage in spontaneous action."[3]

People used to speculate about a thought that destroys the thinker, some unspeakable Lovecraftian horror, or a Gödel sentence that crashes the human logical system. It turns out that the disabling thought is one that we've all encountered: the idea that free will doesn't exist. It just wasn't harmful until you believed it.[4]

Europeans and Americans, especially, prefer to think of the future as a bit like the wide-open frontier of our pioneer mythologies—an empty untamed expanse full of possibility. We love the idea that we are free agents, willful determiners of our lives. We think of ourselves as cars who can go anywhere we please, even off-road, not trains fixed to a single track. If we think of the future as already holding something in store for us, we delimit that something to *destiny,* a kind of dotted line around the person we might become but aren't obliged to, a future self that awaits our freely willed actions to fulfill or not fulfill, depending. It's in sharp contrast to the ancient notion of fate, as a preordained future that will always outwit our best efforts at evasion.

"What's Expected of Us" is a mini *Oedipus Rex* for an age of fidget spinners—bringing us back to that premodern fate-bound worldview. But we don't need to look as far back as Sophocles's Athens for models for the Predictor. The first thing the Predictor reminds me of—and I wonder if Chiang had it in mind when he wrote his story—is a notoriously mind-bending 1983 discovery by neuroscientist Benjamin Libet. The nerves in participants' fingers readied to fire ("lit up," you might say) a fifth of a second before participants consciously decided to move their finger.[5] Libet's discoveries prompted other cognitive scientists to prove that we are not really masters in our house. Experiments by psychologist Daniel Wegner and others seemed to show that we instead take credit for unconsciously willed actions per our culturally ingrained ideas of agency.[6] The ego sees something it likes—a successful motor action, say—and proudly goes, "I did that." It sees something it didn't like, like tripping and falling down icy steps, and chalks it up to accident or to some external force or influence impinging on it.

Like it or not, introspection—and Einstein—teach the same lessons the Predictor does, even without the high tech of a negative time delay. In hindsight, all our freely willed actions appear determined and are immutable; there's always a point of view (such as just a second from now) where that has to be true of you right now, feeling all free. Einstein's discoveries reaffirmed that there's always some other point of view from which our current, freely willed actions are already in the past to another observer, etched in stone or glass. We might as well step into the role of that other observer ourselves—and in fact, this is what our stream of consciousness may really amount to. Dunne, in his sequel to *An Experiment with Time* called *The Serial Universe*, likened philosophy to the perpetual substitution of a mental picture of reality with a frozen picture of ourselves within that reality; it is also an apt depiction of our self-awareness.[7] There's no escaping this endless march of frozen self-representations in a kind of cinematic freeze-frame as our cursor-like consciousness scrolls through the video of our lives. Our moment-to-moment feeling of free will—along with the sense (or wish) we may have of an indeterminate future—is already included in the block universe.

I like to remind my block universe–blocked friends that free will is a Western hang-up, not a universal one. Some wisdom traditions centralize the paradoxical-sounding teaching that contentment comes directly from giving up belief in free will. The Zen masters of China and Japan, for instance, discovered that direct experience of the illusory nature of free will actually leads to liberation: *the less free we imagine we are, the more free we feel.* It's that same joy anyone feels when they become so good at a complex skill that it becomes effortless, performed automatically (unconsciously) in a state of bliss and perfection. Shaolin kung fu masters, who were Zen monks, were not worried about their free will, any more than a fighter pilot is worried about free will when executing a demanding maneuver.

The problem with that immobilized subset of Chiang's Predictor users is that they can't shake their feeling of free will even when they know it isn't real in some larger sense. Lying in bed and not responding to their surroundings doesn't help, since that is just as much an action as getting up and seizing the day in the belief that we are authors of our destiny. Our thoughts and interpretations are just as much enacted as our physical movements; they are just as much parts of that big causal mechanism in the block universe. Frustrated apathy arises from trying to be spontaneous but perpetually feeling maddeningly contrived and self-conscious, because spontaneity is really a performance, a bit of theater. *That's* what's unpleasant about it—a self-conscious awkwardness at playing a theatrical role. It is a lot like being an awkward, angsty, and uncertain teenager.

It is also a lot like being a beginning Zen practitioner. For the latter, if they are persistent, there sooner or later comes a breakthrough moment, a *kensho,* where the free-will/determinism distinction is shattered. At that point they discover that, unburdened from the baggage of thinking about their freedom or unfreedom, their thoughts become more rewarding and their actions and words more skillful. There is a real lightness and efficacy that comes from transcending our worries over free will.

Thus, when I see skeptics draw out their free-will card around the question of precognition, I cheerfully make a pitch for Zen meditation (or any kind of meditative introspection): it is in our power to set aside or outgrow our hang-ups about free will, at least long enough to experience the kinds of joys the precognitive life can bring. The akinetic mutists of "What's Expected of Us" are simply stuck in that awkward, teenager-like training-wheels period. The other two thirds of Predictor users, one imagines, have already arrived at some kind of blissful enlightenment.

I do think something like Chiang's Predictor would be the perfect training tool for Zen monks—a kind of material(ized) koan. When Apple's iWill Touch™ predictive toy goes on sale on Black Friday 2030, I'll be first in line at the Apple Store to buy one. Until then, I'll just sit quietly, with my eyelids lowered, breathe in through my nostrils, and contemplate the precognitive airbag in my 2029 Tesla—it's the same thing.

ALCHEMIST'S GATE

Another story by Chiang, "The Merchant and the Alchemist's Gate," has even more to teach precogs about the block universe, the temporal shenanigans it allows, and the value of traveling through time (physically or mentally) even if we can't actually change history. First published in 2007 and also republished in *Exhalation,* this story is about a medieval Baghdad shopkeeper named Bashaarat who shows a fabric merchant named Fuwaad ibn Abbas some astonishing wares he has made using alchemy, including a portal that will carry an individual twenty years into the future. To help Fuwaad decide whether to use the portal, Bashaarat tells three stories about past clients.

One of those clients, a rope-maker named Hassan, used the portal as a young man and encountered his very prosperous older self, who gave him various bits of strange advice. Following that advice, he lived precisely the auspicious life he saw in his older self. Another client, a weaver named Ajib, traveled through the portal and stole money from his older, pitiful, miserly self, but as a result found himself living precisely the miserly life he had found and pitied. Lastly, Bashaarat tells the story of Raniya, the wife of the first traveler, Hassan, who traveled twenty years into the past, using another portal at his shop in Cairo, to seduce Hassan as a young man. In doing so, Raniya learned that it was her own tutelage that gave her husband his sophistication as a lover, which she had always loved in him. The implications of Raniya's story are what sell Fuwaad on the value of time travel. "I realize now that, even though the past is unchangeable, one may encounter the unexpected when visiting it."

Armed with this insight, the merchant decides to travel twenty years into the past using the Cairo portal to visit his wife, who had died shortly after their marriage and whose death had haunted him his whole life. She had died after being injured in the collapse of a mosque after they had parted in anger. Various accidents on his journey hinder him from reaching her in Baghdad before her death—remember, Novikov's self-consistency laws prevent changing the past—but on his journey he encounters his wife's nurse, who informs him that her last thoughts had been of him and that her short life had been made complete by him. It is a message that releases him from his lifetime of pain and regret and one that he could not have learned without the benefit of time travel.*

THE UNKNOWN PAST

The scientists of the Enlightenment threw out teleology because they couldn't yet imagine a retrocausation that wasn't part of God's singular purpose or divine plan—and that God was traditionally an irrational and cruel one. If there is no plan as such, but just what lies ahead, drawing living things and thinking beings like ourselves toward generally positive outcomes (most basically survival, but also other meaningful connections and rewards), then it creates a new vision of time, one that is always full of hope. The Italian psychologists Ulisse di Corpo and Antonella Vannini use the term *syntropy*: convergence on order and unity.[8] Whatever we call it, it offers a wholly new way of looking at the meaning, and joys, of being a conscious being in a deterministic universe.

Seeing the brain as a tesseract allowing future thoughts and emotions to impact us in the present totally reframes that eternally vexing question of free will, or at least the conscious will that neuroscientists no longer believe in. We simply need to "place" conscious will differently in relation to our actions: it would be in our conscious reflections on our past that something like the causal efficacy of thought actually comes into play. Our conscious will may really be what we experience

---

*"The Merchant and the Alchemist's Gate" puts a positive spin on another famous Baghdad tale about immutable fate, W. Somerset Maugham's 1933 "An Appointment in Samarra." Allegedly based on an old Mesopotamian legend, it is a very short story about a Baghdad servant who encounters Death in the city bazaar. Death makes a threatening gesture to him, so he borrows his master's horse to flee to another town, Samarra. Later, the master goes to the bazaar and asks Death why he threatened his servant. Death replies that his gesture was only a start of surprise. "I was astonished to see him in Bagdad, for I had an appointment with him tonight in Samarra" (Quoted in Žižek 1989, 58).

as our hindsight reflection, specifically on our successes. Getting clearer on this may be what makes the difference between succumbing to akinetic mutism like the Predictor users in Chiang's "What's Expected of Us" and being able to say "carpe diem!" instead.

"The Merchant and the Alchemist's Gate" returns us to the ancient idea of fate, or wyrd, but with a hopeful and modern twist: it shows that whether immutable fate is tragic or redemptive depends on our attitude, not on something external to us like the will of the gods. Ajib, who stole from his future self, lived the impoverished life he saw when he visited the future; Hassan, who saw his future and was pleased by it, willingly obeyed his future self's commands and was duly rewarded. But in the chicken-and-egg universe of time travel, you could also say that their attitudes were symptomatic of their future outcomes at the same time that they were the causes of those outcomes. Ajib saw his future and was displeased, and behaved accordingly; Hassan, pleased by what he saw in the future, was loyal and obedient to his older self. In one sense it does harken back to the Calvinistic predestination doctrine, in which the elect were those whose worldly prosperity was a mark or sign of the fact that God had already decided to reward them in the afterlife. But the block universe of Minkowski and Einstein, unlike the unforgiving one of Calvin, is one where there is always hope for a new discovery that changes everything, about the future as well as the past.

The reason is that while fixed in one sense, the future also isn't predecided by God (or anybody) at the beginning of Creation. It is decided—and continues to be decided—by your own actions as you live your life. Just because you are a miserly thief today doesn't mean you won't perhaps discover something tomorrow that changes your mind about yourself and how to live your life, a discovery that turns you into a humble but empowered precog with an auspicious destiny (or fate). Who knows—if you are reading this book right now, it may be a sign that you are already among the elect in the new precognitive world, a friend and servant of your future surviving, successful self. This is because you are starting to grasp that the symbols and figures in your dreams *are* that self, gesturing in a kind of semaphore across the fourth dimension.

PART 5

THE CARE OF
THE LONG SELF

14
After the Miracle
How Our Thoughts Influence Our Past

People who find the idea of precognition, retrocausation, and time loops interesting are often of an occultist bent, and I am frequently asked how the block universe that allows precognition can be reconciled with the active intention-setting that a magician might utilize, as well as about the idea that thoughts and intentions can directly exert a positive influence over our lives.

In this connection, I often think of my friend Mitch Horowitz, an occult historian, and his writings on New Thought, the distinctively American idea that our thoughts are causative over our reality. Forming an intention of a definite chief aim, persisting toward that aim in an ethical manner, and visualizing the fruits of that pursuit are important aspects of this tradition, which has its roots in the Transcendentalists, Spiritualists, and Christian Scientists of the 1800s. Most people know this tradition better from twentieth-century positive-thinking gurus like Napoleon Hill (*Think and Grow Rich*) and Norman Vincent Peale (*The Power of Positive Thinking*).

At first, the appealing idea that thoughts are causative seems antithetical to the kind of fatalistic determinism I have described—a block universe where the future already exists in such a way that it can act back upon the present, but in which case is not subject to change. Are these framings really in conflict? Sometimes when two ideas seem diametrically opposed, zooming in reveals a closer kinship. I believe the time-loops framework can illuminate how thoughts can be causative; and by the same token, New Thought ideas might even rescue what had seemed like our doomed notion of free will—or at least help compensate for what might appear (to block-universe haters) as a dismal kind of Calvinism.

TIME COLLAPSE

Mitch himself is no stranger to time loops. In his 2018 book *The Miracle Club,* he describes several experiences that caused him to question the simplistic linearity of time and causation that Enlightenment science has always insisted upon. One of them fits right into the Spidey-sense-type experiences described in chapter 12.

Mitch describes that in the summer of 2016, he developed an inexplicable interest in the Monkees, the late-1960s TV band formed as a knockoff of the Beatles. This was a weird band for Mitch to get interested in. Anyone who knows him in person or from his lectures and social media knows that he literally wears his punk musical tastes on his sleeve, always appearing in a Dead Kennedys or Misfits T-shirt or the like. Yet suddenly this punk-styled writer on American occult traditions found himself obsessively listening to jingly pop songs like "I'm Not Your Steppin' Stone" and "Last Train to Clarksville." A retrocausal reason for this odd obsession surfaced a few months later, when Mitch was invited by the *Washington Post* to review a new memoir, *Infinite Tuesday,* by the Monkees' guitarist and songwriter Michael Nesmith. Nesmith, it turned out, was into the Christian Science teachings that Mitch had written about in his books.

It was the kind of impossible coincidence that many people would chalk up to synchronicity, but it seems more like Mitch was feeling his future. In this case, his future had sent him a message via a sudden detour in his musical taste.

The same year, 2016, also brought the fulfillment of a time loop that began with a dream Mitch had two years earlier. Despite his interest in mind power and even in psi research, Mitch had been a doubter about the significance of dreams. He didn't generally write them down and thought of them as "little more than a retread of the day's events, a potpourri of impressions, and a working through of anxieties"[1]—the kinds of assumptions promoted by many popular science books on dreaming as well as by the reductive neuroscientists discussed in chapter 4. Yet one morning in late July 2014, he uncharacteristically wrote down the following dream in a red notebook he kept beside his bed:

Dreamt I was speaking (at A.R.E. [Association for Research and Enlightenment, in Virginia Beach, VA]) to 2 auditoriums—one "New Age" & one like a movie theatre. Joked about it. Both melded into one neat, tidy room following a distraction in the New Age auditorium. I carried a cane—wondering how the audience took it. Did they like it?[2]

Although he later could not remember why, Mitch also jotted with this dream the date of a particular channeled reading by the early twentieth-century clairvoyant Edgar Cayce, the founder of the center he was speaking at in the dream. That reading, "July 15, 1928," had to do with what Cayce had called "the mental as builder."

Mitch forgot all about this dream after he recorded it. But then in April 2016 he went to deliver a talk on Cayce at the A.R.E. His presentation was on "Mind as Builder," the theme of Cayce's July 15, 1928, reading, which had also become a dominant theme in Mitch's own writing and thinking. But incredibly, when being given a tour of the Association's archives, he was shown and allowed to hold a cane that had belonged to the nineteenth-century Spiritualist Andrew Jackson Davis (the man who coined the term *Law of Attraction*). Davis's Magic Staff was a significant artifact of American New Thought history, and holding it was a significant moment for Mitch personally.

It was just a few days after his return to New York from this trip that Mitch happened upon his old red notebook and found that forgotten dream record—one that corresponded to his actual visit both literally (the cane) and symbolically. The dream's theme of speaking to two separate audiences (New Age and mainstream) that merged into one also foreshadowed the major theme of his professional life in 2016, bringing intellectual rigor as a historian to his authentic belief in the positive-mind philosophies of New Thought figures like Cayce and Davis.

Mitch writes, "to rediscover my overlooked dream, and to realize that I had mentally lived out that scene some two years earlier, brought me a stirring sense of time collapse, in which events were playing out in a nonlinear manner."[3] Reality, as he noted in his review of Michael Nesmith's *Infinite Tuesday,* "doesn't travel straight lines."[4]

SEIZE THE YESTERDAY

What sets Mitch apart from some writers in the New Age (a label he embraces) is his rigorous inquiry into possible mechanisms for thought-causation. It is not enough for him to hand-wave about consciousness and synchronicity and leave it at that. The question Horowitz poses in *The Miracle Club* is this: Does the direct efficacy of thought potentially have a physical, not just metaphysical, explanation? "If thought possesses causative properties . . . then what are its means of transaction?"[5] His instinct, which I think is correct, is that something like his "time collapse"—what I would call time loops—plays an important role. Both of the uncanny experiences he described as time collapses seem like examples, albeit inadvertent ones, of the unexpected way our conscious thoughts can be causative over our reality via our past.

If we can be influenced by our future thoughts, whether in dreams or in waking life, then it necessarily implies that our conscious thoughts now influence our prior actions. This I think is one of the most exciting entailments of the time loops model. On one level it is obvious and implicit from everything that we've seen in previous chapters, but it also is so counterintuitive that it is easy to forget or minimize, so I am underscoring it. And I believe it supplies at least a partial answer to Mitch's question about the mechanics of thought causation. That is to say, if our unconscious behaviors are premonitory of what we think of as our will, if what we precognize with our actions and our automatic (unconscious) responses as well as our dreams is our future conscious feelings and realizations, then those are by definition retro-causing our younger selves, like those billiard balls in physicists' thought experiments about wormholes.

If your day is even slightly affected by a dream, even just in the mere act of taking a few seconds to write it down (as Mitch did with his dream about speaking at A.R.E.), and the dream consists of or contains thoughts and emotions from sometime in your future—and again, it is conceivable that all dreams might—then those future thoughts and emotions exert a shaping force on the present—even if you misinterpret your dream, as you are bound to do by the wyrd logic described earlier. This will be the case even if you do nothing more with your dream record than leave it untouched and forgotten in a bedside drawer. According to the famous butterfly effect of chaos theory,[6] that action of remembering and writing down the dream is a minute or two you might have done something else, perhaps making you miss your usual bus or have an encounter in the street you wouldn't have otherwise. These tiny differences add up over a lifetime.

Dreams point to this kind of retrocausation being operative across days, years, and even decades of our lives, but it may also be operative on millisecond or second scales, such as in the presentiment research of Dean Radin.[7] Indeed, it may be pervasive and basic to our cognition and behavior, not just some exceptional thing that happens once in a while. One way of looking at it is that we go through life behaviorally divining successful or rewarding outcomes—orienting to them through that kind of presentimental "wyrdar" from chapter 12—which we then reflect on consciously afterward. Behavior—all behavior—may really be premonitory in some sense. What we interpret in hindsight as our will or intention is thus really the reward of having had an accurate premonition of a future successful action.*

---

*I suggest Benjamin Libet's seemingly free-will-destroying findings about the lag of conscious decisions behind the readiness potential in our motor neurons could reflect the tip of the iceberg of presentimental functioning—precisely what Dean Radin identified in his studies of involuntary (autonomic) responses to imminent stimuli (see Wargo 2018).

Another, simpler way of putting this is that we may be "pulling our meat puppet's strings" from a point further along our timeline, displaced from the action.[8] The relation of our conscious will to our successful actions may be literally a causal loop. Our four-dimensional longbodies or Long Selves may be built of time loops whose closures are powerful, emotionally charged thoughts, including thoughts about our own success.

I suspect—and it is an area that I and a few collaborators have only begun exploring[9]—that a growing understanding of time loops could ultimately give us tools, like life hacks, whereby we sow boons in our future via conscious interventions in our past. Building forward-going habits of dream-honoring would be a crucial part of this. A general habit of honoring is a lot of what many magicians, occultists, and practitioners of New Thought methods actively cultivate, even if they may describe or explain it using a different idiom. And I'd bet it will turn out to be the ethic and driving motivation of our timefaring descendants too, hundreds or thousands of years from now, with their wormholes and *Interstellar*-like tesseracts. We can sow seeds in the past for a better tomorrow.*

It is important to note here that causing or sowing seeds in the past is quite a different thing from *changing* the past—the idea that we could somehow alter our histories or undo past mistakes, the too-easy premise of many classic time-travel yarns. Previous writers on precognitive dreams, such as Robert Moss (in his book *Dreaming True*), have speculated about such possibilities.[10] I think it is absolutely essential though—actually gives the theory its necessary traction—to insist on the distinction between changing the past, which is paradoxical, and influencing or causing the past, which is not.

There is the popular notion, for example, of the Mandela effect: some apparent discrepancy between history as people remember it and real events, which has sometimes been attributed to some glitch in the

---

*One interesting, increasingly popular theory of UFOs is that they may be us, time travelers from our own future (Masters 2019; Wargo 2020a).

Matrix or alteration of the timeline, perhaps through the meddling of a time traveler.* It is that kind of neurotic universe, slipping and sliding and unable to make up its mind, that some parapsychologists are implicitly invoking when they speak of precognition showing us probabilistic rather than actual futures. But in fact, such a universe implicitly nullifies the validity of any dream or potentially precognitive experience in the same stroke that it seems to grant it: is there another timeline where Freud quit smoking after his dream about Anna Hammerschlag and thus didn't get cancer, or another timeline where the woman in Louisa Rhine's story failed to rescue her child from the soon-to-fall chandelier? Maybe, but in that case, we must also suppose that there is another timeline where I forgot to put on my pants before going to work this morning—something that happens frequently in my dreams. Is that, too, a real experience somewhere in an alternate reality (a lot of alternate realities, it seems) that my freely willed actions happened to prevent in this timeline? There is a slippery slope to absurdity in this idea, not to mention the scientist's horror of untestability. There is no way to test whether our counterfactual what-ifs really exist in some parallel universe, even if those counterfactuals—as thoughts or fantasies—are often the targets of our precognitive dreams.

Our awareness of the past is part of our timeline; our memory is part of history. If the past could be changed, how would we ever know? The fact that makes all the difference, though, is what Ted Chiang showed in "The Merchant and the Alchemist's Gate"—that our memory, what we think we know of the past, is often wrong or incomplete. Although it is paradoxical to think we can change the past, through physical or mental time travel, we can learn things about the past that we never knew or suspected, including how we now may be playing (or,

---

*As it pertains specifically to Nelson Mandela, many non–South Africans were surprised to learn that he died in 2013, because they remembered him dying in jail in the 1980s—hence the idea that maybe they are remembering a different timeline. They are more likely confusing or conflating Mandela with Steven Biko, a dissident who was killed in police custody in 1977 and who was the subject of the Peter Gabriel hit single "Biko" in 1980 and a 1987 film, *Cry Freedom,* starring Denzel Washington.

have played) a powerful causal role in shaping our past. (We will see a startling example of this in the next chapter.)

FAILURE IS NOT AN OPTION

Most modern conceptual frameworks for understanding the past make no room for teleology, and thus we think of the past as untouchable by any later influence. But I hope to have convinced you that that's just a modern, post-Enlightenment failure of imagination, not a real limitation on reality. The retrocausation paradigm in physics suggests that everything seemingly random or indeterminate about the behavior of particles on a quantum level may really be where future influence has been hiding, misidentified and mischaracterized in many of the most mainstream interpretations of quantum mysteries over the past century. The famous Copenhagen interpretation, for example, says the particle has no real reality until it is measured, but the retrocausal model reframes it: the particle always had definite properties, and it is specifically the physicist's subsequent measurement that gave it those prior properties.

Again, my hunch is that molecular processes involved in memory and learning are able to scale up quantum retrocausation, turning the brain into a tesseract. One way we already know quantum processes manifest in biology is the phenomenon called quantum tunneling. New Agers are (in)famous for misappropriating quantum ideas to explain miracles, but if there ever was a quantum phenomenon genuinely tailor-made for helping us understand New Thought, it is this one. When they are not interfered with in the act of measurement, particles have a way of fast-forwarding toward their destinations, taking the fastest possible path as though they know where they are headed, and even somehow passing through solid barriers. The retrocausation paradigm implies something very specific about the phenomenon: it is the interaction with the next thing that the particle hits (its destination, perhaps a measuring device) that retro-determines the particle's path. Its path was never random, in other words—it really did "know where it was going" all along.

This quantum fast-forwarding toward what to our eyes appear like intended outcomes could be the X factor separating life from lifeless matter in organic molecules, the missing vital principle underlying life.[11] (It is already known that photosynthesis and enzymatic actions depend on quantum tunneling, for example.[12]) It would force us to reincorporate something resembling purpose—even if not God's purpose—into our understanding of living systems. And it would scale up in nervous systems, which tend to some greater-than-chance degree to gravitate toward survival and other rewards in an organism's future.

What especially excites me about this idea is that it would allow us to flip or at least augment the New Thought idea that success is built on mind, a function of mental attitude. If our presentimentally informed behavior tends to "tunnel" toward optimal outcomes like survival and rewards—and if indeed this tunneling is what thought is on some basic molecular level—then mind is really built on success as much as vice versa. Mind *is* success—a tendency toward the optimum. (To appropriate the idiom of quantum-computing researchers, successful outcomes would be post-selecting the actions leading to them.[13])

Understood retrocausally, the quantum tendency toward the optimum seen in tunneling means there is no other world of "failure" (or missing the target) out there as an option for a particle. In a block universe, there's no alternative path a particle could have taken, and by extension there's no counterfactual history or biography for an organism or person made of those particles. That squad leader with Spidey sense in chapter 12 automatically took the right path, away from the IED, and there was no alternative or counterfactual reality where she took the left path instead. Her making the right choice was not random. Failure is literally not an option in a retrocausal universe. I suspect the tesseract mind-brain scales up this tunneling-toward-the-optimum principle that rules the quantum domain and utilizes it to create the splendiferous four-dimensional formations that are our biographies. On the entropy-dominated human scale, it's not perfect—again, bad things sometimes happen to good precogs, as they happen to anyone—but it makes our lives ever so slightly more right than wrong, just as it makes life intrinsically successful.

Mind—the persistent special sauce of life itself—is indeed a builder, and in the most radical way possible. Through our thoughts, we write/wrote our life stories. But I like that horticultural metaphor of sowing too: our thoughts in the present planted seeds in the past as dreams and other kinds of intuitive actions, and those seeds germinate as boons or positive rewards in the present and still to come.

Imagine how much more we could direct that self-shaping capacity by building habits of attending to our dreams and other inspired or creative thoughts and honoring them, even without knowing what future experiences and events they refer to. Imagine discovering on a weekly or even a daily basis that you really have been retro-shaping your life all along, that you really are the author of your Long Self.

15

A Precog Claims Her Gifts

One Woman's Life-Altering Precognitive Awakening

All the while I thought on the truth of Bashaarat's words: past and future are the same, and we cannot change either, only know them more fully. My journey to the past had changed nothing, but what I had learned changed everything, and I understood that it could not have been otherwise. If our lives are tales that Allah tells, then we are the audience as well as the players, and it is by living these tales that we receive their lessons.

TED CHIANG,
"THE MERCHANT AND THE ALCHEMIST'S GATE"

If the brain is indeed a tesseract, then what Ted Chiang reveals about time travel in "The Merchant and the Alchemist's Gate" must already be true of our lives: while you cannot change your past or future, at any stage of the game you might learn something new that changes everything. It can be humbling to make such a discovery. Sometimes it can be life-altering.

I'll now tell you a true tale of one such life-altering discovery, stranger than the strangest fiction.

Tobi, whom I've mentioned previously, was nineteen, a college sophomore living cheaply in a crowded basement with several friends on a street less than a block away from the campus of the University of Colorado in Boulder. It was the winter of 1988, and she had fallen into a deep depression. She doesn't know what brought on the depression—she attributes it now partly to moving into a dark warren-like apartment, unaware at that point in her life that she was sensitive to light deprivation (the office where she worked on campus also had no windows). At the time, though, she associated her crushing low mood with a series of terrible dreams that occurred over the course of a few weeks that winter.

The dreams were, randomly, about a kid named Michael that she had known in grade school, in a town on the East Coast where her family had lived until she was twelve. In her dreams, he appeared as a kind of giant, looming over her, and she was fending him off weakly with a weapon—extremely uncharacteristic of her nonviolent personality (and also uncharacteristic of Michael, whom she remembered as gentle and harmless, but big). Tobi and her family had moved west to Colorado seven years earlier, and she had no reason to be dreaming of this childhood classmate. Yet these dreams were persistent. Her depression caused her to remain in bed and even forced her to withdraw from her classes and call off her plans to move to California to be with her boyfriend from high school.

Fast forward nearly two and a half decades, to 2011. Now a mother of two in Denver, married to the musician from her creative writing class whom she had begun dating that same winter in 1988 (after calling off her California plans), Tobi had another dream about her grade-school classmate. By this point, she had been keeping a dream journal for several years, so she wrote this one down in detail: Michael met her on the street, led her to his house, and opened it with a key that had been hidden in the mailbox. But standing on the porch, he tried to conceal from her what was inside the house. Peering past him, she could see it was full of, in her words, "wonderful books."

It didn't yet occur to Tobi to do anything else with this dream about Michael, such as Google him (something she of course could not have done at all in 1988). But then seven years later, around the same time of year in 2018, she had another dream, this time about another boy who had been a friend of Michael's:

[Michael's friend] vandalized my house, breaking the outer panes of my double-paned windows and punching holes in my soffits to reveal glimpses of a soaring, sunlit, spacious roof vault and its rafters (a view that wasn't architecturally "real"). It was impossible that he could have or would have done this. Yet he and his mom stood silently on my porch while I wondered what to do about the damage.

Michael was her first association to this dream vandal, whom she only dimly remembered and whose name she did not know. The dream really seemed to be about Michael. It was now three decades since her college nightmares, but this dream finally prompted Tobi to do an online search of Michael's name out of curiosity.

She discovered awful news, and it took a while (and extensive further online research) to confirm that it was indeed the same Michael she had known as a child and had been dreaming about. She learned Michael had been murdered in 2008 (a decade earlier), in precisely the manner she had been trying to fend him off in her distressing college dreams from 1988. She did not record the exact dates of the earliest dreams from college, but the one in 2011—when he was trying to hide something in his house—was on the same day (though wrong year) of his actual death, according to a news story she found.

By this time, Tobi not only had been keeping a dream journal for many years but had become an adept dreamworker. She both recorded and studied her night dreams and practiced a variant of Jungian active imagination, entering and engaging with the dreamworld during the day while typing at her computer—a skill that she learned and honed during a period of illness in 2013. Her records of her night dreams as well as her waking adventures in nonordinary reality were brimming with what she had learned to think of as confirmations of her experiences, signposting her progress. "I thought it was all 'synchronicity,' as if the Universe knew about my dreams and was sending me information, gifts, and jokes after the fact to tell me I was on the right track." But the discovery of this former classmate's murder, in exactly the manner she had dreamed, unsettled her sanguine attitude toward her dreamlife and her belief that this was just synchronicity at work.

In the flurry of online research Tobi did that evening and the following day, it occurred to her to Google the names of her housemates from her sophomore year, all of whom she had lost contact with at various times in the years after college. Among those names was mine—I had been one of her housemates. She had assumed I'd gone on to become an anthropologist, since she knew I'd moved to Atlanta for graduate school in that field after I graduated from CU in 1989. Now she discovered that, amazingly, I'd been writing about precognition and precognitive dreaming for a few years on my blog *The Nightshirt* and had just published—literally a few days before her discovery about Michael—my first book, *Time Loops,* on the subject.

Out of curiosity, Tobi ordered my book. From it, she learned about cases of people having uncanny precognitive dreams about events decades in their future—dreams like Freud's about Anna Hammerschlag or Vladimir Nabokov's about "Harry and Kuvyrkin." She also learned the story of Elizabeth Krohn and her progress coming to grips with her premonitions about air disasters she couldn't prevent. The realization that she, too, was a precog came like an avalanche to Tobi over the following days and weeks—kind of like Chazz Palminteri's mug shattering in slo-mo at the end of *The Usual Suspects.* All of those "synchronistic" dreams she had recorded and printed out in binders took on a new meaning. She also suddenly had new insight into numerous dreams over the previous decade pointing toward a major discovery in her future, about "claiming gifts," that figures in her dreamworld hinted belonged to her. She had even dreamed, "randomly," about me in March 2017. In her dream journal, she had noted "an interaction, possibly with Eric Wargo . . . that demonstrates the presence of non-ordinary worlds/conscious[ness]." In her dreams, she often interacted with figures that she already took to be her older self, but it didn't yet occur to her that they were more than symbolic or figurative.

Recall again that River Lethe that hypnotizes dreamers and other experiencers of wonders. Forget about it. Nothing to see here, move on. It's just coincidence. It's just your brain deceiving you. Or at best (as in

Tobi's case), take it as a pat on the back for a job well done, a sign you are on the right track. Like me and others who awaken to their precognition belatedly, Tobi had nurtured her dreamlife with wide reading in various metaphysical and dream-interpretive traditions that encourage attention to the meaningful coincidences and convergences in our lives, which mainstream psychology resolutely ignores. But those traditions could only go so far in illuminating the dazzling implications—about consciousness, about time, and about her own life story—that her dream corpus was now disclosing. Tobi realized that she was the one creating all those synchronicities. They were time loops. Her life seemed to be full of them. All the hints and symbols in her dream corpus began to fall into place. She was now, as her dreams had been promising, claiming her gifts.

WELCOME TO THE BUNNY PLANET

Tobi's subsequent cautious email, reestablishing contact after almost three decades (subject line: "Um, quit it"), came like an avalanche to me, too. Readers and strangers at parties share their amazing dream experiences with me—it really is the biggest reward of writing about this topic (I was kidding about the fabulous wealth and the Tesla)—but here was someone from my own past whom I knew and trusted and who had a truly mindboggling story to tell. Most amazingly, it was a story that hinged on me, both as someone in her life when she had the dreams and then much later as someone whose writings about precognition were able to help banish the spell of that River Lethe. (Figures in Tobi's dreams leading up to that point had also alluded to an imminent anamnesis or unforgetting of something profound about her story; Mnemosyne, the Greek mythical antidote to Lethe, even was mentioned.)

Over the subsequent weeks, Tobi shared with me by email the news stories she had found about Michael's murder, the court records from the trial of his killer, as well as many of her dream records—including photocopies of those that had been handwritten or printed without being saved. Her night dreams and especially handwritten annotations to her daytime active dream records contained countless synchronicities that on reexamination were clearly time loops inaugurated by precognitive dreams, and she continues to discover new examples every day. We actively collaborated in trying to understand the story of her Michael dreams, their possible connection to our entangled biographies as former housemates reconnecting decades later over a paranormal experience, and what it all teaches about the Long Self. Part of my own (admittedly selfish) reward was it was the perfect case study of everything I'd been writing about until that point.

Tobi and I agreed, first of all, that her dreams in college were not warning dreams or premonitions. They were nothing that could have ever been used to avert the tragedy that befell Michael. Had he not died in the way he did, she would never have found out about it, and thus would never have had those dreams decades earlier. Ultimately, we also decided that the dreams were not really, in the end, about Michael's death—although there was a working-through process for Tobi in coming to this realization. Rather, her belated discovery of that murder was a kind of MacGuffin in her claiming of her own precognitive gifts—that vast, impossible sunlit space in her own attic that Michael's friend revealed with his vandalism, or the library of wonderful books in Michael's house. Her dreams in college seem to have already "known" the significance of this discovery—not only through the enormity of Michael in those dreams, but also through her inability to quite fend him off, as he was looming over her. In that series of dreams, she perpetually failed to kill him with the weapon that she was wielding.

The nexus of experiences in Tobi's life starting with her college dreams and ending with learning about Michael's murder and her own precognition was more than a time loop, it was really a time *knot*. One way to describe it (at least, from my perspective, of trying to fit precognition within a larger theory of memory) is that my being Tobi's housemate in 1987–88 acted as a precognitive prime—not unlike in one of Daryl Bem's experiments. My becoming a precognition writer later (and her ability to find out about that via the internet) sparked a kind of short circuit between these distant periods in her life. But a better metaphor than a short circuit is . . . a wormhole. A wormhole literally folds space-time and brings two spatially and temporally distant points together, and this is what happens in dreams; they fold the spacetime of your biography and bring temporally distant points into brief, blurry contact.

A skeptic, even one open-minded to the possibility of precognition, would balk at aspects of Tobi's story, getting bogged down in various "What are the odds?" sorts of questions. What are the odds one of Tobi's housemates would go on to write about precognition and that Tobi just happened to dream of Michael's death during the time they were housemates? What are the odds she would then discover what happened to Michael just a few days after that housemate published his book? The odds against the last one, in a purely statistical universe governed by chance, would be astronomical. But to even think of this as a question of chance and odds is a misunderstanding rooted in the open-ended-future myth we all grew up with—and, incidentally, that the skeptics' law-of-large-numbers argument is also predicated on. Precognition forces us to throw out those questions of odds and chance where human behavior is concerned.

It is a cliché to say nothing happens by chance, but in the world of time loops, it's true that many things in our lives don't. Tobi had those dreams in college, when I was her housemate, because she would be discovering the precognitive source of those dreams later, right before encountering my book. As impossible as such a thing might sound, it is really consistent with the experiences of other dreamer-precogs, both in the literature and those I correspond with. Even my own humble dreamlife supplies plenty of instances showing exactly the same time-looping principles as Tobi's dream corpus reveals, even if not as constantly or around anything as dramatic as a murder.

One Saturday in December 2018, about a month into my email correspondence with Tobi, I opened my dream journal from 1999 for an unrelated reason, and I discovered by accident that I had dreamed "randomly" about her on November 15 of that year, a decade after I had last had any contact with her or her husband (whom I had remained friends with for a couple years after college). I misspelled her name with a *y*, which is why she had not come up in a previous search for possible appearances of her name. I dreamed that "Toby" was a sibyl—that is, a prophetess—who ran a rabbit farm. Prophecy was nothing I ever would have associated with her during the years I knew her in college, nor anything she would have associated with herself at that point. Literally as I was emailing Tobi about this interesting discovery, an email from UPS popped up in my inbox letting me know a package had arrived. Opening it in front of my computer, I found that it was a Christmas gift that Tobi had sent me and my wife for our young daughter: the book *Voyage to the Bunny Planet,* by Rosemary Wells—a book Tobi's children had enjoyed when they were small.

The temporal-window effect was operative in this old dream, further confirming for me its precognitive (rather than coincidental) nature. I had recorded in my dream journal that to get to "Toby's" rabbit farm, I had to swerve in a U-shape on an icy parking lot. On the day I discovered this old dream and got Tobi's package, my major (and totally unrelated) preoccupation happened to be finishing a paper for an upcoming symposium. The paper centered on a symbol for retro-causation that the physicist John Wheeler had used: an eyeball atop one end of a giant U (for universe), gazing back across the abyss of time toward the Big Bang. For Wheeler, the ultimate rise of intelligence in the universe retro-caused the cosmic past through observation.[1]

Here again, it would be natural to balk at the wild statistical improbability of my just happening to discover this old dream about Tobi precisely at the moment, nearly two decades later, when it came true. But this kind of discovery becomes inevitable if you keep a dream journal long enough, with an eye to time loops. Tobi finds that many of her dreams also seem to "know" if and when they will resurface in her journals. These significant long-range dreams reemerge to awareness right when they are supposed to—not because they exert a special synchronistic force upon us or because some trickster god is orchestrating these discoveries for our edification, but because our finding of these dreams is what retro-caused them in the first place. I only had the dream about "Toby" the sibyl with a rabbit farm, in conjunction with a big U-shape, because I would be finding that dream on that day in December 2018 when all those people, ideas, and images converged. It was a dream about my rediscovery of the dream—the fractal geometry of prophecy at work. And those trivial, almost inconsiderable little details that slip through the nets of most dream observers—the fact that I only discovered this dream when I did because I had misspelled Tobi's name when writing the dream down two decades earlier, as well as a shipping mishap that caused UPS (another U) to deliver *Voyage to the Bunny Planet* on that day instead of two days before, as had been Tobi's intention—end up having played some role in delivering these dream-fulfillments at their appointed time.

Highly specific dreams about experiences or bundles of associated experiences years and decades in the future, such as Tobi's dreams about Michael or mine about "Toby" as a sibylline rabbit farmer, let alone any of the others I've described in previous chapters, quickly put to rest any notion that our dreams show merely possible futures. Rather, they seem to be stunning affirmations that Einstein and Minkowski were right: we live in a block universe where the future, including the distant future, already exists, down to the smallest detail. Your own future experiences already exist—albeit associatively and symbolically—in your tesseract brain right now. Dreams not only show us these experiences, they often already include some symbolic representation of our belated amazement (and sometimes our facepalms) at discovering their future referents. I have come to think that amazement is the most powerful billiard ball that we deflect our younger selves with. But by the laws of wyrd, our younger selves may significantly misinterpret that future amazement. Tobi misinterpreted hers as horror.

Although it only required a slight reframing of what she was already doing as a dreamworker, Tobi's amazed discovery of her precognitive nature in midlife was a kind of giant towering over the landscape of her whole biography. From the naive vantage point of a college sophomore who knew nothing about ESP or the paranormal, that giant had a terrifying manifestation. The mix of emotions her three-decades-older self would feel on learning of Michael's real-life murder were indeed overpowering, including the same mix of excitement and survivor's guilt that seems to be the energy in many premonitory experiences. (In *Time Loops* I call this emotional mélange "jouissance."[2])

Part of the guilt Tobi felt was over using Michael's story, or her knowledge of it, for her own purposes. That her claiming of her precognitive gifts depended on learning of this classmate's death felt to her like a kind of exploitation. It is important to register this ethical concern, because conscientiousness and a sense of responsibility and dutifulness may actually be a prerequisite to the ability to consciously access and use precognition, as opposed to experiencing it as an alien trickster in our lives. We'll address this possibility in the next chapter.

Tobi's dreams about Michael taught me how powerful time loops may be in shaping our biographies. They have also helped me see the full extent of my own precognition by alerting me to possibilities in my dream journals that had never occurred to me or seemed possible. I also think that, just as my presence in Tobi's life three decades ago acted as a precognitive prime for her subsequent awakening, my presentiment of her story likely primed my own later life path toward becoming a researcher and writer on precognition.* Precognition weaves our fates in wyrd ways. I hope that Tobi's story will aid other dreamworkers out there, perhaps alerting them to similarly mind-blowing discoveries awaiting them in their own dream journals.

---

*One of the passages in *Time Loops* that struck Tobi in her initial reading concerned my argument that the careers of precognitive dreamer Elizabeth Krohn and religion historian Jeffrey Kripal, described in their coauthored book *Changed in a Flash* (Krohn and Kripal 2018), were precognitively entangled—that is, that Krohn's story may have subtly shaped Kripal's paranormal interests via his precognition of their later collaboration, just as his writing may have in turn shaped Krohn's experiences retroactively (Wargo 2018). I suspect this may be a general principle in many artistic or creative collaborations.

16
Giants and Angels
The Precognitive Self-Care System

8 JAN 2015. I REACH MYSELF

I'm underwater, digging in the pond bottom with an oar. I know I have a breathing tube that leads up to a lotus-like thing that floats on the surface—I'm getting oxygen that way.

I break through, as if I've penetrated the roof of a cavern from above. I reach in and encounter a hand/arm. It's almost like a mirror—my arm reaching an arm reaching me. I know it's me down there. I pull me through. It's future me! She can speak to me. She is older. She conveys that I am/will do fine (transform). All is unfolding as it should. I think about what I would say to a younger me—I would say the same!

—Tobi, Denver

It may be obvious that I see precognitive dreamwork as a kind of writing—a thick (re)description and (re)inscription of your life story. Even if you don't literally write about your dreams beyond just recording them in your journal, what precognitive dreamwork leads to is an enhanced sense of your life as a composition with a beginning, middle, and end, and as having a rich and unique inner coherence. Just as a well-told story contains surprises but also has dramatic unity and features devices like foreshadowing, so does your life. The reductive psychologies of the past three centuries have denied such a coherence by implying the past is dead and gone and that the future has no direct relevance. At best they have made the coherence of the self depressingly past-deterministic (Freud) or archetypal-deterministic (Jung). Precognitive dreamwork offers a third way, which cuts between these reductions, alerting us in a whole new way to the vastness and irreducibility of our own life story.

For example, my friend Tobi's fuller understanding of her own pre-cognition enabled her to see what had really happened that winter in 1988 that seemed to knock her life off course. She didn't have a murder-ous or psychotic unconscious revealing some dark truth in her horrific dreams. The imagery in those dreams had a meaning she simply had been in no position to understand from her younger vantage point. Her college sophomore self was like the younger Coop in *Interstellar,* unable to make sense of the mess of books falling from his bookshelf. She was unable to imagine that the dreams troubling her sleep were really mes-sages of amazement from her much older self, reaching across more than three decades. Her 1988 brain interpreted that future amazement as horror. The repercussions of this necessary misunderstanding must have added up to a world of difference over the ensuing years: Her depression made her withdraw from her classes and cancel her plans to move out of state. That resulted in her starting to date the musician in her creative writing class who became her husband and the father of her kids . . . and so on.

Intriguingly (and who knows, maybe not coincidentally), a then-popular novel that Tobi and I both admired and discussed in 1988 was Milan Kundera's *The Unbearable Lightness of Being.* It centers on the theme of never being able to know how life might have been different had one taken another course of action at any given time point. The counterfactuals we inevitably compare our lives to are just imaginary.[1] But I cannot help but see Tobi's 2018 amazement about her own pre-cognitive nature as a billiard ball that deflected her younger self toward the future she lived, in which she could make that intensely reward-ing and life-changing discovery in midlife. Thus, a certain amount of youthful trauma and pain was the price of her later success. The dreams about Michael alone may not have caused her college depression, nor the actions and decisions that followed from it, but they played a role—they exerted a significant nudge.

CROSSING THE JABBOK

Tobi reminds me of linguist-precog Louise Banks from *Arrival,* but her story also reminds me of another, much older myth, that of the biblical dreamer Jacob.

Famously, while on a journey from Canaan to Haran, Jacob dreamed of angels ascending and descending a ladder to heaven and hearing God's blessings from above; he then anointed the rock he was using for a pillow, calling it *Beth-el,* meaning "house of the Lord." But the episode in this Canaanite shaman's life with more application to Tobi's story was his later, all-night wrestling match with a shadowy, silent figure on the banks of the river Jabbok, from Genesis 32:22–28 (ESV):

> The same night he arose and . . . crossed the ford of the Jabbok. . . .
> And a man wrestled with him until the breaking of the day. When
> the man saw that he did not prevail against Jacob, he touched his
> hip socket, and Jacob's hip was put out of joint as he wrestled with
> him. Then he said, "Let me go, for the day has broken." But Jacob
> said, "I will not let you go unless you bless me." And he said to him,
> "What is your name?" And he said, "Jacob." Then he said, "Your
> name shall no longer be called Jacob, but Israel, for you have striven
> with God and with men, and have prevailed."

Any ordeal in a myth that lasts all night and ends with the daybreak is likely referring to a dream. Jacob thought he was struggling with God—different versions of the story describe it as a man or an angel—but was it really his own future self? Are they the same thing? J. W. Dunne would have suggested as much. He thought our dreaming higher consciousness was equivalent to the God of the mystics.

I don't make any grand theological claims for the dreaming mind, but I do think that in our dreams we are like Jacob on the shore of the

Jabbok, wrestling with a presence that is unrecognized and unknown and that may even injure us slightly, yet in some obscure way does so for our greater good. It is our own future self we are wrestling with. It is only a wrestling match, a striving, when we don't grasp its identity, and thus see it as an enemy or an alien trickster in our life. When we more correctly perceive its intent as one of care and compassion, looking out for our well-being and our success, then it may truly assume a more angelic aspect.

Encounters with one's self at other times happened to be a recurring theme in the life and work of science-fiction writer Philip K. Dick. His numerous precognitive dreams and stories, uncannily foretelling later events in his life, have been described by various biographers.[2] Lawrence Sutin highlights one story Dick related to an interviewer in 1977:

Back at the time that I was starting to write science fiction, one night I was asleep and I woke up and there was a figure standing at the edge of the bed looking down at me and I grunted in amazement and all of a sudden my wife woke up and started screaming—she could see it too—and I recognized it and I reassured her by saying it was just me that was there, not to be afraid. . . . That was, say, 1951, and within the last two years I've dreamed almost every night that I was back in that house and I have a strange feeling that back then in 1951–52 I saw my future self who had somehow in some way that we don't understand . . . that I crashed backwards as my future self through one of my dreams now of that house, going back there and seeing myself again. That would be the kind of stuff I would write as a fantasy in the early Fifties.*[3]

By now, we should be able to see that the idea of visiting oneself in the past and being visited by one's future self is more than just a

---

*According to Sutin, Dick's wife at the time, Kleo, remembered this event, but says she realized that what had frightened both of them was really the moon's reflection in the glass door to their bedroom. Her husband may have fashioned a precognitive hallucination around his misperception.

clever science-fictional conceit. It may indeed be a potent interpretation not only of the kinds of precognitive experiences described in previous chapters but also many spiritual experiences, including encounters with helping spirits and guardian angels.

Dick incorporated his remembered encounter with his future self into the novel he was working on in the mid-1970s, *Radio Free Albemuth*—an early (and only posthumously published) incarnation of what became his masterpiece *Valis*. The main character, a musician named Nicholas Brady, experiences being visited at night by a figure standing next to his bed and gazing down benevolently. "He had the impression that the figure, himself, had come back from the future, perhaps from a point vastly far ahead, to make certain that he, his prior self, was doing okay at a critical time in his life. The impression was distinct and strong and he could not rid himself of it."[4]

In his classic 1954 book about a profound experience using mescaline, *The Doors of Perception,* Aldous Huxley speculated that the brain served as a kind of filter or reducing valve for a more expanded, potentially omniscient consciousness he called Mind at Large.[5] Increased understanding of the brain, altered states, and sleep states since that time has made it possible to push the kinds of questions Huxley asked about that reducing valve, and the special situations that may open or widen it, as well as the precognitive nature of some perceptual distortions and hallucinations, such as those that Dick chronicled and drew upon for his fiction. Expanding on Huxley's insights, the writer Anthony Peake speculates that so-called REM intrusions in semi-awake states on the edge of sleep—as well as waking hallucinations experienced most commonly by people with neurological disorders and mental illness—reflect openings to our vaster consciousness, an inner guide he calls the Daemon.[6] The Daemon, he notes, is often precognitive (among other things).

What I am calling the Long Self is analogous to Peake's Daemon, but I am placing greater emphasis on the biographical dimensions of this expanded sense of who we are. What precognitive dreams and dream-like phenomena suggest to me is the possibility that what

Huxley called Mind at Large, and what mystics and shamans have often described as other realities and spirit worlds, may (at least partly) be our own transfigured lives, our biographies as they still lay untraversed and unlived ahead of us, including all the people and situations and emotions we have yet to encounter and experience. The reducing valve, in other words, might be a temporal thing, reducing our Long Self to something manageable by the mind in the moment, reflecting and refracting our entire biography through the present moment of conscious awareness.

People who experience visitations by guardian protectors in dreams or waking visions may be unlikely to interpret these experiences as encounters with their future selves. It's not an intuitive idea. They may interpret them instead in spiritual terms, as divine messengers. The Jungian tradition in psychotherapy, on the other hand, interprets them as split-off parts of the self. The Jungian analyst and writer Donald Kalsched describes an inner self-care system through which patients traumatized in childhood cordon off and protect a portion of the self from harm.[7] That sequestered "regressed self"[8] may reappear in dreams throughout life as a child or spirit animal (the hooded child on the beach in the patient's dolphin dream, chapter 9, is one example). Dissociated from this preserved inner child, the "progressed self"[9] adapts to the world, adopting a compliant personality as a kind of self-armor. The progressed self may appear in dreams and visions as a kind of guardian angel but also as a persecutor. Kalsched notes that encounters with this inner resource of the "mytho-poetic psyche" often go hand in hand with uncanny psychic phenomena.

Seeing the self as internally split in this way makes intuitive (and probably clinically useful) sense, but arguably it is another example of the Jungian (as well as Freudian) tendency to turn time into space. The precognitive, Phildickian interpretation that the self now is interacting with future versions of itself—always with some degree of misinterpretation—greatly simplifies the picture.

In *Trauma and the Soul,* for instance, Kalsched describes a case originally reported by English Jungian analyst Esther Harding: "A mother sent her young daughter to her father's study one morning to deliver an important note, written on a piece of paper. The little girl went off to deliver the note. Shortly thereafter the daughter came back in tears and said 'I'm sorry mother, the angel won't let me go in.'" Irritated, the mother kept sending the child back, only to have her keep returning with the same excuse. Finally, the mother took the daughter and marched her to the father's study with the message. "As they entered . . . the mother saw her husband slumped in his chair, his drink spilled on the floor, dead from a heart attack."[10] It's very much like Freud's similarly heartbreaking story of the father and his burning child recounted in chapter 5. Like Freud, Kalsched strains to fit the remarkable narrative within the coordinates of his preferred theoretical framework. He writes, "This story brings home to us the miraculous and daimonic powers of the archetypal psyche in its efforts to preserve what I have called the imperishable personal spirit or soul."[11] But framing it this way cannot account for its "impossible" dimension: How did the child know that there was something wrong beyond the door?

We need no longer appeal to "miraculous and daimonic powers" to understand how the self looks after itself. Remember that the precognitive unconscious personifies its messages whenever possible. It seems in this case that the girl's future self appeared to her as an angel barring entry until she could enlist the protective help of her mother. It was just like that predeployed airbag, buffering somewhat against a terrible, life-altering discovery. The discovery beyond the door was still a trauma, but without her mother there with her, one imagines it could have been far more life-shattering.

However we explain what happened in this and in many other similar cases in Kalsched's book, he is right to see these uncanny phenomena as part of a self-care system. The Long Self cares for itself literally across its timeline. The future surviving self extends a guiding hand to its younger self, especially during times of trauma, guiding it toward survival (physical and emotional). The younger self may not grasp the beneficial results of this trans-temporal intervention. Consequently, these self-interventions are never recognized for what they are, and may often be misinterpreted, even as something fearful and oppressive. The giant looming over Tobi in her college dreams, for instance, was not really her classmate. It was more likely a manifestation of Tobi's own future, protecting, caring self, guiding her through and past the depression she was enduring and toward her successful and eventually self-consciously precognitive future.

Similarly, I think we should see Freud's Irma dream as a manifestation of his future self (as a caring Anna) guiding him toward the life of success he lived, despite a certain quota of suffering. The dream may have represented a conscious wish from his future self that he'd done a few things different when he was younger, including quitting smoking and being less adamant that dreams were only disguised fulfillments of repressed wishes (and not premonitions). Yet the actions he took on the basis of his youthful misinterpretation of that dream-wish—writing *The Interpretation of Dreams* and not quitting smoking—was the foundation for his entire life achievement and the basis of his immortality. Had he permanently quit smoking, on his friend Fliess's advice, he probably would not have gone on to develop cancer, and would thus not have had the dream that made him famous in the first place. But he also probably would not have lived any longer than he did. Having not put himself on the scientific map with *The Interpretation of Dreams* in 1899, the relatively little-known psychiatrist Sigmund Freud might not have been able to relocate with his family to London in 1938 with the help of an international community of followers; in that case, he as well as his entire family might have perished in the Holocaust.

Was the Anna Hammerschlag of Freud's dream a manifestation of his precognitive Long Self, protecting not only himself but his entire family? I like to look at it that way. But per Kundera, there is no way to know. Life is unbearably light that way—and this is one of the perpetual frustrations, but also fascinations, of precognitive dreamwork and lifework. Amazing discoveries come along with a heavy dose of uncertainty, raising as many questions as they answer.

MOTHER HOLLE

Tobi had figured out the self-care aspect of precognition by the time she contacted me in November 2018, and it is one of the insights about this topic I credit to her. "I think that precognition is a caring function," she explained in one of her early emails. "You have to attend and care to do it. This points to why [the brothers Grimm's] 'Mother Holle' is such a crucial fairy tale for precognitive dreamers."

"Mother Holle" tells of an unloved but dutiful stepdaughter who chases a spindle down a well, finding herself in a meadow where she tends conscientiously to various tasks for an old woman, Frau Holle, and is magically rewarded. She is followed by her selfish stepsister, who seeks the rewards without doing the duties presented to her. "The step-daughter that falls down the well into a different realm is rewarded because she can't turn away from caring," Tobi wrote in her email. "She shakes the overladen apple tree to relieve it of too much weight. She pulls the loaves out of the oven so they will not burn. She serves Mother Holle with care. She is showered with gold. Then her stepsister hankers for the same reward and she has no trouble entering the realm or hearing the calls from the apple tree and loaves. But she does not care and leaves them to their own devices. . . . And she is showered with dark pitch at the end of her time there." Note that the juxtaposed stories about Hassan and Ajib in "The Merchant and the Alchemist's Gate" can be seen as versions of this same dichotomy.

An attitude of care for oneself and others is what creates the fertile ground for precognition to manifest, and a conscientious, ethical mindset goes along with this. A growing body of psychological research in the area of prospection (thinking about the future) is worth mentioning here. The extent to which people feel a sense of connection to their future selves appears to predict how well they make life decisions like saving for retirement, taking care of their health, and so on.[12] Prospection includes anticipating how we will think back on our present from a future standpoint—for instance, imagining future regrets—and this kind of thinking has implications for ethical decision-making too.[13]

The real (versus just imaginal) reality of precognitive/retrocausal self-interaction across time in both directions—influencing one's own past as well as being influenced by one's own future—elevates this ethical dimension of prospection to paramount importance in the life of the precognitive dreamworker and lifeworker.* Chiang's thought experiment in "The Merchant and the Alchemist's Gate" suggests that we relate to our Long Self with the same mindset that we treat other people—with care and compassion (like Hassan) or else instrumentally and exploitatively (like Ajib)—and that our life choices reflect that basic attitude with which we approach other-as-self and self-as-other. It benefits our own success and that of our fellows to be able to imagine ourselves as Long Selves.[14]

A principle can be formulated here, and it's Principle #22:

Conscientiousness and an attitude of care (for self and others) may be essential for manifesting precognition, or at least for doing so consistently.

CLAIMING YOUR COUNTRY

Jacob limped after his wresting match with his angelic future self, because his battle left him wounded in the hip. Yet his fate was highly auspicious—he assumed the name Israel after this encounter.

We all have it in us to be pioneers in exploring and laying claim

---

*Future research on the personality traits that facilitate precognitive awareness should examine the role of conscientiousness, one of the Big Five personality trait dimensions. When she read about Daryl Bem's experiments in my book *Time Loops,* Tobi realized that her own good test scores in school may have been a result of her conscientiousness in investigating the correct answers to tricky questions after taking standardized tests. Were her scores reflective of her post-test studying? It would be the same thing Daryl Bem called retroactive facilitation of recall in his "Feeling the Future" experiments (Bem 2011). Studies of ESP aptitude have often focused on two other trait dimensions, extraversion and openness to experience (Carpenter 2012).

to our own country. We all have it in us to be Jacobs. The sooner we can face the bizarre fact that we make our past in the process of finding it, and find it in the process of making it, the sooner our attitude can become one of care for our Long Self in the block universe. Dream journaling with an eye to precognition—precognitive dreamwork—is the first step. But you may find, as you build up a corpus of precognitive dreams and come face to face with the reality of that Long Self on a daily or near-daily basis, that mapping out those dream connections and reexploring what may have seemed like dead-and-gone territory—your past life, however meandering it may have seemed at the time, however traumatic it may have been, even—starts to brings even more amazing rewards and insights than just identifying discrete precognitive dream hits. This is because even if we can't change the past or future, precognition (and the retrocausation it implies) changes everything we thought we knew about both. It is redemptive.

We see our past and future selves unclearly and obliquely. But in fact, the distance between you now and you decades from now, or decades ago, may be just a wrinkled piece of cellophane. When we realize that our major upheavals in the second half of life may actually have been the billiard balls deflecting us when we were younger, it compels a new kind of sympathy and understanding for that immature being we once were—and by extension, a new kind of loyalty to the person we will become.

The Long Self is truly an epic composition, and you are the one composing it. Like a writer of your soul, your aesthetic decisions now turn out to have shaped yourself long in the past, and your decisions in your future are shaping your experience now. Tobi characterizes it this way: "I believe we are involved in creating the already-written lives that we enact." To consciously manifest and realize this amazing fact, you must build habits of self-care. Recognize that care for yourself at other ages is not just an attitude but has a real effect, a real outcome in the past—and via the past, in your future. "This is the part of the route without a short cut," Tobi insists. "You must do the tasks, you must care."

Tobi wrote in another email: "It delights me to think that all those times I wished aloud to my family that I could go back and assure my younger self and the younger selves of my family members that we got through that time, that all would be well, that we survived, *that I actually was doing that.*"

17

Look Back in Amber

Time Gimmicks and Dream Paleontology

Because precognition can only be confirmed in hindsight and dreams can only be studied after they have been written down, precognitive dreamwork is, ironically, a retrospective, archaeological, or even paleontological endeavor. It is a venturing into one's own past, even one's deep past, and in a way that literally has a creative power to shape that past. It is a way to simultaneously find and make the shape of your biography.

One of the most sublime and surprising rewards of this self-paleontology via dreamwork is discovering a fossil of one's present consciousness in a dream record—be it from the previous night or longer ago. To my knowledge, this has never been described in books on precognition and dreams, but it is literally like prying open a piece of limestone from an ancient sediment and finding a fossilized imprint of your face as it looks right now. Appropriately, it was in a paleontology-themed dream that I was first confronted with this marvel of the dreamlife.

Although I love dinosaurs, I hardly ever dream about them. In roughly a quarter century of keeping an electronic dream diary, I have on a handful of occasions recorded dreams with trilobite-like, vaguely prehistoric sea invertebrates. Dinosaur-related books or films have appeared in a few dreams in my journals over the years. I once dreamed of a mammoth. I once dreamed of a plesiosaur frozen in a glacier. (That was pretty cool, I'll admit.) But the number of times live dinosaurs or similarly charismatic prehistoric creatures have appeared in my dream journal can be counted on the fingers of one hand of a T. rex.

Consequently, a dream in late January 2018 excited me greatly. I found myself flying over what I knew was a prehistoric landscape, toward a pair of mid-sized quadrupeds that seemed (from a distance) to be sauropods of some sort. Even better, it was a lucid dream. I can never control my flight when I am flying in a lucid dream, but I was at least fully conscious that this was a dream. I thought, all right, finally— a *Jurassic Park*–like experience! (We'll have more to say about lucid dreams in the final section of this book.)

It was thus with a little disappointment that, as my dream-self sped nearer to the creatures, I saw that they weren't dinosaurs after all. As I landed between them, I saw they were instead sort of boring, squat, vaguely-but-not-quite-reptilian animals that I associated with some earlier period preceding the dinosaur era. The one on my right was brown and cat-like, with a squarish head and long canines but a lizard-like fat tail; it was advancing on the creature on my left, which was slower, lumpier, squat, and black, more evil and reptilian-looking. I found I was forced to intervene, holding the muzzles of both animals at arms' reach to keep them from attacking each other. As I strained to keep them apart, I was transfixed by a red dot, as from a laser pointer or laser gunsight, fixed immovably on the body of the reptilian creature on my left. Although I tried, I couldn't turn my head to see what hunter was targeting this animal.

I jotted down notes on this in my notebook immediately after I awoke from this dream—it was probably around 6:00 a.m.—and then I wrote a paragraph describing the dream in more detail in my electronic dream journal later that morning. The amazing fulfillment of this dream came about twelve hours later, right after I opened my mailbox that evening after work. There, I was pleasantly surprised to find the new (Winter 2018) issue of *Prehistoric Times,* a sort of quarterly fan magazine about dinosaurs, dinosaur art, and dinosaur culture (toys, collectibles, and so on). I had purchased a subscription to this magazine the previous fall after buying an issue at the gift shop of a small dinosaur museum in my hometown of Morrison, Colorado. I thought it would be fun showing dinosaur pictures and toys to my small daughter, but it also stoked my midlife nostalgia for my own dinosaur-saturated childhood.

The Winter 2018 issue was my first issue since subscribing, and I had forgotten all about this magazine and my subscription by that point. When I sat down with my daughter to peruse the issue, I was amazed to encounter, on page twelve, a big color picture of the exact scene in my dream the night before. It showed, side by side, the same two creatures that had moved to attack each other and that I had struggled to keep apart. From the picture's caption, I learned that the saber-toothed creature on the righthand side of the image was a sauroctonus and that the squat, reptilian-looking animal on the left (the one with the laser dot in my dream) was a scutosaurus.

The picture was the first illustration in a feature about therapsids. Therapsids (I quickly learned) were the vaguely dog- or cat-like proto-mammals of the Permian period, the period preceding the dinosaur-dominated Mesozoic era. I dimly remembered such animals from my childhood as the boring early land quadrupeds shown at the beginning of some dinosaur books, preceding the exciting Mesozoic animals every kid is really interested in. The feature was specifically on therapsid paintings by a Czech illustrator named Zdeněk Burian, an influential paleo-artist from the middle years of the last century.

By the time I had recorded this dream about a Permian battle, I had identified a couple hundred Dunne dreams in my journals, but this one was probably the most crystal-clear example of dream precognition so far in my life. No amount of Freudian free association was necessary to unpack the dream's connection to the next day's experience. There were no apparent puns or other substitutions. I quite literally dreamed that picture, with the embellishment that I was in the scene, interacting with those two animals. (Remember, the mnemonic brain creates an immersive experience and adds drama whenever and wherever it can.) Not only the two animals in my dream but also the dream setting had been exactly like what was in this Burian painting—a flat area below a low hill.*

The only odd dream detail not in the actual picture was the laser dot, but it proved to be the most significant element in this dream and the reason I am telling this story.

As my excitement over this precognitive dream hit settled, I scrutinized the various therapsid pictures in the *Prehistoric Times* article, expecting maybe to find something like that laser dot, perhaps a printer's blemish on one of the images. I also looked through the rest of the magazine for something like it. But just a moment's free association revealed its significance: the first thing it reminded me of was the red dot of a laser gunsight on the forehead of Sarah Connor (Linda Hamilton) in James Cameron's 1984 film *The Terminator*. In that movie, Arnold Schwarzenegger plays a time-traveling robot assassin from the mid-twenty-first century trying to hunt down the mother of a future resistance leader in mid-1980s Los Angeles. In a memorable scene, he tracks Sarah Connor down in a crowded bar and advances on her with a gun, the red dot from its laser gunsight trained on her forehead. She is rescued in the nick of time by another time traveler sent back to protect her.

I hadn't thought about *The Terminator* in years, yet what is that movie but a story about a hunter from the future traveling back in time to target someone in the past? In my dream, I couldn't turn my head to see who was targeting the scutosaurus. As I sat on the couch next to my daughter the following evening, with *Prehistoric Times* open on my lap alongside my open dream journal, I had the dumbfounded realization that the out-of-sight hunter in the dream had been me *at that moment,* about twelve hours ahead in my timeline from the dream. The dream had symbolically pre-presented my own retrospective scrutiny of these dream fauna

---

*I had never seen this picture before, nor did any of the dinosaur books I had bought for my daughter contain pictures of these creatures. That night, I also verified that there was no "in the next issue" teaser in the issue I had bought in Colorado, which might have tipped me off. Visiting the magazine's website, I was additionally able to confirm that it showed only the cover of this issue, not the picture I am claiming I precognized. Thus I could not have seen the picture at the site when subscribing.

from the point of view of my amazed future self, sitting on that couch.

The laser dot, recorded right there in my dream journal, was literally my look back at this dream, as though trapped in shale or amber, albeit in the associative mnemonic code used by dream precognition to present associations to future events. It induced a kind of vertigo. My daughter must have wondered why daddy had fallen weirdly silent as he stared into his dream notebook, as into some wormhole, that January night.

OBJECTS IN MIRROR ARE
CLOSER THAN THEY APPEAR

Once alerted to this mind-bending possibility in dreams, I soon discovered that it is actually common to find a fossil of one's future gaze preserved in a past dream. The precognitive nature of the dream is represented within the dream, like a fractal. You will only discover such fossils, however, in dreams that you recognize as being precognitive at or near the time when the confirming event comes to pass, rather than at some time later. The reason goes back to that temporal-window principle described in chapter 7, that dreams bind together experiences within a narrow window of time, usually an hour or few hours of waking life. If your realization that your dream was precognitive coincides with the experience being precognized, your realization will likely be included (symbolically) in the dream. On the other hand, if you only discover a precognitive dream sometime after the precognized experience, outside that (possibly ill-defined) window, you would not expect to find your retrospective gaze preserved associatively among its images and symbols, because your realization did not happen within the set of proximate experiences the dream was bundling.

Principle #23 of this book is:

Dreams that turn out to have been precognitive often contain some symbolic representation of the act of returning to the dream to verify its precognitive character.

The tip-off is *time gimmicks,* a term introduced by psychoanalyst/ parapsychologist Jule Eisenbud in a 1982 book called *Paranormal Foreknowlege.** In my experience, dreams pre-present my future hindsight gaze via some element in the dream having to do with or associating to time travel, perhaps a time-travel movie or story (such as *The Terminator*), with anachronisms of some sort, with some juxtaposition of old and new, or with something metaphorically giving the idea of going back or looking back. My U-shaped swerve on ice on my way to visiting "Toby the sibyl" (chapter 15) is another example—it related to a symbol for retrocausation used by the physicist John Wheeler, a giant eyeball on one tip of the U (for universe) *looking back* at the Big Bang. We also saw an example in chapter 7: I had already realized my dream about hoodlums converging on a neighbor's home was precognitive when I got the email from my mother with the mountain lion video; then, after I fell down the steps, I opened my dream journal to refresh my memory of the dream's images. Consequently, besides the other events bundled in the dream (the mountain lion video, my fall, and thoughts about crying wolf) was my own looking back to the dream record in my journal, represented as my viewing the events in a rear-view mirror. My first free association to that rearview mirror was, incidentally, to another movie that is metaphorically about time travel and dinosaurs: *Jurassic Park*. A typically Spielbergian shot shows a pursuing T. rex in the rearview mirror of a jeep, with the manufacturer's sticker visible: "Objects in mirror are closer than they appear."

As you look at a recorded dream that contains your own gaze in it, you realize you are quite literally looking at yourself across time. Your own past is also closer than it may appear. Whether we're talking a span of a few hours or days or a few decades, such an idea has no place in mainstream psychology or philosophy. Just imagine what it could do for our sense of self to have such experiences more frequently.

---

*Eisenbud used the term *time gimmick* in connection to a strip from the 1970s newspaper comic *B.C.* that appeared in a seemingly precognitive dream of one of his patients (see Wargo 2018, for discussion of this case). He did not recognize the wider prevalence of time anachronisms as symbols of dream precognition within dreams.

Discovering some past dream representation of oneself looking back at the dream in hindsight is the most powerful validation of precognitive dreamwork as a gnosis: *the knower is literally included in the known.* There's that serpent devouring its own tail, again. It is also yet another startling confirmation of the solid, block-like nature of spacetime: the past is still here, and more amazingly, the future is already here. The evidence is there for those who merely have the patience to write their dreams down in their journals and routinely go back to their dream records. The act of inscription is crucial, though. Even though I might well have remembered my Permian-battle dream from the night before without a written record, I would never have been sure of my memories, or sure I wasn't somehow deceiving myself, and I would easily have forgotten a small but pertinent detail like the laser dot.

One of my free associations to the dream after I discovered its pre-cognitive target was Keats's "Ode on a Grecian Urn," a poetic image expressing the idea of stasis and eternity and permanence: two painted figures locked in a permanent chase, unable to escape their situation. Its last stanza is famous:

> *O Attic shape! Fair attitude! with brede*
> *Of marble men and maidens overwrought,*
> *With forest branches and the trodden weed;*
> *Thou, silent form, dost tease us out of thought*
> *As doth eternity: Cold Pastoral!*
> *When old age shall this generation waste,*
> *Thou shalt remain, in midst of other woe*
> *Than ours, a friend to man, to whom thou say'st,*
> *"Beauty is truth, truth beauty,—that is all*
> *Ye know on earth, and all ye need to know."*

The scutosaurus and the sauroctonus were like those marble men frozen in time; my dream animated them, but my presence from the future dramatically kept them apart. My dreaming brain, you could even say, portrayed itself as an emissary of the block universe, preventing history from being different than it was. You will increasingly have these kinds of sublime realizations about the block universe and your own unconscious role in fulfilling your fate the more you become attuned to precognitive dreaming.

PAY IT FORWARD

Earlier I mentioned the possibility of sowing seeds in our past for a better tomorrow via establishing habits of honoring our dreams and other potentially precognitive experiences. Among the positive values of Jung's writings and teachings was his emphasis on honoring and commemorating the miraculous in one's life. He encouraged his patients to draw or paint their dreams, for instance, and he commemorated his own synchronicities in the grand style that his and (mostly) his wife's wealth allowed. For instance, during a period in 1933 when he was studying the relationship between Christianity and Alchemy, he encountered a snake that had choked to death trying to swallow a fish. This seemed to him like a concrete symbol of the fatal inability of both systems of thought—the Christian fish and the Alchemical serpent—to integrate each other. He honored this synchronistic discovery with a stone engraving that can still be seen at his Bollingen tower retreat on the shore of Lake Zurich, where he had found the animals.[1]

Developing personal habits and rituals to honor our dreams is an important part of precognitive dreamwork. Writing dreams down in the morning in a notebook dedicated for the purpose is the most fundamental part of it. But drawing or painting striking images from dreams is also a common practice. However you choose to honor your dreams, such honoring is a crucial feed-forward component helpful in manifesting precognition with regularity. As with any habit or skill we wish to improve upon, it is important to build positive associations with it, so these little celebratory acts of honoring can contribute to those associations and in some cases even serve as the target of our precognition. Some of these targets may become powerful personal symbols and associations that you will then find have fed back into your prior dreamlife.

Freud had something of the same mentality Jung did around honoring his accomplishments, and it seems to have fed back into his dreamlife in important ways that he could not or would not consciously (or publicly) admit. After his dream about Anna Hammerschlag, he suggested to his friend Wilhelm Fliess, only half in jest, that one day a plaque would be displayed at the villa where he had had the dream, announcing that "In this house, on July 24th, 1895 the secret of dreams was revealed to Dr. Sigm. Freud."[2] In fact, he actually did go on to honor the dream in a more concrete way: he named his next child after Anna. As I suggested in chapter 5, this may have been hugely significant in the dream's "choice" of messenger about the then-far-off events that would shape the last decade and a half of his life.

I like to keep souvenirs. After my Permian-battle dream, I purchased small plastic toys of both of the creatures in the dream, a scutosaurus and a close relative of sauroctonus called inostrancevia, ostensibly for my daughter (who already had many such toys) but really as much for myself. We live in an amazing modern world where the most obscure prehistoric creatures, even from the boring Permian period, are now made into inexpensive toys you can purchase online or even at your local toy store. (As an unfrozen caveman writer from the 1970s, I am perpetually amazed by this.) This purchase, it later turned out, fed back into that dream in a significant way.

A year and a half after the dream, my nightly game with my now three-and-a-half-year-old after putting her in bed was amusing her by making shapes on the ceiling with a laser pointer cat toy. One evening, after she had fallen asleep and I was dozing in my bed, I for the first time thought about this laser pointer in the context of that old dream, its association with *The Terminator*, and so on. I turned my head to look at my bedside table where I had placed the laser pointer, and I was stunned—and delighted—to see that the laser was right next to, and pointing at, the plastic scutosaurus. My daughter's dinosaur toys ordinarily live on a shelf in another room, but randomly, this one toy somehow found its way to my bedside table that day (toys tend to wander, with a three-year-old) and was juxtaposed with the laser.

I would obviously not have given the juxtaposition between a scutosaurus toy and a laser cat toy a second thought or even a first thought but for my dream association to both objects and the fact that I was just then thinking about that dream (and indeed, my "random" train of thought may have been precognitive of this discovery). But its memorability must, I also realized, have projected into the past, creating an associative connection between these two objects a year and a half earlier in that dream, a connection that wouldn't otherwise have existed in my tesseract head.

The more we build the habit of allowing ourselves to be deflected by dreams that fascinate us but that we cannot yet understand—that is, the more we pay attention to and appreciate our dreams upon waking without knowing their meaning—the more we will find, later, that we have been actively shaping our past through our amazement at our precognition and what it reveals about our biography. And the more we honor our precognitive hits or confirmations, for instance through art or by keeping or making souvenirs, the more exciting they are and the more they will become a target of our dreams, and the more we will notice precognition happening. By building a habit of honoring your dreamlife, you will sow the seeds for amazing discoveries in your future, which then feed into and shape your past.

THE IRRATIONALE OF THE DREAM

There is an interesting footnote to Freud's dream theory—literally a footnote—that is highly relevant here. It is often assumed that Freud intended us simply to decode our dreams, find the latent dream thought, and that was that. In fact, his theory was much more subtle, and even he didn't quite realize that subtlety when he was drafting his book, which is why an interesting clarification ended up in a footnote to later editions of *The Interpretation of Dreams*:

[N]ow that analysts at least have become reconciled to replacing the manifest dream by the meaning revealed by its interpretation, many of them have become guilty of falling into another confusion which they cling to with equal obstinacy. They seek to find the essence of dreams in their latent content and in so doing they overlook the distinction between the latent dream-thoughts and the dream-work.

At bottom, dreams are nothing other than a particular form of thinking, made possible by the conditions of the state of sleep. It is the dream-work which creates that form, and it alone is the essence of dreaming—the explanation of its particular nature.[3]

Again, Freud meant something different by dream-work than the act of interpreting the dream, the now more common usage of the term *dreamwork* and the one I am using in this book. He meant the unconscious mind's own process of transforming some thought into the particular, singular images found in the dream. It is one thing to say that your dream of riding a polar bear into Walmart to buy gum drops is really about wanting to sleep with your mother. The question is, why did the dream pick those specific symbols to represent that secret thought?* The real interesting matter in the dream, in other words, is not the thought that you can arrive at by decoding it—often enough the latent thought, even in a Freudian reading, isn't that surprising or shameful (e.g., the professional anxieties Freud thought were symbolized in his Irma dream). What really matters is the specific form taken by the dream, what you might call its "irrationale," for selecting *those particular* symbols, images, and motifs to represent the thought, and not any of the other possible symbols, images, and motifs it might have used.[4]

If Freud thought that it was in this irrationale, the dream-work, that the real hidden thought was to be discovered, I suggest instead that

---

*Often enough, as in his dream of Irma's injection, the repressed thought was not really repressed at all. Freud knew perfectly well he felt professional anxiety over malpractice.

it is in that irrationale that an added and perhaps even more important prophetic dimension in the dream is hiding. Here is where, even beyond Dunnean precognitive content in our dreams—the individual episodes being pre-mnemonically encoded—we need to look to that larger field of the unconscious, shaping and bending those future thoughts in very particular ways. The unconscious is a kind of four-dimensional skein of associations extending across our whole life, from childhood to old age. Nightly dreams refract the diffuse meaning-glow of the Long Self, bringing into focus specific resonances between recent experiences and future experiences.

I have reiterated throughout this book the basic principles that dreams represent future thoughts using preexisting associations in memory and that they generally bundle experiences within a narrow (perhaps a few hours) window of waking time. Now that you have made it nearly to the end of the book, you are ready for a further revelation that your younger self couldn't yet have comprehended and that would only have frightened and confused you: some features or aspects of a dream, including its "choice" of symbols (or its irrationale) may arise from associations formed subsequent to the future experience or experiences being targeted.

The singular question that had lingered in my mind after my Permian-battle dream and my discovery of the time gimmick in it was this: Why was the laser dot specifically on the scutosaurus, not the sauroctonus? (Nerd problems, I know. Imagine being married to me.) Excitedly finding the toy juxtaposed with the laser pointer all that time after the dream not only may have determined the seemingly arbitrary fact of which animal was being targeted by my future self in the dream, but (it seemed) it also may have helped determine that dream's entire choice of time gimmick. It could just as easily have been a rearview mirror (as in *Jurassic Park*) or any number of other movie anachronisms, but it happened to be a laser dot—which, true to the polyvalent or double-entendre nature of most dream symbols, could point both to a cat toy and to a gunsight of a time-traveling assassin.

Dreams are clever that way. They seem to be drawing on our whole lifetime's stock of mental associations. They have a lot of good stuff to work with.

Principle #24 is:

The associative language used in a dream, or its choice of symbolism, is partly shaped or at least constrained in interesting ways by subsequent experiences and by its connection to other dreams across the course of life.

DREAM DAISY-CHAINS

You will discover as your dream journal grows that your dreams are interconnected in a vast web or, again, skein of associations. A metaphor my collaborator Tobi uses comes from the *Arbai Trilogy* of science-fiction writer Sheri S. Tepper. The Arbai device is a vast mycelia-like communication network linking individuals all over a planet. Tobi sees the intertwining associative strands in her precognitive dreamlife as a kind of Arbai device binding and linking the many far-flung corners of her own biography. Mapping it out, in light of her belated understanding of how this device truly transcended time, has become a major autobiographical project for her.

What diligent precognitive dreamworkers discover is that multiple dreams over successive days or weeks (and in some cases years) may all relate to the same later event, sometimes even "daisy-chained"—a dream pointing to a later dream, which in turn points to the (even later) salient waking experience, or else reveals an aspect of the later dream's symbolism. As I was completing this book, Tobi sent me two daisy-chained dreams she had recorded in 2017 and that now clearly pointed to mortality-related concerns she would experience in the early months of the COVID-19 pandemic in 2020. First, on March 31, 2017, she dreamed she was supervising an archaeological excavation in her yard:

In the back right corner of the yard, I'm supervising a dig. The hole is just like the one in a history-of-women documentary I watched this week— the excavation of a burial mound/kurgan (Ukraine steppes) of a powerful warrior woman shaman buried with weapons, a silver mirror, goods.

Above us to the right, almost as if on a transparent platform, is a dragon (a living, fire-breathing one). Unlike other dragon dreams, with Asian dragons, this is the European-looking type, as in alchemical plates. The dragon may be white. Seems to be a protector guardian.[5]

The next day, Tobi appended to this dream record the following quote from Jung that she heard on a podcast, referencing the protective role of dragons in symbolism. "So whenever life means business, when things are getting serious, you are likely to find a saurian on the way."[6] It seemed to her like a synchronicity.

Then in mid-September of that year, she recorded a further dream:

A plague or chemical was going to hit and there was a possibility of mass death in Denver. We needed to prepare the girls in case [my husband] and I didn't survive. I wanted our oldest daughter to know about financials—passwords, how to pay bills. But we also dug a huge grave in the back right corner* of the yard—didn't want the girls to have our dead bodies to dispose of (city services would be overwhelmed). I consider how the girls would get us to the graves. I decide we should have the worn-out linen sheets at hand. In fact, maybe we will wrap ourselves in the sheets and sit against the wood chip pile (next to the grave) while the event "hits." Then I'm worried—what if [our youngest daughter] is the only survivor?[7]

She noted with an asterisk that the graves were exactly where the archeological dig of the ancient woman (with protective white dragon) was located in the previous dream.

On March 23, 2020, the day Denver announced its stay-at-home order and a week shy of three years after the initial excavation-and-dragon dream, Tobi found herself laundering a basketful of worn-out linen sheets to occupy her time while shut in with her family during the pandemic. The sheets were clean but had been gathering dust, and she had been putting off this laundry task for a long time. The same day, prompted by the parental-mortality fears of her oldest daughter, she decided to discuss passwords and financial affairs in the unlikely event something happened to her and her husband. As she was doing this, she naturally wondered what would happen if only their youngest survived. It was two days later, when searching her dream records for possible precognitive referents to COVID-19, that she discovered these forgotten dreams from 2017 and their match to her concerns and activities on that single day during her family's home isolation.*

Intrigued by the Jung quote about saurians appearing "whenever life means business," Tobi consulted a reference work, Juan Edwardo Cirlot's classic *Dictionary of Symbols,* where she found the following under the entry for "Dragons": "For [Henri] Dontenville, who tends to favour an historicist and sociological approach to the symbolism of legends, *dragons signify plagues which beset the country* (or the individual if the symbol takes on a psychological implication)."[8]

What these daisy-chained dreams suggest is a temporally impossible narrative: the prior excavation of a subsequent burial (and of a shaman, no less—one of the recurring themes of my emails to Tobi was my suggestion that she was in fact an "urban shaman"). One way of looking at them is that the initial dream precognized Tobi's hearing of a significant Jung quote the next day, the same way Maggy Quarles van Ufford dreamed of scarab jewelry just before Jung's discourse on scarabs. Yet that Jungian dragon archetype was principally significant because of a subsequent discovery (three years later) of its traditional symbolic relation to plagues in a time of heightened emotion and anxiety for Tobi and her family during a pandemic.

---

*Tobi took a screenshot of a CNN page on April 3, 2020, that also seemed related to her dreams three years earlier about overwhelmed city services and bed linens. The headline read "Bodies left in streets in this overwhelmed city," and the accompanying photo showed a body placed outside a home, covered with a white household linen like a bedsheet.

Note how tempting it would be to adopt a Jungian archetypal reading here: that somehow dragons (saurians) objectively symbolize plagues and life getting serious, as though hard-wired in the collective unconscious or some Platonic realm of ideal forms. But given the fact that Tobi's dreams related clearly to her concerns on a very specific day nearly three years after the initial dream (the linens, the passwords), why not include Tobi's learning of the traditional symbolism of dragons from Cirlot's dictionary within that bundle of precognitive associations?

Archetypes are cultural meanings encoded in oral and written traditions. Their force over our dreams comes from our actual, real-life engagement with those texts and traditions (such as consulting a symbolism dictionary). That engagement may be subsequent to their appearance in our dreams, giving the illusion—since no one believes in precognition—that those meanings were somehow there already in a stock of collective symbols in the unconscious.

SINEWS OF THE LONG SELF

Over the span of the decade since I first turned my attention to precognitive dreaming, it has gone from being a perplexity I didn't quite believe in to a fascinating intellectual exploration to (now) something a little bit like a personal religion. The original meaning of religion is re-linking—that is, linking back to some spiritual source from which we feel ourselves sundered. In Sanskrit, *yoga* has the same root: to yoke, as one yokes a cart to the cow pulling it. What precognitive dreamwork yokes me to, repeatedly and with always unexpected force, is my own biography, my life as a single, more-unified-than-I-ever-knew landscape.

It has led me to believe that biography, not psychology, should be the operative term in the humanistic science—or scientifically informed humanism—of the twenty-first century. To characterize our inner self as a psyche is to slightly miss what is really happening, the nature of this thing, this source in us. This source "in" us is really the completeness of us, our wholeness . . . which means our whole story, from birth to death, as it is refracted through that moment-to-moment cursor consciousness. Bringing to light the hidden ways our biography—including our future biography—shapes the landscape of our lives now, and the way our lives now shaped our past, even perhaps our childhoods, is a truly sublime and awesome project of conscious, and conscientious, self-care.

It is indeed a path of gnosis. And like any other gnosis, there's an ecstatic component to it. Every precognitive dream hit is a bit like a hit from a kind of psychedelic drug, an exhilarating, vertiginous, spiritual and life affirmation. It's like zooming in on a fractal, where the fractal is your life. Every day can bring new discoveries about the precognitive significance of a perplexing symbol in an old dream, if not the full-on closure of a time loop that began a day, a year, or even decades in your past. It's always something unexpected, but it will be something that adds to the wonder and strangeness of your existence.

The trick—and what precognitive dreamwork teaches—is focusing on and learning to be amazed by the haphazard, trivial details of your life that most people overlook, the Chazz Palminteri-dropping-his-mug stuff. As you build your spacetimeship, your dream corpus, you will start to find that a surprising portion of the seemingly random mess in the office of your life has fed back into your past and shaped who you were, and thus who you have become. It's not really random at all.

It makes sense that ritualistically honoring both our dreams and our realizations about the Long Self is a kind of sacrament. Besides acting like a bait attracting your dream precognition, it also acts a bit like a coloring dye in microscopy, revealing hidden associative structures that would be invisible otherwise. Those time loops are like cells of the Long Self. And the chains of association that unfold over years are like its sinews.

Besides honoring our dream hits, it is equally important to honor dreams' mystery and not hasten toward facile answers to what your still-unidentified dreams mean, as though the answer is always findable. Dreams never completely make sense, even after precognitively targeted experiences come to pass. Our dreams can never fully be understood, because our lives are not yet done. (That, above all else, is worthy of celebration.) Those associative skeins that run through our lives are still pointed in directions we cannot yet know, and consequently our dream-work is never (and could never be) finished.

We are never done with our dreams, and our dreams are never done with us.

PART 6

SPACETIME TRAVEL IN THE BORDERLANDS (GAMES FOR ADVANCED PLAYERS)

18
Possessed by Your Future
Out-of-Body Experiences, Lucid Dreams, and Sleep Paralysis

A warm summer breeze came in the window over my desk, and there was the sound of cicadas from the big magnolias surrounding the house. I couldn't tell if it was day or night—night I assumed, because I looked down and saw I had on pajamas. The computer was off, the desk a mess (as always). Piles of papers and books covered the floor. And oddly, I was holding in each hand a grease pencil, a red one in my left hand, a white one in my right.

The sound of the cicadas turned to hissing, loud, like steam from a boiling kettle. And that was when I felt a terribly evil presence enter my body. I could not disobey what it was making me do, though I tried. This force made me bring the tips of the two grease pencils near to each other, and I felt a surging energy as I tried to resist this compulsion. I could not resist, and my hands, controlled by this evil presence, brought the white tip into contact with the red, like closing some evil circuit.

The energy flowing through my body was electric and powerful—I could not defy it. I knew, somehow, that this spirit possessing me was connected to Papua New Guinea, and a remote village in its western lowlands I had visited for a few months six years earlier.

Still under its total power, I dropped the white pencil and held up the red one, and I held a nearly closed fist up to my eye and peered at the tip of the red grease pencil through the narrow gap created by my curled fingers. I felt the spell breaking, and this gesture seemed important in breaking it.

The next thing I knew, my wife was shaking me awake. "Eric, Eric!" I calmed down. I was lying in bed, not in the study at all.

"You were snorting like a pig," my wife said.

When I rose from bed in the morning after my extremely vivid nightmare of being possessed by a presence from Papua New Guinea, curiosity drove me straight into the study, to confirm that indeed every physical detail in my dream had been correct: not just the mess on the desk and floor, and the open window over the desk, but also the presence, among countless other random items, of grease pencils in various colors that I used to mark drafts of my dissertation.

As I sat in my study chair and surveyed the scene, remarking on how exactly that dream (if that's what it was) had got it right, I picked up two grease pencils—red and white—and held one in each hand, just as I had done in my sleep. I brought the white one into contact with the red, again just as in the dream. Of course, this time there was no electric feeling of closing some evil circuit—just mild self-consciousness, a feeling of being slightly absurd, like I was acting a part in a play.

I also held my loose fist up to my eye, as in the dream, and—again feeling stupid and self-conscious—peered through it as through a telescope. The ability of a tiny hole to magnify light was something my father had told me when I was a child. Either he had said, or I had inferred, that you could turn your fist into a telescope, or a microscope, this way. Nothing seemed magnified, and indeed I saw no white spot on the tip of the red grease pencil through the tiny gap made by my loose fist.

This experience happened in 1998, in Atlanta. Several years earlier, as I said, I had spent a few months in a very remote village in the western lowlands of Papua New Guinea. Magic and mysticism had not then been among my interests, but there were two healers in the village—an older woman and her husband—and one of my first paranormal experiences was during an evening I and my companion (my then-wife, who was doing fieldwork in the village) visited their house at the edge of the village, near a path leading to a stream, with a couple of young local men who spoke a little English and could translate for us.

I was not able to follow much of what was happening, but after animated discussion in the local language, the woman went into some kind of trance and all of us seated around the floor (including the woman's husband, who didn't say much and whose powers I was led to believe were less than hers) heard an insistent rapping on the house. No one seemed very surprised by this, but I was spooked. In the dim light I looked at everyone's motionless hands and couldn't see how this trick was being done. I was sure there was nobody outside making the sounds. Houses there are built of slats of bamboo, high up on stilts, and anybody walking around outside would have been readily seen and heard.

Although this strange rapping had perplexed my companion and I, I had not thought much more of it after that evening. One-off "impossible" experiences, when they have no prior or subsequent context, often fall prey to that River Lethe. But now, several years later, sitting in my pajamas in my study in Atlanta, I thought back to that evening and was captivated—and a little scared—by the remote possibility that I might have actually been "witched," remotely possessed or controlled by a Melanesian sorcerer—perhaps that woman. Had she somehow extracted my soul from my body and made it into her puppet for a scary minute or two on a summer night?

It was captivating because, I mean, what a great idea for a novel: sorceress controls anthropologist from afar, uses him to do her bidding. I had recently read Whitley Strieber's *Communion* for the first time and had admired the writer's ability to turn a baffling nocturnal abduction (whatever it was and whatever it meant) into a riveting paranormal bestseller. As I sat in my study hating my dissertation and longing for something more fun to write, I wondered if I should try my hand at that genre. (Alas, I never did.)

But of course, it was scary too, because what if that possession was real?

NOBODY EXPECTS PRECOGNITION

If you are a Monty Python fan, you will recall the recurring sketch "Spanish Inquisition": someone in the course of a mundane argument will huffily say, "Well, I didn't expect a Spanish Inquisition . . .", and red-robed Inquisitors will leap from behind a door shrieking, "Nobody expects the Spanish Inquisition!" Well, obviously, one of the themes of this book is that nobody expects precognition, and our blind spot to retrograde causal relationships leads to all kinds of alternative framings of the baffling experiences generated by the tesseracts in our heads.

For example, the spatial immersiveness of dream experiences has led people from time immemorial to think that the dreamworld could be a real alternative reality, or that our spirits are leaving our bodies in our sleep and traveling this world or other worlds. The pagan cultures of Europe in antiquity, for instance, believed that our dreams were real nocturnal journeys out of our body in spirit form.[1] Whether it is possible for the spirit or soul, or what we now usually call consciousness, to detach from the body is hotly debated among people who study out-of-body experiences, near-death experiences, and shamanic experiences, and it is a debate mostly beyond the scope of this book. But it is important to remember that the imaginal capability of the brain—that special-effects studio—is vastly greater than we may suspect, especially if we are not used to paying attention to dreams, imagination, or altered states. As we saw in chapter 7, we naturally turn an "impossible" temporal feat (seeing into the future) into a much less baffling spatial one (seeing or being influenced across space)—but precognition could provide a better explanation for some paranormal experiences associated with the edge realms of sleep, including out-of-body experiences, lucid dreams, sleep paralysis, and hypnagogic/hypnopompic states.

A common feature in the literature on out-of-body travel, for instance, is that the experiencer will subsequently encounter some kind of confirmation of their experience. They will visit a location seen out-of-body and find more or less the exact thing they saw, or may instead read or learn something that confirms what they witnessed in their altered state.[2] (Such verifications after the fact make these experiences veridical, or truthful, in the language of parapsychologists.) These confirmations are common in near-death experiences as well, and they constitute a reasonable basis for the belief that consciousness could exist independently of the brain and thus survive the death of the body. But because no one expects precognition, people seldom consider whether the subsequent "confirmatory" episode could sometimes be the *source* of the prior experience. According to the logic we have explored throughout this book, and that J. W. Dunne identified in his book on dreams, precognition is an alternative explanation that may shed light on some out-of-body–type experiences.

It was my reading of Dunne and my growing experience with precognitive dreamwork a decade and a half after my weird experience in Atlanta that finally put to rest any notions that I had been remote-controlled via some kind of spirit possession or Melanesian magic. As with all things precognitive, it was necessary to set aside my natural causal bias and do just a little interpretive detective work: tracing my waking thoughts about the dream backward to see how those thoughts might have been pre-presented within the dream itself. Once I saw the key element, I did a facepalm: my sleep apnea had made me "snort like a pig," which my wife told me as she shook me awake.

Papua New Guinea was in 1998, and still is today, my first and most immediate association to the word *pig*. The societies there, including the village I had stayed in, revolve around the hunting, gifting, and cooking of pig meat. I still cannot pass by a barbecue restaurant without being brought back vividly to that village, where the smell of smoke and pig fat seeped into everything. I believe it was the embarrassed thought that I had been snorting like a pig, hovering over my mind as I went into the bedroom to confirm what I had experienced in my dream (including going through absurd motions with the grease pencils), that colored the prior dream experience, made it somehow "from New Guinea." My dreaming brain interpreted this vivid, almost video-quality precognitive experience as being an out-of-body experience associated with that far-off, exotic land, and some kind of possessing sorcery would have been a natural inference to make in that confused altered state. It was also a time loop, since I would not have gone through those motions in waking life had I not been consciously (very self-consciously) trying to confirm the verisimilitude of the dream afterward.*

TO MARS . . . AND BEYOND

The belief in a detachable spirit double that wandered abroad while we slept remained a common folkloric belief in Europe even after the spread of Christianity. Sharing such a belief with the wrong people, of course, was a good way to get yourself a surprise visit from Michael Palin in red robes and hat. But in the late nineteenth century, belief in consciousness as a separate body from the physical body became something of a fashion among inquiring minds.

Astral travel (or astral projection) was a staple of the quasi-spiritualist movement known as Theosophy—a blend of Eastern religion and Western mysticism that acquired a wide following and strongly influenced popular culture due to the charisma of its founder Helena Blavatsky. The pulp science-fiction writer H. P. Lovecraft, for instance, cribbed heavily from Blavatsky and her followers, putting his distinctively dark spin on the idea of ancient higher beings from other planets traveling astrally to ours and slumbering in the remote regions of the Earth.[3] The much more literary Franz Kafka, who appears to have had spontaneous out-of-body experiences as a young man, was also interested in and influenced by Theosophy via the writer and speaker Rudolf Steiner.[4]

The science-fiction writer Edgar Rice Burroughs describes astral projection quite vividly in his first Mars novel, *A Princess of Mars*. After his

---

*As I was self-consciously going through the motions of touching the white grease pencil to the red one, I remembered something one of the men in my graduate program had said when presenting his fieldwork among East African pastoralists, about the symbolism of blood and milk, and specifically the fact that you can easily turn milk red with a little bit of blood but it is hard to whiten blood by adding milk to it. I no longer remember what the significance of this fact was supposed to be, yet it seemed to relate to the nexus of ideas swirling in my head at that moment: of sorcery and pigs and grease.

prospecting companion is killed by Apache natives, Civil War veteran John Carter takes refuge in an Arizona cave, where he falls asleep and experiences the classic symptoms of sleep paralysis, which often precede the experience of leaving the body: he awakens but finds his body frozen, hearing a noisy presence behind him that he cannot see. Eventually he gains use of his body, but finds that it is merely his astral body—his physical body is still lying on the cave floor. Discarnate, Carter goes to the front of the cave, where he sees Mars on the horizon—as a warrior, it is his personal star—and he focuses his attention and will upon it. "I closed my eyes, stretched out my arms toward the god of my vocation and felt myself drawn with the suddenness of thought through the trackless immensity of space."[5] Through many adventures over the ten years while his Earth body is slumbering in the Arizona cave, the Martian avatar of John Carter has many adventures in the Martian land of Barsoom, marries a princess, and eventually becomes Barsoom's ruler.

I can't vouch that there are cities and marriageable Frank Frazetta princesses on the Red Planet, but as part of my early efforts to explore and exercise my psychic ability, I purchased and read several guides to achieving out-of-body experiences, such as the classic *Journeys Out of the Body* by Robert Monroe, and one of my first not-quite successes was a trip to Mars. One night in late December 2014, after meditating on the edge of sleep—a standard practice to induce out-of-body experiences and lucid dreams—I found myself in the bell tower of a cathedral, looking out across space at Mars, and I willed my consciousness there, just like John Carter did. Specifically, I willed myself to visit the Curiosity rover, which had landed in Gale Crater, near the Martian equator, two years earlier.

My consciousness was obedient . . . sort of. I didn't experience this as being out-of-body, but as a lucid dream—that is, a dream in which you are aware of dreaming and can exert some measure of control over your actions and even, in some cases, the dream environment. (Failed astral journeys—and almost all of them fail, in my experience—may result in lucid dreams as a kind of consolation prize.) After willing myself to Mars, I found my point of view filled with the Martian terrain from a high altitude, as though in orbit. I zoomed down lower and lower over rust-colored ripples and valleys, searching for the Curiosity rover, even though I was conscious that this wasn't the true Mars and that the rippled terrain wasn't at all like the photos Curiosity was sending back from Gale Crater. I zoomed down, down, down and also seemed to get smaller and smaller as I did so. I at last slowed and stopped mere millimeters or less above the surface, where tiny animal figurines were scattered about on their sides, as though dead. Most were clear or colored glass as if made of tiny fused-glass beads. It was strange and memorable, and of course, I wrote it down in detail when I woke up from this vision.

As often happens—and as by then I should have predicted—my adventure in the psychic dream realm that was intended to bring me information about something tens of millions of miles away in space really ended up bringing me a symbolic representation of a reading experience less than forty-eight hours ahead in my future. Two days after this Mars trip, I became engrossed in a new book called *Death on Mars*, speculating about ancient civilizations on that planet, and came to a chapter on Martian meteorites, some of which contain colorful volcanic glasses and possible microfossils believed by the book's author to be Martian microbes.* In the middle of the paragraphs discussing these microfossils (i.e., dead tiny animals) was the book's color photo section, with images of Martian features and microfossils distinctly resembling the images in my dream. I realized that my astral journey had in fact been a kind of CGI movie trailer of my excited reading of this book chapter.†

---

*In the dream, there was also a plastic baby hippo on its side among the glass animals. Years later, I found exactly such a tiny baby hippo toy in the grass near my office and brought it home for my daughter. Because I'd forgotten this detail about my Martian adventure, it didn't occur to me to check whether the date of this find coincided with that of the dream.

†The author of *Death on Mars*, John Brandenburg, was a former NASA scientist whose thesis was that an ancient civilization on Mars had been destroyed by nuclear war, based on radioactive isotope levels gases trapped in these Martian meteorites. In the end, I was not convinced by that thesis, nor by his speculation that this holocaust had been motivated by some faraway civilization's attempt "to prevent the birth of Christ in this solar system" (Brandenburg 2015, 337). But the possible evidence for microbial life on that planet, including in those meteorites, is not easily ignored.

It was a subsequent experience, however—one even more similar to my New Guinea witchcraft nightmare—that really convinced me that many seeming out-of-body experiences are very often highly precognitive lucid dreams instead. About a year after the Martian adventure, I was again performing a series of meditative exercises in bed designed to induce out-of-body experiences, although this time without any specific intention of a destination. Maybe that was a mistake. With some astonishment I found my point of view hovering down near the floor of a hall closet next to our bedroom, where my wife and I keep our medicines. My astral face was basically pressed down against my wife's shoes.* This was a very odd and undignified place to have projected to, as I'm not that into my wife's footwear (not that there's anything wrong with such a fetish). There was, as in my experience in Atlanta, an intense fear and specifically a sense of black magic possessing me. Although I couldn't see her, I interpreted my immobility near the floor as being physically weighed down by one of our two black cats, a slightly overweight (but harmless and sweet) cat named Cindy.

I excitedly recorded this weird experience upon waking and then largely forgot about it. But exactly a year later (calendrical resonance), I physically found myself crouched down in the hall with my head by the floor of that same medicine closet, sifting among my wife's shoes. I was hunting for an Advil I had dropped, fearing that Cindy had eaten the lost pill. It resulted in a stressful multi-day hospital stay for her—the same cat who had been weighing me down in the out-of-body experience. It was quite an upheaval and a blow to my dignity and bank account, although one that we all (including Cindy) survived. (On my blog I describe another linked experience the same night that

---

*Theosophical writers drew a distinction between etheric travel in real physical reality and astral travel in higher planes of existence, so a pedant might quibble that it was really my etheric body that was hovering near the floor of our closet. Robert Monroe called out-of-body experiences in recognizable physical reality "Reality 1" (Monroe 2001); the writer Robert Bruce, whose method I was following on this particular occasion, calls it the "real time zone" (Bruce 2009).

also turned out to be a vivid precognitive dream of an unusual in-body experience on the same weekend as the undignified Advil hunt.[6])

The weight of these spontaneous and deliberate lucid-dream experiences and experiences "out of body" has led me to strongly suspect that astral travel may very often be time travel, not space travel. The appealing "flying through space" metaphors used for these experiences, reinforced by the terms used to describe them ("out of body," "astral projection," and so on) cause us to overlook such a possibility.

Principle #25 of this book is:

_____

Lucid dreams and seeming out-of-body experiences are sometimes vivid, almost video-quality previews of subsequent in-body experiences in waking life.

_____

I can by no means say, simply from my own dream journals, that this is true of *all* alleged out-of-body experiences. But practitioners and anyone researching these phenomena should consider it a possibility to be studied further.

GREAT FEAR

The feeling of intense fear that often accompanies sleep distortions is directly relevant and important to this argument. Early writers on astral travel frequently noted its continuity with what was then called catalepsy: waking up paralyzed, experiencing vibrations and frightening noises, and only with difficulty separating the astral body from the physical, just as Edgar Rice Burroughs describes in *A Princess of Mars*. The modern term for catalepsy is sleep paralysis, and it is a commonly reported sleep disturbance. People all over the world report it, and a common feature is intense fear. The experiencer awakens—or often is in the transitional phase on the way to falling asleep—and finds herself conscious, aware of her surroundings, but unable to move. Some cultures have elaborated folkloric beliefs about this state. In Newfoundland, they call it Old Hag: a spectral presence is believed to be sitting on the chest and immobilizing the individual.[7] I'm a lifelong sufferer, although I've never seen the Hag.

Sleep paralysis has been a common debunking explanation for phenomena like alien abductions, and it is often explained reductively as a brain glitch. The individual's brain partly wakes up but the brain centers responsible for immobilizing us during sleep (so we don't hurt ourselves or act out our dreams) are slow to get the message.[8] It may take what feels like several seconds to a minute to become mobile, and during this time the waking brain's confusion trying to make sense of its paralyzed situation draws the (incorrect) inference of a malevolent presence, perhaps just outside the range of vision. Meanwhile, an overactive amygdala generates the intense fear.

There is a less reductive and much more interesting possibility for sleep paralysis, consistent with what I have argued about out-of-body experiences as potentially a kind of video-quality precognitive experience. If we are in a lucid state and previewing an imminent experience in our familiar physical environment—such as being awake and lying in bed, or some experience elsewhere in our home after rising—we naturally think we should be able to control our bodies. We don't realize we are really only getting a closed-circuit video feed from our awake future. Think of the scene in *Being John Malkovich,* when puppeteer Craig Schwartz (John Cusack) first enters the celebrity vessel body of famous actor John Malkovich and cannot yet control it. Sleep paralysis and out-of-body experiences may be like virtual-reality experiences not through another person's eyes but through our own eyes, sometime in our imminent future. (After years of sleep paralysis experiences, I gradually became aware that my eyes were not actually open, even if it seemed I could see my bedside table or the ceiling of my bedroom.)[9]

The fear experienced in many sleep paralysis, lucid dream, and out-of-body experiences is, I suspect, the same feeling that would accompany being immobilized or forcibly restrained in real life, unable to move and thus highly vulnerable. Because we don't understand that what we are seeing is a preview of something in our future, we feel distress and fear that is readily attributed to some external controlling presence, one that may be just out of view. The brain may reach into an available stock of cultural images to help interpret the situation (e.g., the Old Hag), or it may reach for some more immediate, personal association relevant to the real-life situation being precognized—a New Guinea sorcerer perhaps, or a black cat symbolically associated with black magic.

Principle #26 is:

Feelings of overwhelming fear in nightmares,
sleep paralysis, and lucid dreams may sometimes
be signals of receiving a kind of video feed from
a future waking experience.

How widely the principle applies—that is, whether extreme terror might always be a signal of receiving or downloading messages from our future—is one of those questions that armies of precognitive dreamworkers can help answer. I do wonder whether the intense fear sometimes paired with precognitive experiences on the edge of sleep could contribute to the cultural taboos that have always surrounded divination and prophecy.

Here is another disclaimer: this hypothesis is not meant to debunk alien abductions or other beliefs about nocturnal paranormal abuse. That the brain can confusingly overlay future experiences on present ones is no disproof of alien beings or other paranormal forces at work in our lives. But again, the perpetually unexpected and overlooked possibility of precognition is one that both experiencers and researchers should remember and consider, to see if it doesn't shed some light.

I believe that sleep paralysis offers a particularly important clue to what exactly Aldous Huxley's famous reducing valve (chapter 16) is reducing and, consequently, to why exceptional experiences associated with altered states of consciousness are . . . exceptional. If we were always bombarded by thoughts and sensory impressions from other times in our life, how would we ever act effectively in a given instance? Just as Dunne argued in *An Experiment with Time,* the situation of being asleep (and immobile) may be the ideal opportunity to allow those experiences and thoughts from other times in our life to rise to slight awareness and mingle with present concerns and priorities. This intermingling may occur in semi-awake states and waking states as well—those REM intrusions that may in many cases really be imaginal semaphore from our own future.

If the unconscious as described by psychoanalysts is, as I argued earlier in this book, equivalent to our Long Self, then the reducing valve could also be the same thing as Freud's famous censor. What that valve/censor is imperfectly but mostly repressing is not forbidden thoughts like wanting to sleep with your mother, but the vast array of our thoughts and sensory experiences that don't pertain to the present moment of the body, its senses, and its pressing survival-necessary motor tasks.

I suspect that in terrifying episodes of sleep paralysis, we not only are seeing why our conscious awareness is ordinarily so restricted to a narrow frame of our unfolding movie-like life but also are gaining an important perspective onto that most vexing of philosophical questions, the problem of free will in a deterministic or block universe. Our belief in free will, which we saw is somewhat incompatible with a larger, four-dimensional, Einsteinian perspective on our lives, may be an essential implication or aspect of the reduced, agential, cursor self (what Anthony Peake calls the Eidolon or Eidolonic consciousness[10]). In other words, this seemingly marginal, trivial, and (usually) rare nuisance to people who may be undergoing especially stressful periods in their life may be rich with philosophical implications about the tesseract brain and the block universe it inhabits.

I still wonder whether the terror that accompanied my dream adventure in my study in Atlanta in 1998 was related to my intensified self-consciousness and feeling of absurdity when acting out the same motions during waking life less than an hour later. I similarly wonder whether my terror as my astral body hovered down by my wife's shoes that evening in 2014 was related to my troubled emotions on a night exactly a year later when my physical body found itself in precisely the same strange position: absurdity and indignity coupled with growing anxiety that I needed to rush my cat to the emergency room due to a ridiculous mishap with a pain reliever.

So often in precognitive dreamwork, we are faced with the stunning juxtaposition between the sublime and the trivial, the cosmic and the comic. Here is where a future science of precognition may call upon not only the writings of Freud but also those of the philosopher Jean-Paul Sartre, who prioritized the absurdity of existence in his existentialist writings. Remember the Predictor users immobilized by an absurd futility in the story "What's Expected of Us"? It may be no accident that people are particularly prone to out-of-body experiences and sleep paralysis during existentially angsty adolescence and young adulthood. It is a time in our waking lives when we feel the most absurd and self-conscious, which in some ways is a kind of dissociation from reality. Teens and young adults may more readily come unstuck in time, like Kurt Vonnegut's time-traveling WWII soldier Billy Pilgrim does in his novel *Slaughterhouse Five*. So might people who find themselves in impossible situations more generally, perhaps as a result of trauma or stress, such as in combat. (Out-of-body and other paranormal experiences are often associated with trauma, for example.) All these are questions that future research—and future citizen science by dreamworkers—can help find the answers to.

19
Liminal Precognition
Hypnagogia, Active Imagination,
Creativity, and Meditation

The best evidence for something transcendent about us lies in the unconscious realm, which by the laws of wyrd we can never probe directly nor encompass with our conscious awareness. The precognitive unconscious is the smartest, best thing in us. It is one reason I am distrustful of the current parapsychological fashion to focus on "consciousness" as the antidote to reductive materialism. Whatever, wherever, *when*ever the unconscious is, it evades and eludes our conscious knowing and is our deepest mystery. It speaks to us and through us only obliquely. I sometimes liken it to a horse we may learn to ride and even master to some degree, but no matter how well we are acquainted with it, no matter how much we understand it, it will always seem to have a mind of its own. It will always be slightly other, or alien.

The distinction between consciousness and the unconscious, and between waking and dreaming, is much more permeable than is often imagined. In addition to REM-intrusive states like sleep paralysis, another especially rich zone for precognitive exploration is hypnagogia. Hypnagogic and (in the morning) hypnopompic experiences, or what dream writer Jennifer Dumpert calls "liminal dreams," occur on the boundary between waking and sleep.[1] They often consist of a brief, surreal scene or two and some verbal phrase or snippet of dialogue, and they are classically associated with artistic and scientific inspiration. Salvador Dali actively harnessed the power of hypnagogia by napping in a chair holding a heavy key over a plate on the floor. On falling asleep, the key dropped to the plate, waking him and enabling him to capture the bizarre image he had just seen. August Kekulé's famous story of seeing snakes eating their own tails while nodding off in front of the fireplace, which he said gave him the idea of the benzene ring, would have been a hypnagogic vision.*

Sensory-deprivation techniques used in ESP research such as "ganzfeld"—taping half ping-pong balls over the eyes and feeding white noise through noise-canceling earphones—can facilitate hypnagogic images. These simple, beautiful, and incredibly surreal tableaux are in my experience very often precognitive of things seen or encountered soon afterward or the following day, and the fact that nobody expects precognition contributes to misinterpreting these experiences as one of ESP's usual suspects, like clairvoyance, telepathy, or communication with some other, discarnate intelligence.

A case of apparent mind-to-mind contact during a hypnagogic reverie described by Brian Inglis in his book *Coincidence* is nicely illustrative. A man named Sebastian Earl submitted the following story to Inglis's parapsychology research center in Edinburgh, the Koestler Foundation, about an episode that happened when he was fifteen:

> One night while drifting off to sleep I was startled by the sentence "Why do crazy rabbits jump into electric chairs?" popping into my thoughts. I was so amazed by the oddity of this that I told it to [my best friend] Adam the next day at school. He was very shaken; he explained that he had read that sentence in the book he had been reading the night before.[2]

The book was Ken Kesey's *One Flew Over the Cuckoo's Nest,* which Earl's friend recommended he read. When he did, he was able

---

*Although hypnagogia does give creative insights, there are reasons to believe Kekulé may have had ulterior motives for telling this "snakes" story the way he did (see Wargo 2018).

to confirm the amazing similarity of his hypnagogic sentence to a passage in the book. Earl could not fathom how this happened. "What it is remarkable for is the fact that there is no so-called 'scientific' or 'logical' theory that can explain why I 'picked up' what my friend was reading in Wimbledon while I was in Kensington."[3] Leaping out from behind the door, a Precognition Inquisitor would point out to Earl that he was probably not picking up what Adam was reading the same evening but, instead, precognitively orienting toward a meaningful moment of connection with his friend the next day. Earl's decision to share his liminal dream with his friend elicited the "confirmation" about Kesey's book, per the same time-looping logic we have seen again and again around precognitive dreams.

Don't worry, I've made the same mistake Sebastian Earl did and have been visited by the same Precognition Inquisition. Late in the evening on Friday, August 29, 2014, I was propped up against a tower of pillows in my bed, fitfully nodding off and awakening with a start. I had had surgery that morning to fix my deviated septum—the reason I sound like a pig sometimes when I sleep—and was unable to lay flat, lest it restart the bleeding in my nose. (The surgeon warned me that getting any rest this first night might be difficult.) The result was that I kept drifting into hypnagogia. In one of my brief hypnagogic reveries, I felt a portal open up straight to the brain of the filmmaker and artist David Lynch. It was just like in *Being John Malkovich,* but the celebrity vessel body was way more dark and interesting. In that quick vision I saw a succession of paintings by Lynch, including a huge mud-brown diptych, and his distinctive Midwest voice explained that he intended his paintings to be used as objects of meditation, "like corpses."

In real life, I was, and am, a huge David Lynch fan. But while I did know he was a painter in addition to his work in film and TV, at that point I'd only ever seen a few of his works in that medium, and I had no memory of seeing the pictures I saw in my brief hypnagogic vision. What he said about corpses fascinated me—it reminded me of the Buddhist practice of meditating in graveyards—and when I jerked awake (it had probably just been a couple seconds, total), I reached over from my propped-up pillows and wrote this "telepathic connection to David Lynch" down in my notebook. It was the only rewarding moment in that long, miserable day.

I don't know if I really thought I'd found a telepathic portal to my artistic hero—I sort of half thought it, the way I'd half thought I'd been possessed by a sorcerer (a quite Lynchian idea, by the way) that morning in Atlanta years before. Two days later, though, the truth came in the form of the Arts section of the Sunday *New York Times*. The main feature was on a new exhibition of Lynch's paintings in Philadelphia, the city where he had studied as a young artist in the late 1960s. The top picture was a photo of Lynch working on a painting in his atelier, and leaning behind him were the right two panels of a huge mud-brown triptych—the left panel was cut off at the edge of the photo. The visible panels were the "diptych" I had seen when nodding off in my hypnagogic state. The article discussed Lynch's well-known Transcendental Meditation practice. What I didn't know and learned in that article was that when Lynch was an art student, he got permission to go into the Philadelphia morgue near his apartment late at night to spend time studying the cadavers. In the article, he talked about his fascination with decay.[4]

It was a beautiful example of precognitive hypnagogia, in other words, and one that also nicely illustrated the principle identified by Dunne with his dream of Lieutenant B.'s crash: what may immediately feel like a connection to another mind across space (as if we would really know what such a connection felt like, in any case—remember that problem of source monitoring) is more likely going to turn out to be a preview of some interesting or unsettling experience, often a reading experience, in one's near future. It also illustrated the power of the hypnagogic state for coming unstuck in time, like Vonnegut's Billy Pilgrim. I have since found that many of my most vivid, short-range precognitive experiences (proving veridical within a day or two) involve this fascinating liminal dream state.

Principle #27 is:

_____

Hypnagogic and hypnopompic images
frequently bear precognitive fruit,
often within a day or two.

_____

Working with hypnagogia presents several challenges. The first is learning to notice these liminal dreams when they are occurring. We all experience them on the way to and from sleep, but we are generally not aware of them because we forget them afterward. It is necessary to develop a knack of catching yourself in the act of following a particularly bizarre (but in the moment, completely sensible-seeming) train of thought, and then recording it right away. Meditation and mindfulness techniques are especially helpful for cultivating a detached, critical awareness of one's own mental processes. Dumpert's *Liminal Dreaming* is an outstanding guide to entering hypnagogic states and developing the ability to remain on the edge of sleep and, most importantly, remember these visions afterward.[5] Nose surgery also does the trick, but I don't recommend it.

The other, maybe even bigger challenge, is simple willpower. The seductions of imminent slumber all too often overpower any intention to rise and write down what you have just seen while drifting off. Often the sleepy brain will even trick you by ensuring you that you will remember—how could you not remember something amazing like David Lynch talking to you about corpses, or some equally singular and strange vision? You may even find yourself dreaming or semi-dreaming that you have in fact written down your brilliant hypnagogic or hypnopompic vision in your notebook, only to find the next morning that it was pure wish-fulfillment—you wake up to find nothing in your notebook and totally unable to recall what you saw or heard. By being resolute, though, you will be handsomely rewarded.

CREATIVITY

The same bootstrapping toward our future success that is operative in intuition and Spidey sense is, I believe, also the basis of literary and artistic creativity. This is a huge topic, one that I can only touch on here, but again, many artists find inspiration in liminal, hypnagogic, and hypnopompic images, and writers very often produce ideas and images that prove amazingly prophetic of later events or later experiences or upheavals in their own lives. The creative flow state is an "altered state" that may be rich with precognitive material, if only we have eyes to look for and recognize it.*

The most famous example is Morgan Robertson's 1898 novel *Futility,* about a biggest-ever ocean liner called *Titan* that strikes an iceberg on an April night and sinks in the North Atlantic with too few lifeboats to save the passengers. The very similar real ship *Titanic* sank fourteen years later, in April 1912, under very similar circumstances. This novel has been the subject of much speculation, as well as attempts—never quite convincing—at debunking.[6] But Robertson's novel is really only the tip of the iceberg, so to speak, of literary precognition.

In 1951, after a long creative struggle with a novel that felt perpetually unrealistic to him, Norman Mailer published *Barbary Shore,* about a writer like himself living and working in a Brooklyn Heights rooming house with a colorful mix of artist neighbors, one of whom turned out to be a KGB spy. The novel was panned by critics and Mailer even gave up being a novelist, temporarily. But a few years later, after a stint in Hollywood, Mailer returned to Brooklyn Heights, where he rented a room in a building to work on his next novel. One day he was stunned to encounter a *New York Times* headline about a top KGB colonel named Rudolf Abel who had just been caught running a massive spy ring out of the same building he used for his office. He had known the spy as Emil Goldfus, the "guitarist" who worked one floor down from his studio. It was uncannily like what he had written about in his panned novel.

As mentioned in chapter 16, strange precognitive experiences like

---

*A successful and secretive engineer, ufologist, and inventor, given the pseudonym Tyler in Diana Pasulka's book *American Cosmic,* describes getting inspiration for new biotechnologies in such a state (Pasulka 2019). Tyler interprets it as actually an interaction with an alien intelligence; I see the possibility of interacting with his own successful future self as more likely.

this were the norm for science-fiction writer Philip K. Dick. To take just one of many examples, in 1962 he wrote a story about an android simulacrum of Abraham Lincoln, but he couldn't find a publisher so the story languished unread in his desk drawer. Two years later, Disneyland unveiled one of their most perennially popular exhibits, their animatronic Abraham Lincoln. When he read about this new exhibit, Dick clipped the article from the paper as proof that he was a precog straight out of one of his stories.[7]

A list of similar literary and artistic prophesies could fill a book (rubbing my temples and squinting, I prophesy that it will). Yet even when they are accepted as more than coincidence, it seldom occurs to people to consider such anomalies as providing a valuable clue about the missing source of creative inspiration itself, the dark matter that bends the lives and works of artists. I believe that doing art, in whatever medium, is channeling your own future, and that it may work very similarly to dreams: future thoughts get expressed using the materials—including artistic influences—already at hand.[8] And because these inspirations tend to be so personal, and then get worked over in the processes of revision and polishing, even artists themselves very often fail to notice their own prophecies.

If you are an artist of any kind, or a creative writer, go back and look at your old works, even especially your amateurish or abandoned attempts. For instance, if (like me) you consider yourself a failed fiction writer and have a hard drive full of old unfinished stories or never-persevered-with novels, brace yourself and look at them again with fresh eyes. You may find they contain uncanny foreshadowing of events or situations that followed in your life.

There may even be an inverse relationship between the significance or quality of a work of art and its prophecy quotient. One thing Morgan Robertson's *Futility,* Norman Mailer's *Barbary Shore,* and Phil Dick's *We Can Build You* (the title under which his story about an android Lincoln was finally published, about a decade later) have in common, besides being uncannily prophetic, is that they are really bad. Take courage from this. Dick famously said that messages of the divine are to be found in the "trash stratum"⁹; the same seems to be true of prophecy—it is in the dirt and mess and debris that our future is written most clearly. Learn to love the mess.

ACTIVE IMAGINATION, TRANCE, AND ACTIVE DREAMING

Harnessing the creative flow state for self-insight and the exploration of one's own unconscious is the basis of Jung's method called active imagination, and it is sometimes likened to dreaming while awake. It is widely used by artists and writers, although it goes by many different names. J. R. R. Tolkien wrote the source material for his fantasy epics and the mythology of *The Silmarillion* in a creative-imaginal state he called "Faërie," for instance.[10] Franz Kafka seems to have written some of his early stories in a similar state.[11] It may be no different from shamanic trance—shamans were probably the first artists, after all. Active imagination and shamanic trance are rich states for accessing precognitive material, mining the brain for what it already knows about the future.

There are different approaches to active imagination, and it may not even be a single thing but a kind of spectrum. In *Liminal Dreaming*, Dumpert describes it as a kind of controlled hypnagogia and provides instructions for entering and working with this state that are based on Jung's writings and those of the writer Robert A. Johnson. Essentially one enters an imaginal or lucid dream realm from the edge of sleep, interacting actively with images and symbols that arise, and expressing those interactions through writing, drawing, painting, sculpture, or some other medium.[12]

My precognitive collaborator Tobi developed a facility for active imagination during a period of illness and now regards it as even more central to her dreamwork (as well as more precognitive) than her night dreams. In her case it is not exactly hypnagogia—she describes it as literally dreaming while awake. She begins by sitting at her computer, typing out an intent for her dream, one that registers an openness to learning something new. "Open my eyes to what I couldn't see before" is what she types for a general active dream. Normally, a random thought soon flashes to mind and she follows it without judgment. For example, if there's a suggestion of a leaf, she turns her attention to that with curiosity and anticipation; the restless mind quickly gets bored and will typically produce an action or scene associated with a leaf right away, and she focuses on this. If she has a thought suggesting that the leaf blows across her shoe, for instance, she notices what her shoe looks like, where she's standing, and what's around her. Before she knows it, it becomes a dream environment, but one in which she is lucid and can interact with figures in this realm at will while touch-typing a description of her interactions and the dialogues that ensue.

It's easier said than done, of course. Tobi explained to me that her active dreaming evolved from experimentation with lucid dreaming and repeated practice in lucidly re-entering dreams during the night, as well as facility with using relaxing visualizations during the time she was raising two small children. Visualizing a pleasant retreat (a restaurant where she would order food, eat, and enjoy herself) was the only way to be alone and "go on vacation," and after many nightly visits to this imaginary retreat, someone spontaneously popped into it and spoke to her. She hadn't deliberately imagined this figure the way she imagined eating a meal. It was a deeply shocking experience, and she considers it her initiation into the action of active dreams.*

Tobi's typed records of her active dreams read like shamanic journeys à la Carlos Castaneda, and indeed her descriptions of her early explorations in active dreaming are very similar to shamanic exploration as described by the writer and teacher Michael Harner in books like *The Way of the Shaman*.[13] Harner recommends beginning a shamanic journey to the "lower world" by imaginatively descending through some familiar hole in one's environment. Although she had not read Harner,

---

*Tobi also considers active dreaming to be not that dissimilar from the kinds of rumination that people who suffer depression are familiar with. It suggests an interesting continuum or connection between depression and the facility with mental imagery cultivation that is central to shamanism (Noll 1985). This would be a fascinating realm for future research to explore.

Castaneda, or any other shamanic guidebooks when she developed this skill, in her early efforts Tobi also imagined herself descending into a well, pretending she was the stepdaughter in "Mother Holle," her favorite fairy tale as a kid. (Jung also imagined descending through a hole when he began his interactions with his unconscious.) Harner's method uses drumming to facilitate these journeys, and there are now any number of apps with shamanic drumbeats, binaural beats, and white noise that can be used to facilitate trance and that some might find helpful as active-imagination aids. Jung never used any external aids, nor does Tobi. For her, this altered state somewhat resembles the intensely absorbed semi-trance that artists and writers may settle into when they are in a flow state with their work.*

The resulting narratives are sometimes demonstrably prophetic—veridical, in the parapsychological idiom. Again, although Tobi originally interpreted this veridicality as synchronicity, she now regards these waking interactions with her dreamworld as interactions with her future self.[14] Frequently her experiences relate to future conceptual or life upheavals, the dreams creatively acting out or dramatizing concepts she hasn't yet encountered. Others bring her previews of imminent events.

At the end of an active dream in March 2016, for instance, a figure called Tobi a raven-lover and promised her the gift of a raven, adding cryptically, "but you may keep the cardinals too." The dream ended with a raven call. A few hours later, she received a shipment of two raven statues for her garden. Although she had ordered them, these ravens weren't expected for weeks, and she had not received a shipping notice alerting her that they were on the way. After six weeks of weathering, the finish on the ravens proved to be flawed, so she asked for unfinished replacements from the vendor. "The vendor didn't want the

---

*If you can identify at all with bad writer Jack Torrance (Jack Nicholson) in Stanley Kubrick's 1980 horror film *The Shining*, angry at his family's interruptions when he's in the creative zone—even if all he ended up writing was, "All work and no play makes Jack a dull boy" 10,000 times—you already know this semi-trance. Tobi told me that her family knows not to interrupt her when she is actively dreaming at the computer, or to expect a blank stare when they try to talk to her.

original ravens back (too heavy to ship), so I ended up with four raven statues—two black and two white—and I think of them collectively as 'the cardinal directions.'"

Sometimes Tobi's active dreams relate to something important or interesting she will encounter in her reading over the following days. For instance, in an active dream in October the same year, she recorded the following:

> *Though there is no ground beneath my feet I sense I "have footing" and begin walking with determination. As I do this, the sky rotates—a scene one would experience in a planetarium. . . . There's a sense that the non-material sphere beneath my feet is small, and a dynamo that I am charging. I am making energy with my walking. . . . The movement of the stars is showing me that I'm turning the dynamo and accumulating charge.*

Dynamo was not a word she would ordinarily have used, so it seemed significant that it was part of her understanding in and of this active dream vision. Two days later, she handwrote beside this narrative a passage from Sri Aurobindo that she spontaneously came across: "Purified from all that is Asubha (evil), we have to act in the world as dynamos of that Divine Electricity and send it thrilling and radiating through mankind, so that wherever one of us stands, hundreds around us may become full of His light and force, full of God and full of Ananda."

Although active dreaming and active imagination are not states that come naturally to most people, they are skills that at least some people can learn and develop with practice. Dumpert's book offers valuable instruction, and the shamanic journeying methods of Harner can also be adapted. Like working with hypnagogia more generally, it requires practice to access and then remain in these altered states and then remember the experiences well enough afterward to write them down. Tobi's knack of writing as she goes is relatively unique, as far as I know, but I am eager to hear from readers who may have their own experiences with active dreaming and this form of dreamwork.

Automatic writing is another psychic and Surrealist modality that could produce similar effects, and for some beginners, might possibly serve as a bridge to active dreaming. The ability to turn off the inner censor is key to this practice, as it is to dreaming more generally. The beginner could even approach active dreaming as a kind of automatic writing without any ego or critic attached, not worrying if the images are in any way literary or original. Tobi likens her own early active dream accounts to the flatness of fairy tales: "Fairy tales are not very visual; they aren't writerly; they're full of (what became) clichés. If you're a writer, you want to be imaginal, writerly, original, avoid tired tropes. Since I clearly wasn't [doing creative] writing, I could accept it if a bearded wizard showed up. If I was writing a story, I couldn't. So I was off the hook, not responsible for the story, and just went with what happened without judgment."

MEDITATION AND THE MOMENT OF PRECOGNITION

Meditation is another fruitful approach for tapping into precognition. I have found Zen and mindfulness-based practices to be particularly useful. The more the mind is placid but alert, the more we can focus on small perturbations of thought, and detect oddities in our train of thought that reflect the possible subtle magnetic attraction of some imminent experience or upheaval. Precognitive flashes arise not infrequently during meditation, and as with hypnagogia, recording them as soon as they happen is necessary or they will be forgotten.

Recording visions that occur during meditation defeats meditation's other purposes, of course, and in fact such visions (called *makyo* in the Japanese Zen idiom) are generally regarded by meditation teachers as distractions to be ignored. Traditional contemplative traditions may be just as reductively materialistic and hostile to paranormal possibilities or heretical dimensions of the soul as the mainstream sciences. I believe that paying attention to these distractions as part of your precognitive awake-work is a worthwhile, albeit defiant, trade-off.

Even though it isn't usually described in those terms, using mindfulness for precognition is what many remote viewers are doing. It was the remote-viewing research at SRI in Menlo Park in the 1970s that gave us some of our best methods for accessing psi reliably and consistently, and in a focused, directed manner. The pioneer of the method, Ingo Swann, developed the famous protocols that help occupy the active analytical mind as a way of allowing those more spontaneous images to arise in consciousness. The preparatory phase for a remote-viewing session may involve relaxation or even (for some viewers) entering a kind of meditative trance.[15] Again, whether remote viewing is anything more than precognition remains an open and hotly debated question. But at the very least, those protocols can be applied to accessing information in your future, just as dreaming can be used in remote viewing.

In their book *The Premonition Code,* Theresa Cheung and Julia Mossbridge provide guidance in what they called controlled precognition, based on methods used in remote viewing.[16] It is a method that can be applied without prior experience in meditation, trance states, hypnagogia, or active imagination. What Cheung and Mossbridge call the higher self in their book is more or less what I am calling the unconscious—the Long Self refracted through the present moment.*

The trick with remote viewing as well as less directed meditation or mindfulness is learning to distinguish thoughts that feel like one's own ordinary deliberate thought-stream from spontaneous thoughts and images that are unexpected, that feel alien or uncaused. Again, thoughts that are potentially precognitive may come as fleeting and faint flashes or impressions. I believe they feel alien precisely because of that inabil-

---

*For example, a precognitive method called associative remote viewing was developed by some of the early remote-viewing researchers and is now being taught in workshops, applied in Las Vegas, and even used in higher-stakes financial settings. It is called "associative" because the psychics aren't trying to predict an outcome directly (such as whether a certain stock will rise or fall) but rather are trying to predict an arbitrary object or signal they will later receive in response to the outcome of interest. Psychics work as a team—you can't do it alone—but it removes some of the biasing noise that otherwise makes remote viewing unreliable. Damien Broderick's 2015 book *Knowing the Unknowable* discusses this method.

ity to engage in source-monitoring with precognitive information, discussed in chapter 7. Central to the method described by Cheung and Mossbridge is learning to distinguish this information delivered by the higher self (or unconscious) from the filling-in-the-blanks cognitive process that remote viewers call analytical overlay. Getting a feel for alien thoughts versus our more analytical mental processes is helpful in utilizing hypnagogia for precognition and creativity as well. And again, when people don't expect (or even have a concept of) precognition, such alien-feeling thoughts will readily be attributed to other sources like real alien intelligences, telepathy, and so on.

I find that a mindfulness-like tool created in the field of ecological psychology, called experience sampling, is also helpful in accessing the precognitive unconscious. In experiments, participants are prodded at random times throughout the day using a pager, at which points they record or report what they were just thinking in the preceding moments.[17] Observing their thought-stream is at first a challenging task for people who are unused to introspecting. Once they get the hang of it, participants often find it not only surprising but rewarding, even simply as a window into their own moods. (For instance, depressed people sometimes find that their actual thoughts throughout the day are far less negative than they imagine they are, and vice versa.)

However, you don't need a pager to do it. The basic idea of experience sampling is just to get in the habit of stopping and noticing what you were just thinking a second or a few seconds ago. It is in those innocuous, perhaps "random" thoughts just before you decided to pay them any real attention that precognitive associations to imminent experiences (as well as answers to not-quite-formulated questions) can often be found. I think of this pre-conscious window as the moment of precognition. When you are thinking but are not (yet) conscious of thinking, it is more or less like dreaming—a free, private, and uninhibited, thus creative, phase in mental life. Learning to catch yourself in the act of thinking greatly increases the number of synchronicities in your day, and it may persuade you (if you still need persuading) that synchronicity is nothing but your own precognitive nature that you have until now failed to recognize or own.

The challenge in working productively with any state of consciousness, be it sleeping or waking or any of the various states in-between, is that your experiences, thoughts, or impressions need to be written down, drawn, or otherwise recorded. Otherwise they are forgotten, or at the very least our memory of them is not trustworthy. Our passing thoughts while awake are just as evanescent as our dreams. Again, the business—the work—in both precognitive dreamwork and precognitive awake-work is the writing-down part. It cannot be passed over. So, besides keeping a dream journal next to your bed, carry a small notebook or sketchbook with you throughout the day.

CONCLUSION
The Long Self Revolution
A Call to Action

> *"I swear I shall make good use of these riches that Allah*
> *has blessed me with," said the younger Hassan.*
> *"And I renew that oath," said the older.*
>
> TED CHIANG,
"THE MERCHANT AND THE ALCHEMIST'S GATE"

We are at the cusp of a revolution in our thinking about time and mind. Advances in physics and computing that point to the reality of retrocausation are being mirrored in popular culture with an explosion of novels, films, and TV series about precognition, time travel, and time-loopiness in various forms. The complexities and confusions around time and causation seem a bit more manageable than they did in previous decades. People are ready to think in new ways about these topics, rather than simply avoid them because they cause headaches. You can call it the Long Self Revolution.

As I've written and spoken on time loops over the past few years, I have met more and more people actively exploring the Long Self in one way or another, through dreams or active exploration of synchronicity or magical practice or other approaches. Those whose dreams I've shared in the previous chapters are only some of them. There is a growing community of precogs out there, people conscious of how their mind-brains reach into their future as well as of how their present consciousness may shape their past.[1] Somebody reading this book right now—possibly you—could be realizing, like my friend Tobi did, that all those synchronicities you have experienced around your dreams are really manifestations of a superhuman ability—or really, a human superability—that you never imagined really existed and that has been operating in the background your whole life, shaping that life in astonishing ways.

Be prepared, though. Not everyone is ready for such realizations.

Another magazine I subscribe to and read avidly (although not to my preschooler) is *New Scientist*. In a July 2018 issue, one of its editors, Rowan Hooper, penned a "Field Notes" piece about his visit to the 35th annual International Dream Conference in Phoenix. He visited the "interdisciplinary" (his scare quotes) conference to learn about the latest in scientific psychology and neuroscience of dreaming but found himself in a surprisingly diverse group that included New Agers, psychoanalysts, and parapsychologists expressing what was to him a profoundly distressing panoply of beliefs about dreams—including the belief that they may foretell future events. Hooper writes that he nearly choked on his burrito when a psychoanalyst he was dining with told him he believes dreams can be precognitive.

Many people at that meeting, he lamented, expressed their belief in precognitive dreams, and for this science editor it represented a challenge to his faith in cultural and scientific progress. "Our fascination with dreams goes back millennia, with many ancient cultures believing they carried messages from spirits or spoke to us of the future," Hooper writes. "How sad that thousands of years later, we are still bogged down in such mysticism, when we could instead be probing what truly generates dreams, and what they tell us about consciousness and how our brains work."[2]

In other words, despite the continued mystery, even to scientists, of dreams and dreaming, this editor clearly went in knowing all he needed to know about dreams: they're not "mystical," they don't speak of the future, and so on. He had hoped to find a homogeneous set of scientists upholding some narrowly materialistic consensus on this. "Call me naïve," Hooper writes, "but it was a shame to find an 'us versus them' attitude among the non-scientists." The psychoanalyst he had lunch with might have called that projection, since Hooper himself clearly took such an attitude toward those non- or para-scientific others and their "mumbo jumbo," as he put it.[3]

Lest any *New Scientist* readers in 2018 be on the fence about the possibilities of precognitive dreaming, Hooper provided the standard explaining-away. "No matter that with so many people dreaming each night, this is quite likely to happen by chance."[4] Again, the law of large numbers argument that skeptics like Hooper always rest their cases on depends on the phenomenon in question happening rarely. I hope you are convinced by now that whatever precognitive dreaming is, it ain't rare.

It is elusive and slippery, though. Most alleged precognitive dreams, because their relationship to a claimed target event consists of highly personal associations, understandably hold little weight with skeptics, who are as hostile to untestable psychoanalytic premises as they are to parapsychological ones. The fact that a dreamer is an *n* of 1, dreaming in a unique way about unique life experiences, makes it very hard to gather massive, verifiable data for any theory of dream meaning, including the most radical theory I have put forward in this book—that dreams very often and possibly even always show us "memories" of future experiences in a kind of symbolic language. But in fact, the only readily tested hypothesis about dream meaning is that there is no meaning—it's a bias that's built right into the scientific method. Whenever a scientist debunks the meaning(fulness) of anything, remember that meaning cannot readily be caught in science's nets.

The fact that meaning-centered phenomena resist purely scientific approaches has put the study of dreams (like the study of other psychic and paranormal phenomena) at an impasse for decades. It is why every popular science piece proclaiming the answer to why we dream (It's nocturnal therapy!, It prepares us for threats!, and so on) sounds vaguely unconvincing and then is replaced by a new answer a few months later, and nobody in science pays attention to the growing number of books and memoirs providing compelling, albeit anecdotal, evidence for dream precognition.

So far, no scientist with access to research dollars has been ready to jeopardize their career by studying the question of dream precognition in a way that might produce extraordinary evidence, and until that happens, the whole topic will remain exiled to the disreputable realm of ESP books or small studies in parapsychology journals that mainstream scientists readily ignore. Hooper writes that his head was in his hands by the end of a keynote address by Stanley Krippner, who conducted what are still the best-known dream-ESP studies a half century ago,[5] but those were tiny studies and thus hold zero scientific weight in the world of big-budget science Hooper is used to.

Debates between ESP believers and skeptics are thus a lot like the prehistoric quadrupeds in my Permian-battle dream, or the attic figures on Keats's Grecian urn: ancient combatants frozen in time, locked in an eternal dispute that goes nowhere. Somewhere in the block universe, an open-minded psychoanalyst is still calmly explaining dream precognition to a *New Scientist* editor choking on his burrito—a scene on endless loop.

This is why real dreamers need to get into the act, not just academics and scientists. The grass-roots, citizen-science movement I'd love to help foment with this book is to force a conversation in mainstream psychology and the wider culture by convincing enough people, perhaps even a few sleep scientists, that this is a topic that can no longer be simply dismissed and ridiculed. If that happens, it may finally be possible to do the big, interdisciplinary work that would put precognition and precognitive dreaming on the scientific map once and for all, moving it out from those paranormal shadows. The implications would be transformative. In *Time Loops,* I likened it to dismantling a wall that has separated us from a whole half of time that has been gathering scientific dust, regarded as a forbidden realm that is off-limits. The Not Yet—

the future as it impacts human behavior, art, and everything else in the present—is truly undiscovered country. And my bet is also that, in the end, our relation to the Not Yet will turn out to be not just some minor, nifty icing on our mental cake. Precognition could be fundamental, the basis of many mental processes that have until now been explained in boringly linear ways.

To get to that point, dreamers can't just make vague claims. We need to show our work. Those bulging dream journals, punctuated with exclamation marks next to the roughly 25 percent of dreams that, I'll wager, you'll discover are possibly or clearly precognitive, will ultimately wear away at societal doubts. You don't need to take on the big dragons—or the scientists. You can start just with the doubts of spouses and associates. Making converts among your family members and trusted colleagues and friends on social media will ultimately go a long way toward changing the cultural conversation.

Dreamers may end up with an overflowing gallery of precognitive dreams that will make the skeptics choke on their burritos—or better yet, broaden their minds. Sooner or later, it won't just be the occasional astronomer dreaming of a future discovery. Some psychologist or neuroscientist is going to catch herself having an experience that she clearly, "impossibly" dreamed about days or weeks or years earlier and will be brave enough to study the problem with real funding and tools to supply the extraordinary evidence for the once-absurd—but in fact, totally ordinary—idea that dreams bring us messages from our future.

BE LONG TOGETHER

The larger goal of the Long Self Revolution is not just convincing skeptics, or contributing to the advancement of science, as important as those things are. There's a bigger, human reason. By reawakening us to our own lives' vastness and value, precognitive dreamwork and the lifework it makes possible can lead us to better appreciate the vastness and value of other people as well. It helps us imagine (without ever knowing) the epic stories that they are made of.

(Re)awakening to the wonder of our common humanity feels like the most important project we could undertake as the traumatic second decade of the twenty-first century closes and we embark on an uncertain third. The COVID-19 pandemic that decimated the United States when callousness, irresponsibility, and greed trumped public health revealed starkly the lack of humanity among the powerful. At the time of this writing, 200,000 people have died in the United States from a virus whose transmission was significantly preventable. Many of those people died alone, on ventilators, unable to be with their loved ones.

The same terrible year, 2020, we watched the Long Self of an innocent man, George Floyd, cut short under a police officer's knee. Rather than show contrition and resolve to finally address racism in their ranks, those appointed to serve and protect our communities engaged in further violence against Black Americans over the ensuing months, as well as nightly displays of unapologetic—indeed deliberate, performatively cruel—brutality against Black Lives Matter protesters.

Cruelty and injustice are nothing new. It has always been easy to export violence and suffering to the rest of the world when we don't imagine that the victims are real people leading real lives that matter. Weirdly, the very technologies that made the world a smaller place, that were supposed to create a global village, have only made it easier to dehumanize—to unmatter—poor people in the more remote corners of that village. Soldiers launch drone assassinations halfway around the globe from the comfort and safety of video-game consoles on American military bases.* Pixelated videos of innocents blown to bits in mistaken air strikes elicit yawns by those who pull the trigger and tough-minded

---

*The sci-fi-sounding idea that reality is a simulation, increasingly popular in Silicon Valley, appeals to many as an explanation for paranormal phenomena and synchronicities; yet at the same time, it potentially reinforces the view that other people could be NPCs (non-player characters) in some big cosmic game (Virk 2019). The moral and ethical endpoint of such video-game thinking is horrific to contemplate, given the genocides of the past century.

excuses by the generals who consider such collateral murders necessary sacrifices in the ever-more-nebulous War on Terror.

There's a common theme in all this. The unmattering of Black, or brown, or transgender, or Muslim lives reveals an ever-more-defiant and deliberate refusal to imagine or care. It is a cancerous empathy deficit that could destroy our species if it is not confronted with some antidote, and a vaccine to halt its further spread. This empathy deficit may be as urgent an existential threat as the climate crisis, even if it is harder to perceive and define. I think it is what really lies at the root of that ecological catastrophe.

I see the Long Self Revolution as a revolution of imagination and care, of empathy and anti-cruelty. When you directly experience your own self as a vast and sublime and unique four-dimensional formation in the block universe, you realize that every fellow traveler on this planet is similarly vast and sublime and unique—like threads in a tapestry, both irreducibly individual and completely interdependent. Precognitive dreamwork (and lifework) makes it impossible to ignore or deny the worth, value, and real reality of other, embodied lives—including lives very distant and different from ours.* Our planet is a splendid, multi-colored tapestry woven from the intertwining of Long Selves. (Probably our universe is too, in ways we will discover in a few thousand years.)

Caring for the future of the earth first requires imagining that each of its inhabitants has a future. That's what a Long Self is: someone with a future. Thus the Long Self Revolution is incompatible both with cruelty and with the resentful apocalypticism of those who deny that our planet and our species are going somewhere, and going somewhere better.[6] In a way, it recruits the future to save the present.

Who knew that your dreams—your literal night dreams—could be political? But there you are . . . and here we are. There is a future. After you've witnessed its presence in those dreams, you cannot deny

---

*Animals too. A beetle showing up at the window of a famous therapist, or a big cat striding by a writer's woodpile, is a real individual being with its own place in the world and its own life story, its own Long Self, not just a materialized archetype whose comings and goings serve mainly to edify or reward the person who encounters it.

it. It is speaking to you and through you every night. Pay attention.

I hope that the adventure of precognitive dreamwork does for you what it has done for me: I hope it helps you imagine your future, and makes you care—for your self, for other selves, and for our world—in a new and humbling and empowering way.

APPENDIX
Precognitive Dreamwork Principles

1. Precognition isn't about events in the future; it is about our own future experiences, including reading or learning experiences.

2. Precognitive dreams do not necessarily feel special or numinous. Record all your dreams.

3. Dreams symbolically show us our future conscious thoughts in response to upheavals and learning experiences.

4. Dreams build future towers out of past bricks.

5. Peripheral figures in our lives who appear in our dreams, as well as celebrities, may be stand-ins for associations about those individuals, action figures in a symbolic allegory or tableau.

6. A recent situation or experience may spark a dream about a future experience that resembles it somehow (thematic resonance).

7. The drama quotient in a dream may be wildly out of proportion to the significance of the experience or upheaval that it targets.

8. It is associations to our dreams and not their manifest content that often reveal the links to later experiences.

9. Assume (without ever being able to prove it) that all your dreams may be precognitive.

10. Dreams often encode experiences within a single temporal window of waking time, although not necessarily to just one emotionally salient occurrence during that window.

11. Dreams sometimes pre-present significant experiences exactly (or almost exactly) a year or multiple years in the future (calendrical resonance).

12. Synchronicity is what it feels like when we precognitively orient toward rewarding miracles, gifts in the landscape of our life, and are unaware that our actions played some role in leading us to (and even creating) those miracles.

13. In one way or another, dreams lead us to the future that they prophesy.

14. A dream may pre-present the dreamer's later thoughts about the dream, or its value to the dreamer, in a kind of fractal fashion.

15. A precognitive dream may be unimportant in itself; what matters, what it is really about, is what it leads you to do in your life, or the connection it helps you make.

16. Precognition often orients us to experiences that challenge our prior beliefs or worldviews.

17. The thought "but I survived" is a very common target of precognition.

18. Experiences that cause some chagrin because they are somewhat embarrassing or humiliating are a common target for precognitive dreams.

19. Dreams obliquely and symbolically pre-present actual experiences rather than literalistically pre-presenting future possibilities.

20. Dreams cannot directly represent nonbeing, but they nevertheless are often about nonbeing, our thoughts about loss or the possibility of loss.

21. It is not your fault if you have a premonition that comes true.

22. Conscientiousness and an attitude of care (for self and others) may be essential for manifesting precognition, or at least for doing so consistently.

23. Dreams that turn out to have been precognitive often contain some symbolic representation of the act of returning to the dream to verify its precognitive character.

24. The associative language used in a dream, or its choice of symbolism, is partly shaped or at least constrained in interesting

ways by subsequent experiences and by its connection to other dreams across the course of life.

25. Lucid dreams and seeming out-of-body experiences are sometimes vivid, almost video-quality previews of subsequent in-body experiences in waking life.

26. Feelings of overwhelming fear in nightmares, sleep paralysis, and lucid dreams may sometimes be signals of receiving a kind of video feed from a future waking experience.

27. Hypnagogic and hypnopompic images frequently bear precognitive fruit, often within a day or two.

Notes

INTRODUCTION. THEY DREAMED

1. Dossey 2009, 54.
2. Kalas 2018, 55.
3. Books approaching psychic claims from a skeptical perspective include Wiseman 2010; Gardner 1998.
4. White 2017.
5. See, for example, Hooper 2018.
6. Mossbridge and Radin 2018.
7. Priestley 1989.
8. Jung 1973b.

CHAPTER 1. UNMANNED:
MY PSYCHIC DUE DILIGENCE

1. Feather and Schmicker 2005.
2. Freud 1965.
3. Freud 1965, 49.
4. Freud 1974.
5. Bem 2011.
6. Rhine 1961, 1967.
7. Dunne and Jahn 2003.
8. Joe McMoneagle, interviewed in Mungia 2019.
9. Radin 1997.
10. Mossbridge et al. 2012, 2014; Tsakiris 2017.

11. Honorton and Ferrari 1989.
12. Mossbridge et al. 2012.
13. Utts 1995.
14. Ronson 2007.
15. Bem et al. 2016.
16. Dixon et al. 2009.
17. Haynes 2019.
18. See Wargo 2018.
19. Sheldrake 2011.
20. The physicist Paul Davies, a pioneer in the study of life's emergence and its informational properties, has even speculated as much. See Davies 2004.
21. Sagan 1997.

CHAPTER 2. VAAL AND REDEMPTION: HOW A *STAR TREK* EPISODE TAUGHT ME MEMORY GOES BACKWARD

1. McMoneagle 1993, 2002; Smith 2005; Targ 2004.
2. Graff 1998, 2000.
3. Cushman 2014.
4. Dunne 1952.
5. Dunne 1952, 44.
6. Dunne 1952.
7. Minkowski 2012.
8. Dunne 1955.
9. Dunne 1952, 51.
10. Krohn and Kripal 2018.

CHAPTER 3. PSYCHIC CITIZEN SCIENCE: TAKING THE J. W. DUNNE CHALLENGE

1. See, for instance, Mole 2016.
2. See, for example, Domhoff 2003; Rock 2004.
3. Moss similarly argues that trivial precognitive dreams reveal the routineness of our precognitive faculty. See Moss 2000.
4. Notes discovered after Tolkien's death and made public by his son

Christopher contain references to Dunne and graphs from his books. See
Flieger 1997.

5. Nabokov 2018.

6. Nabokov 2018, 43.

7. Nabokov 2018, 59.

8. Nabokov 2018, 59–61.

9. Siegel 2017.

10. Paquette 2011.

11. Lewis 1977, 22–23.

CHAPTER 4. THE TECHNICOLOR ELEPHANT:
FREUD AND THE ART OF MEMORY

1. Freud 1965, 139.

2. Freud 1965.

3. Freud 1965.

4. Blechner 1998.

5. Hobson and McCarley 1977.

6. Crick and Mitchison 1983.

7. Wamsley and Stickgold 2010.

8. Freud 1965.

9. Wamsley and Stickgold, 2010.

10. Llewellyn 2013.

11. Carruthers 1996; Foer 2011; Yates 1996.

12. Llewellyn 2013.

CHAPTER 5.
FUTURE TOWERS FROM PAST BRICKS:
BASICS OF DREAM PRECOGNITION

1. See also Wargo 2018.

2. Dunne 1952, 207.

3. Freud 1965, 547–48.

4. Faraday 1974, 69.

5. Rhine 1961.

6. Faraday 1974, 320.

7. Faraday 1974, 316.

8. Dossey 2009.
9. Moss 2009.
10. Siegel 2017, 36.
11. Anzieu 1986.
12. Freud 1965, 139.
13. Wargo 2018.

CHAPTER 6. THE UNUSUAL SUSPECTS OF THE DREAMWORLD: APPLYING FREE ASSOCIATION AND THE MNEMONIC THEORY

1. *Knife in the Water* was a 1964 film by Roman Polanski.
2. Freud 1965, 659.
3. Yates 1996.
4. Siegel 2017.
5. Dunne 1952.

CHAPTER 7. RULES OF THE GRAIL KINGDOM: DREAM SPACE AND DREAM TIME

1. Wagner 1962, 7.
2. Swain 1993.
3. Buonomano 2017.
4. Carruthers 1996.
5. Barber and Barber 2006.
6. Jeffrey Kripal, personal conversation.
7. See Noll 1985.
8. Noll 1985.
9. Carruthers 1996.
10. Cepelewicz 2019.
11. Ramachandran et al. 2016.
12. This is an argument I make at greater length in *Time Loops*. See Wargo 2018.
13. Watari n.d.

CHAPTER 8. LIBRARY ANGELS AND SCARAB BEETLES: SYNCHRONICITY, RETROCAUSATION, AND THE TESSERACT BRAIN

1. Jung 1973b.
2. Moss 2009.
3. Jung 1973a, 1973b.
4. Jung 1973a, 110.
5. Jung 1973a.
6. Jung and Pauli 2001.
7. Koestler 1972.
8. Dixon et al. 2009.
9. Aharonov and Tollaksen 2007.
10. McFadden and Al-Khalili 2014.
11. Atmanspacher et al. 2014; Brainerd et al. 2013; Wendt 2015.
12. Ouellette 2016.
13. Hameroff and Penrose 2014.
14. Kripal 2017, 2019. See also Peake 2016.
15. Kelly et al. 2010.
16. See Wargo 2018.
17. De Moura 2014.
18. Wargo 2018.
19. Dean 2002, 113–14.
20. Dean 2002, 109–10.
21. White 2018.

CHAPTER 9. BEYOND ARCHETYPES: THE FRACTAL GEOMETRY OF PROPHECY

1. Tolkien 1997, 255.
2. Gefter 2014.
3. Jung 1973a, 109.
4. Wargo 2018.
5. Jung 1985.
6. De Moura 2014.
7. Jung 1985.
8. Wargo 2018.

9. Jung 1973b, 28.

10. Kalsched 2013, 67.

11. Kalsched 2013, 66.

12. Jung 1965, 178.

13. Main 2007.

14. De Moura 2014.

15. Beitman 2016.

16. See Wargo 2016b.

17. Pasulka 2019.

18. Jung and Pauli 2001; Moss 2009.

19. Jung and Pauli 2001, 163.

20. Moss 2009, 229.

21. Moss 2009, 229.

22. Moss 2009, 230.

23. Moss 2009, 230.

24. See, for instance, Douglas 1993.

25. Jansen 2003, 225.

26. "Real magic" is a term used by Dean Radin. See Radin 2018.

CHAPTER 10. "BUT I SURVIVED": UNDERSTANDING PREMONITIONS

1. Kripal 2010.

2. Twain 2010; see also Charman 2017.

3. Stevenson 1974.

4. Chapter 1 of *Time Loops* discusses the *Titanic* and Aberfan premonitions and debates surrounding them. See Wargo 2018.

5. Paquette 2011.

6. "Predictions Hit Bullseye" 2002; Channel 5 2003; Peake 2012.

7. Graff 2000, 55.

8. May and Depp 2015.

9. Marwaha and May 2015.

10. Graff 2000, 43.

11. Aristotle as paraphrased by Ernest Becker 1973, 2.

12. This is a point made by Dossey 2009.

13. Moss 2000.

CHAPTER II.
FOUR-DIMENSIONAL BILLIARDS: TIME TRAVEL AND MEANING IN A SELF-CONSISTENT UNIVERSE

1. Krohn and Kripal 2018.
2. Knight 2019.
3. Rhine 1961.
4. Feather and Schmicker 2005.
5. Rhine 1961, 187.
6. L'Engle 2007. See White 2018.
7. Novikov 1998.
8. Echeverria et al. 1991.
9. Nick Herbert, personal communication.
10. Lloyd et al. 2011, 3.
11. Freud 1984b.

CHAPTER 12. THE WYRD OF DOCTOR WTF: THE REAL SUPERPOWERS OF THE UNCONSCIOUS

1. Wargo 2018.
2. See Wargo 2018 for a summary of this evidence.
3. Freud 1965, 336.
4. Cheung and Mossbridge 2018.
5. Wargo 2018.
6. Beidel 2014.
7. McMoneagle 2002.
8. Wargo 2019.
9. Wargo 2018.

CHAPTER 13. WHAT'S EXPECTED OF US IN A BLOCK UNIVERSE: NEW MYTHS FOR PRECOGS

1. Chiang 2002.
2. See Krohn and Kripal 2018.
3. Chiang 2019, 59.
4. Chiang 2019, 59–60.
5. Libet 2004.

6. Wegner 2002.

7. Dunne 1941.

8. Di Corpo and Vannini 2015.

CHAPTER 14. AFTER THE MIRACLE: HOW OUR THOUGHTS INFLUENCE OUR PAST

1. Horowitz 2018, 158.

2. Horowitz 2018, 158.

3. Horowitz 2018, 160.

4. Horowitz 2018, 157.

5. Horowitz 2018, 153.

6. Gleick 1987; For extended discussion of the butterfly effect as it relates to precognition and time travel, see Wargo 2018, chapter 5.

7. Radin 1997, 2018.

8. For extended discussion of this idea, see Wargo 2018, chapter 7.

9. Watari n.d.

10. Moss 2000.

11. Wargo 2018.

12. McFadden and Al-Khalili 2014.

13. Wargo 2018.

CHAPTER 15. A PRECOG CLAIMS HER GIFTS: ONE WOMAN'S LIFE-ALTERING PRECOGNITIVE AWAKENING

1. See Davies 2006; Gefter 2014.

2. Wargo 2018.

CHAPTER 16. GIANTS AND ANGELS: THE PRECOGNITIVE SELF-CARE SYSTEM

1. Philips 2012.

2. See Peake 2013; Sutin 2005; Wargo 2018.

3. Sutin 2005, 79–80; see also Peake 2013, 182.

4. Dick 1985, 10.

5. Huxley 1954.

6. Peake 2016.

7. Kalsched 2013.

8. Kalsched 2013, 71.

9. Kalsched 2013, 71.

10. Kalsched 2013, 28.

11. Kalsched 2013, 29.

12. Urminsky 2017.

13. Sheldon and Fishbach 2018; Zeelenberg 2018.

14. For a similar idea, see Strickler 2019.

CHAPTER 17. LOOK BACK IN AMBER: TIME GIMMICKS AND DREAM PALEONTOLOGY

1. Cambray 2009.

2. Freud 1965, 154.

3. In Žižek 1989, 14.

4. Žižek 1989.

5. Watari n.d.

6. The quote is from Jung's Seminar on Dream Analysis, Lecture V (4 June 1930). Retrieved from Blogarama. Posted September 19, 2017.

7. Watari n.d.

8. Cirlot 1971, 86 (my italics).

CHAPTER 18. POSSESSED BY YOUR FUTURE: OUT-OF-BODY EXPERIENCES, LUCID DREAMS, AND SLEEP PARALYSIS

1. Lecouteux 2003.

2. Robert Monroe's *Journeys Out of the Body,* for instance, contains examples of both kinds of after-the-fact confirmations. See Monroe 2001.

3. Price 1982.

4. Leavitt 2012.

5. Burroughs 1979, 10.

6. Wargo 2016a.

7. Hufford 1982.

8. Peake 2016.

9. Peake discusses the phenomenon of "false awakenings" in similar terms. See Peake 2016.
10. Peake 2016.

CHAPTER 19. LIMINAL PRECOGNITION: HYPNAGOGIA, ACTIVE IMAGINATION, CREATIVITY, AND MEDITATION

1. Dumpert 2019.
2. Inglis 2012, 75.
3. Inglis 2012, 75.
4. Sheets 2014.
5. Dumpert 2019.
6. Wargo 2018.
7. Peake 2012; Wargo 2018.
8. Wargo 2020b.
9. Dick 2011.
10. Flieger 1997.
11. Leavitt 2012.
12. Dumpert 2019.
13. Harner 1990.
14. Watari n.d.
15. Schnabel 1997.
16. Cheung and Mossbridge 2018.
17. Larson and Czikszentmihalyi 1983.

CONCLUSION. THE LONG SELF REVOLUTION: A CALL TO ACTION

1. Cheung and Mossbridge 2018.
2. Hooper 2018.
3. Hooper 2018.
4. Hooper 2018.
5. See Krippner et al. 2002.
6. See DeLay 2019.

References

Aharanov, Yakir, and Jeff Tollaksen. 2007. "New Insights on Time-Symmetry in Quantum Mechanics." arXiv.

Anzieu, Didier. 1986. *Freud's Self-Analysis*. Madison, Wisc.: International Universities Press, Inc.

Atmanspacher, Harald, Thomas Filk, and Hartmann Romer. 2004. "Quantum Zeno Features of Bi-stable Perception." *Biological Cybernetics* 90:33–40.

Barber, Elizabeth Wayland, and Paul T. Barber. 2006. *When They Severed Earth from Sky*. Princeton, N.J.: Princeton University Press.

Becker, Ernest. 1973. *The Denial of Death*. New York: Free Press.

Beidel, Eric. 2014, March 27. "More than a Feeling: ONR Investigates 'Spidey Sense' for Sailors and Marines (Media Release)." Arlington, Va.: Office of Naval Research.

Beitman, Bernard D. 2016. *Connecting with Coincidence*. Deerfield Beach, Fla.: Health Communications, Inc.

Bem, Daryl. 2011. "Feeling the Future: Experimental Evidence for Anomalous Retroactive Influences on Cognition and Affect." *Journal of Personality and Social Psychology* 100:407–25.

Bem, Daryl, Patrizio E. Tressoldi, Thomas Rabeyron, and Michael Duggan. 2016. "Feeling the Future: A Meta-Analysis of 90 Experiments on the Anomalous Anticipation of Random Future Events [version 2; peer review: 2 approved]." *F1000Research*, 4:1188.

Blechner, Mark J. 1998. "The Analysis and Creation of Dream Meaning: Interpersonal, Intrapsychic, and Neurobiological Perspectives." *Contemporary Psychoanalysis* 34:181–94.

Brainerd, Charles J., Zheng Wang, and Valerie F. Reyna. 2013. "Superposition of Episodic Memories: Overdistribution and Quantum Models." *Topics in Cognitive Sciences* 5:773–99.

Brandenburg, John E. 2015. *Death on Mars.* Kempton, Ill.: Adventures Unlimited Press.

Broderick, Damien. 2015. *Knowing the Unknowable.* Vancleave, Miss.: Surinam Turtle Press.

Bruce, Robert. 2009. *Astral Dynamics.* Charlottesville, Va.: Hampton Roads.

Buonomano, Dean. 2017. *Your Brain Is a Time Machine.* New York: W. W. Norton & Company.

Burroughs, Edgar Rice. 1979. *A Princess of Mars.* New York: Del Rey.

Cambray, Joseph. 2009. *Synchronicity.* College Station, Tex.: Texas A&M University Press.

Carpenter, James C. 2012. *First Sight.* Lanham, Md.: Rowman & Littlefield Publishers.

Carruthers, Mary. 1996. *The Book of Memory.* Cambridge, UK: Cambridge University Press.

Cepelewicz, Jordana. 2019, February 12. "How the Brain Creates a Timeline of the Past." Quanta Magazine.

Channel 5. 2003. "The Man Who Painted the Future." *Extraordinary People* (Season 1: Episode 1).

Charman, Robert A. 2017. "Re-evaluation of Samuel Clemens' Dream Precognition Case—Did He Foresee the Future Funeral Casket of His Younger Brother Henry?" *Journal of the Society for Psychical Research* 81: 17–25.

Cheung, Theresa, and Julia Mossbridge. 2018. *The Premonition Code.* London: Watkins.

Chiang, Ted. 2002. *Stories of Your Life and Others.* New York: Vintage.

———. 2019. *Exhalation.* New York: Alfred A. Knopf.

Cirlot, J. E. 1971. *A Dictionary of Symbols.* London: Routledge.

Crick, Francis, and Graeme Mitchison. 1983, July 14. "The Function of Dream Sleep." *Nature* 304:111–14.

Cushman, Marc. 2014. *These Are the Voyages TOS: Season Two.* Los Angeles, Calif: Jacobs Brown Press.

Davies, Paul C. W. 2004. "Quantum Fluctuations and Life." arXiv.

———. 2006. *The Goldilocks Enigma.* London: Penguin.

Dean, Barbara. 2002. "Intersection: A Meeting with a Mountain Lion." In Cass Adams, ed., *The Soul Unearthed.* Boulder, Colo.: Sentient Publications.

DeLay, Tad. 2019. *Against*. Eugene, Ore.: Cascade Books.

De Moura, Vicente. 2014. "Learning from the Patient: The East, Synchronicity and Transference in the History of an Unknown Case of C. G. Jung." *Journal of Analytical Psychology* 59:391–409.

Dick, Philip K. 1985. *Radio Free Albemuth*. New York: Arbor House.

———. 2011. *Exegesis*. Boston: Houghton Mifflin Harcourt.

Di Corpo, Ulisse, Antonella Vannini. 2015. *Syntropy*. Princeton, N.J.: ICRL Press.

Dixon, P. Ben, David J. Starling, Andrew N. Jordan, and John C. Howell. 2009. "Ultrasensitive Beam Deflection Measurement via Interferometric Weak Value Amplification." *Physical Review Letters* 102:173601, 1–4.

Domhoff, G. William. 2003. *The Scientific Study of Dreams*. Washington, DC: American Psychological Association.

Dossey, Larry. 2009. *The Power of Premonitions*. New York: Dutton.

Douglas, Claire. 1993. *Translate this Darkness*. New York: Simon & Schuster.

Dumpert, Jennifer. 2019. *Liminal Dreaming*. Berkeley, Calif.: North Atlantic Books.

Dunne, Brenda J., and Robert G. Jahn. 2003. "Information and Uncertainty in Remote Perception Research." *Journal of Scientific Exploration* 17:207–41.

Dunne, J. W. 1941. *The Serial Universe*. London: Faber and Faber.

———. (1927) 1952. *An Experiment with Time*. London: Faber and Faber.

———. 1955. *Intrusions?* London: Faber and Faber.

Echeverria, Fernando, Gunnar Klinkhammer, and Kip S. Thorne. 1991. "Billiard Balls in Wormhole Spacetimes with Closed Timelike Curves: Classical Theory." *Physical Review D* 44:1077–99.

Eisenbud, Jule. 1982. *Paranormal Foreknowledge*. New York: Human Sciences Press.

Faraday, Ann. 1974. *The Dream Game*. New York: Harper & Row.

Feather, Sally Rhine, and Michael Schmicker. 2005. *The Gift*. New York: St. Martin's Press.

Flieger, Verlyn. 1997. *A Question of Time*. Kent, Ohio: The Kent State University Press.

Foer, Joshua. 2011. *Moonwalking with Einstein*. London: Penguin.

Freud, Sigmund. (1899) 1965. *The Interpretation of Dreams*. New York: Avon Books.

———. (1901) 1965. *The Psychopathology of Everyday Life*. New York: W. W. Norton & Company.

———. (1899) 1974. "A Premonitory Dream Fulfilled." In G. Devereux, ed., *Psychoanalysis and the Occult*. London: Souvenir Press.

———. (1920) 1984a. "Beyond the Pleasure Principle." In Sigmund Freud, *On Metapsychology*. London: Penguin.

———. (1925) 1984b. "Negation." In Sigmund Freud, *On Metapsychology*. London: Penguin.

Gardner, Martin, ed. 1998. *The Wreck of the Titanic Foretold?* Amherst, N.Y.: Prometheus Books.

Gefter, Amanda. 2014. *Trespassing on Einstein's Lawn*. New York: Bantam Books.

Gleick, James. 1987. *Chaos*. New York: Penguin Books.

Graff, Dale E. 1998. *Tracks in the Psychic Wilderness*. Boston, Mass.: Element.

———. 2000. *River Dreams*. Boston, Mass.: Element.

Hameroff, Stuart, and Roger Penrose. 2014. "Consciousness in the Universe: A Review of the 'Orch OR' Theory." *Physics of Life Reviews* 11:39–78.

Harner, Michael. 1990. *The Way of the Shaman*. New York: Harper Collins.

Haynes, Korey. 2019, March 13. "Scientists used IBM's quantum computer to reverse time, possibly breaking a law of physics." Astronomy.

Hobson, J. Allan, and Robert W. McCarley. 1977. "The Brain as a Dream State Generator: An Activation-Synthesis Hypothesis of the Dream Process." *The American Journal of Psychiatry* 134:1335–48.

Honorton, Charles, and Diane C. Ferrari. 1989. "'Future Telling': A Meta-Analysis of Forced-Choice Precognition Experiments, 1935–1987." *Journal of Parapsychology* 53:281–308.

Hooper, Rowan. 2018, July 14–20. "Field Notes: Nightmares from the Fringe." *New Scientist* 239 (3186):10.

Horowitz, Mitch. 2018. *The Miracle Club*. Rochester, Vt.: Inner Traditions.

Hufford, David J. 1982. *The Terror that Comes in the Night*. Philadelphia, Pa.: University of Pennsylvania Press.

Huxley, Aldous. 1954. *The Doors of Perception*. New York: Harper & Row.

Inglis, Brian. 2012. *Coincidence*. Guildford, UK: White Crow Books.

Jansen, Diana Baynes. 2003. *Jung's Apprentice*. Einsiedeln, Switzerland: Daimon Verlag.

Jung, C. G. 1965. *Memories, Dreams, Reflections*. New York: Vintage Books.

———. 1973a. "On Synchronicity." In *Synchronicity*. Princeton, N.J.: Princeton University Press.

———. 1973b. "Synchronicity: An Acausal Connecting Principle." In *Synchronicity*. Princeton, N.J.: Princeton University Press.

———. 1985. "The Realities of Practical Psychotherapy." In *The Practice of Psychotherapy*. Princeton, N.J.: Princeton University Press.

Jung, C. G., and Wolfgang Pauli. 2001. *Atom and Archetype*. Princeton, N.J.: Princeton University Press.

Kaku, Michio. 2005. *Parallel Worlds*. New York: Anchor Books.

Kalas, Paul. 2018. *The Oneironauts*. Author.

Kalsched, Donald. 2013. *Trauma and the Soul*. London: Routledge.

Kelly, Edward F., Emily Williams Kelly, Adam Crabtree, Alan Gauld, Michael Grosso, and Bruce Greyson. 2010. *Irreducible Mind*. Lanham, Md.: Roman & Littlefield Publishers.

Knight, Sam. 2019, March 4. "The Premonitions Bureau." *The New Yorker*.

Koestler, Arthur. 1972. *The Roots of Coincidence*. New York: Vintage.

Krohn, Elizabeth Greenfield, and Jeffrey J. Kripal. 2018. *Changed in a Flash*. Berkeley, Calif.: North Atlantic Books.

Kripal, Jeffrey J. 2010. *Authors of the Impossible*. Chicago, Ill.: The University of Chicago Press.

———. 2011. *Mutants and Mystics*. Chicago, Ill.: The University of Chicago Press.

———. 2017. *Secret Body*. Chicago, Ill.: The University of Chicago Press.

———. 2019. *The Flip*. Chicago, Ill.: The University of Chicago Press.

Krippner, Stanley, Montague Ullman, and Charles Honorton. (1971) 2002. "A Precognitive Dream Study with a Single Subject." In M. Ullman, S. Krippner, and A. Vaughan, eds., *Dream Telepathy*. Charlottesville, Va.: Hampton Roads.

Larson, Reed, and Mihaly Czikszentmihalyi. 1983. "The Experience Sampling Method." *New Directions for Methodology of Social & Behavioral Science* 15:41–56.

Leavitt, June O. 2012. *The Mystical Life of Franz Kafka*. Oxford, UK: Oxford University Press.

Lecouteux, Claude. 2003. *Witches, Werewolves, and Fairies*. Rochester, Vt.: Inner Traditions.

L'Engle, Madeleine. (1962) 2007. *A Wrinkle in Time*. New York: Farrar, Straus and Giroux.

Lewis, C. S. 1977. *The Dark Tower*. London: Collins.

Libet, Benjamin. 2004. *Mind Time*. Cambridge, Mass.: Harvard University Press.

Llewellyn, Sue. 2013. "Such Stuff as Dreams Are Made On? Elaborative Encoding, the Ancient Art of Memory, and the Hippocampus." *Behavioral and Brain Sciences* 36:589–607.

Lloyd, Seth; et al. 2011. "Closed Timelike Curves via Postselection: Theory and Experimental Test of Consistency." *Physical Review Letters* 106:040403.

Main, Roderick. 2007. "Ruptured Time and the Reenchantment of Modernity." In A. Casement, ed., *Who Owns Jung?* London: Karnac Books.

Marwaha, Sonali Bhatt, and Edwin C. May. 2015. "The Multiphasic Model of Precognition." In E. C. May and S. B. Marwaha, eds., *Extrasensory Perception Vol. 2.* Santa Barbara, Calif.: Praeger.

Masters, Michael P. 2019. *Identified Flying Objects.* Butte, Mont.: Author.

May, Edwin C., and Joseph G. Depp. 2015. "Entropy and Precognition: The Physics Domain of the Multiphasic Model of Precognition." In E. C. May and S. B. Marwaha, eds., *Extrasensory Perception Vol. 2.* Santa Barbara, Calif.: Praeger.

May, Edwin C., Victor Rubel, and Loyd Auerbach. 2014. *ESP Wars East & West.* Palo Alto, Calif.: Laboratories for Fundamental Research.

McFadden, Johnjoe, and Jim Al-Khalili. 2014. *Life on the Edge.* New York: Crown Publishers.

McMoneagle, Joseph. 1993. *Mind Trek.* Charlottesville, Va.: Hampton Roads.

———. 2002. *The Stargate Chronicles.* Charlottesville, Va.: Hampton Roads.

Minkowski, Hermann. 2012. *Space and Time.* Montreal, Quebec, Canada: Minkowski Institute Press.

Mole, Beth. 2016. "Sweet drug clears cholesterol, reverses heart disease—and was found by parents." arsTechnica.

Monroe, Robert A. 2001. *Journeys Out of the Body.* New York: Broadway Books.

Moss, Robert. 2000. *Dreaming True.* New York: Pocket Books.

———. 2009. *The Secret History of Dreaming.* Novato, Calif.: New World Library.

Mossbridge, Julia, Patrizio Tressoldi, and Jessica Utts. 2012. "Predictive Physiological Anticipation Preceding Seemingly Unpredictable Stimuli: A Meta-Analysis." *Frontiers in Psychology* 3(390):1–18.

Mossbridge, Julia A., Patrizio Tressoldi, Jessica Utts, John A. Ives, Dean Radin, and Wayne B. Jonas. 2014. "Predicting the Unpredictable: Critical Analysis and Practical Implications of Predictive Anticipatory Activity." *Frontiers in Human Neuroscience* 8(146):1–10.

Mossbridge, Julia A., and Dean Radin. 2018. "Precognition as a Form of Prospection: A Review of the Evidence." *Psychology of Consciousness: Theory, Research, and Practice* 5(1):78–93.

Moye, David. 2014, July 15. "Lottery Winner Must Share $1.7 Million Jackpot With Psychic Waiter." Huffington Post.

Mungia, Lance. 2019. *Third Eye Spies* (film). Conscious Universe Films.

Nabokov, Vladimir. 2018. *Insomniac Dreams*. Princeton, N.J.: Princeton University Press.

Noll, Richard. 1985. "Mental Imagery Cultivation as a Cultural Phenomenon: The Role of Visions in Shamanism." *Current Anthropology* 26(4):443–61.

Noll, Richard. 1994. *The Jung Cult*. Princeton, N.J.: Princeton University Press.

———. 1997. *The Aryan Christ*. New York: Random House.

Novikov, Igor D. 1998. *The River of Time*. Cambridge, UK: Cambridge University Press.

Ouellette, Jennifer. 2016, November 2. "A New Spin on the Quantum Brain." *Quanta Magazine*.

Paquette, Andrew. 2011. *Dreamer*. Winchester, UK: O Books.

Pasulka, D.W. 2019. *American Cosmic*. Oxford, UK: Oxford University Press.

Peake, Anthony. 2012. *The Labyrinth of Time*. London: Arcturus.

———. 2013. *A Life of Philip K. Dick*. London: Arcturus.

———. 2016. *Opening the Doors of Perception*. London: Watkins.

Phillips, Adam. 2012. *Missing Out*. London: Picador.

"Predictions Hit Bullseye: The Seer of Sudbury Hill." 2002 (April). *Fortean Times* no. 156: 16.

Price, Robert M. 1982. "Lovecraft's Use of Theosophy." *Crypt of Cthulhu* 1(5).

Priestley, J. B. 1989. *Man & Time*. London: Bloomsbury Books.

Radin, Dean I. 1997. "Unconscious Perception of Future Emotions: An Experiment in Presentiment." *Journal of Scientific Exploration* 11:163–80.

———. 2018. *Real Magic*. New York: Harmony.

Ramachandran, Vilayanur S., Melissa Vajanaphanich, and Chaipat Chunharas. 2016. "Calendars in the Brain: Their Perceptual Characteristics and Possible Neural Substrate." *Neurocase* 22:461–65.

Rhine, Louisa, E. 1961. *Hidden Channels of the Mind*. New York: William Morrow & Company.

———. 1967. *ESP in Life and Lab*. London: Collier Books.

Rock, Andrea. 2004. *The Mind at Night*. New York: Basic Books.

Ronson, Jon. 2007. "Sylvia Browne: Is she for real?" *The Guardian*.

Sagan, Carl. 1997. *The Demon-Haunted World*. New York: Ballantine Books.

Schnabel, Jim. 1997. *Remote Viewers*. New York: Dell.

Sheets, Hilarie M. 2014, August 31. "David Lynch, Who Began as a Visual Artist, Gets a Museum Show." *New York Times*.

Sheldrake, Rupert. 2011. *Dogs That Know When Their Owners Are*

Coming Home and Other Unexplained Powers of Animals. New York: Three Rivers Press.

Sheldon, Oliver J. and Ayelet Fishbach. 2018. "Anticipating and Overcoming Unethical Temptation." In Gabriele Oettingen, A. Timur Sevincer, and Peter M. Gollwitzer, eds., *The Psychology of Thinking about the Future*. New York: The Guilford Press.

Siegel, Bruce. 2017. *Dreaming the Future*. Los Angeles, Calif.: MetaStory Books.

Smith, Paul. 2005. *Reading the Enemy's Mind*. New York: Forge.

Stevenson, Ian. (1960) 1974. "A Review and Analysis of Paranormal Experiences Connected with the Sinking of the Titanic." In W. H. Tantum, ed., *The Doomed Unsinkable Ship*. Riverside, Connecticut: 7 C's Press.

Strickler, Yancey. 2019. *This Could Be Our Future*. New York: Viking.

Sutin, Lawrence. 2005. *Divine Invasions*. New York: Carroll & Graf Publishers.

Swain, Tony. 1993. *A Place for Strangers*. Cambridge, UK: Cambridge University Press.

Targ, Russell. 2004. *Limitless Mind*. Novato, Calif.: New World Library.

Tepper, Sheri S. 1989. *Grass* (the first book in the *Arbai Trilogy* series). New York: Doubleday.

Tolkien, J. R. R. 1997. *The Hobbit*. Boston: Houghton Mifflin Company.

Tsakiris, Alex. 2017. "Men Like To Be Right—Duh! Novel Experiment Demonstrates Link with Psychic Abilities." *Skeptiko*.

Twain, Mark. 2010. *The Autobiography of Mark Twain Volume 1*. Berkeley, Calif.: The University of California Press.

Urminsky, Oleg. 2017. "The Role of Psychological Connectedness to the Future Self in Decisions Over Time." *Current Directions in Psychological Science* 26(1):34–39.

Utts, Jessica M. 1995. "An Assessment of the Evidence for Psychic Functioning." *Journal of Parapsychology*, 59:289–320.

Vallee, Jacques. 1975. *The Invisible College*. New York: E. P. Dutton & Co.

Virk, Rizwan. 2019. *The Simulation Hypothesis*. [N.p.]: Bayview Books.

Wagner, M. W., and M. Monnet. 1979. "Attitudes of college professors toward extra-sensory perception." *Zetetic Scholar* 5:7–17.

Wagner, Richard. 1962. *Parsifal*. United Kingdom: G. Schirmer.

Wamsley, Erin J., and Robert Stickgold. 2010. "Dreaming and offline memory processing." *Current Biology* 20(23): R1010-3.

Wargo, Eric. 2016a. "Psi's Big Guns: Sleep Paralysis and Astral Time Travel." *The Nightshirt*.

———. 2016b. "Stories Latent in the Landscape: Spirits, Time Slips, and 'Super-Psi.'" *The Nightshirt.*

———. 2018. *Time Loops.* Charlottesville, Va.: Anomalist Books.

———. 2019. "In Defense of the Water Witches." *The Nightshirt.*

———. 2020a. "Time Portals, Time Drones, and Timeships." *The Nightshirt.*

———. 2020b. "Where Was It Before the Dream?" *The Nightshirt.*

Watari, Tobi. n.d. *Unearth the Ancient Woman—A Precography.* Unpublished manuscript.

Wegner, Daniel. 2002. *The Illusion of Conscious Will.* Cambridge, Mass.: The MIT Press.

Wendt, Alexander. 2015. *Quantum Mind and Social Science.* Cambridge, UK: Cambridge University Press.

White, Christopher G. 2018. *Other Worlds.* Cambridge, Mass.: Harvard University Press.

White, Gordon. 2016. *The Chaos Protocols.* Woodbury, Minn.: Llewellyn Publications.

White, Jonathan W. 2017. *Midnight in America.* Chapel Hill, N.C.: The University of North Carolina Press.

Wiseman, Richard. 2010. *Paranormality.* Author.

Yates, Frances A. (1966) 1996. *The Art of Memory.* London: Pimlico.

Zeelenberg, Marcel. 2018. "Anticipated Regret: A Prospective Emotion about the Future Past." In Gabriele Oettingen, A. Timur Sevincer, and Peter M. Gollwitzer, eds., *The Psychology of Thinking about the Future.* New York: The Guilford Press.

Žižek, Slavoj. 1989. *The Sublime Object of Ideology.* London: Verso.

Index